A Brave [...]
GLOBAL [...]
IN A CHANG [...]

This new series of short, accessibl [...] ...g global issues of relevance to humanity today. Intended for the enquiring reader and social activists in the North and the South, as well as students, the books explain what is at stake and question conventional ideas and policies. Drawn from many different parts of the world, the series' authors pay particular attention to the needs and interests of ordinary people, whether living in the rich industrial or the developing countries. They all share a common objective: to help stimulate new thinking and social action in the opening years of the new century.

Global Issues in a Changing World is a joint initiative by Zed Books in collaboration with a number of partner publishers and non-governmental organizations around the world. By working together, we intend to maximize the relevance and availability of the books published in the series.

PARTICIPATING NGOS

Both ENDS, Amsterdam
Catholic Institute of International Relations, London
Corner House, Sturminster Newton
Council on International and Public Affairs, New York
Dag Hammarskjöld Foundation, Uppsala
Development GAP, Washington DC
Focus on the Global South, Bangkok
Inter Pares, Ottawa
Public Interest Research Centre, Delhi
Third World Network, Penang
Third World Network–Africa, Accra
World Development Movement, London

About this Series

'Communities in the South are facing great difficulties in coping with global trends. I hope this brave new series will throw much-needed light on the issues ahead and help us choose the right options.'
Martin Khor, Director, Third World Network

'There is no more important campaign than our struggle to bring the global economy under democratic control. But the issues are fearsomely complex. This Global Issues series is a valuable resource for the committed campaigner and the educated citizen.'
Barry Coates, Director, World Development Movement (WDM)

'Zed Books has long provided an inspiring list about the issues that touch and change people's lives. The Global Issues series is another dimension of Zed's fine record, allowing access to a range of subjects and authors that, to my knowledge, very few publishers have tried. I strongly recommend these new, powerful titles and this exciting series.'
John Pilger, author

'We are all part of a generation that actually has the means to eliminate extreme poverty worldwide. Our task is to harness the forces of globalisation for the benefit of working people, their families and their communities – that is our collective duty. The Global Issues series makes a powerful contribution to the global campaign for justice, sustainable and equitable development, and peaceful progress.'
Glenys Kinnock, MEP

To our families,
that they might live in a better world

ABOUT THE AUTHORS

PAUL TODD read philosophy at the University of East Anglia and has a doctorate from the University of Middlesex. A historian of the Cold War specialising in Middle East issues, he has done research at the US National Security Archives and was editor of the monthly *Gulf Report* at the Gulf Centre for Strategic Studies in London. He is the author of *World Power and Global Reach: US Security Policy in Southwest Asia*.

JONATHAN BLOCH was born in Cape Town, South Africa. He studied law at the University of Cape Town and the London School of Economics. He was politically active in South Africa and remains involved in Southern African causes. He is now a London-based businessman and is a Liberal Democrat councillor in the London Borough of Haringey. He co-authored *British Intelligence and Covert Action* and *KGB/CIA*, and was also a co-author of three chapters of *Dirty Work 2: The CIA in Africa*.

A GLOBAL ISSUES TITLE

GLOBAL INTELLIGENCE
The World's Secret Services Today

Paul Todd and Jonathan Bloch

University Press Ltd
Dhaka

White Lotus Co. Ltd
Bangkok

Books for Change
New Delhi

Fernwood
Nova Scotia

David Philip
Cape Town

Zed Books
London and New York

Global Intelligence
was first published in 2003 by

In Bangladesh: The University Press Ltd, Red Crescent Building,
114 Motijheel C/A, PO Box 2611, Dhaka 1000

In Burma, Cambodia, Laos, Thailand and Vietnam:
White Lotus Co. Ltd, GPO Box 1141, Bangkok 10501, Thailand

In Canada: Fernwood, 8422 St Margaret's Bay Road (Hwy 3),
Site 2A, Box 5, Black Point, Nova Scotia B0J 1B0

In India: Books for Change, 139 Richmond Road, Bangalore 560 025

In Southern Africa: David Philip (an imprint of New Africa Books),
99 Garfield Road, Claremont 7700, South Africa

In the rest of the world:
Zed Books Ltd, 7 Cynthia Street, London N1 9JF, UK and
Room 400, 175 Fifth Avenue, New York, NY 10010, USA

www.zedbooks.demon.co.uk

Copyright © Paul Todd and Jonathan Bloch 2003

The rights of the authors of this work have been asserted by them
in accordance with the Copyright, Designs and Patents Act, 1988.

Cover design by Andrew Corbett
Set in 10/12.6 pt Monotype Bembo by Long House, Cumbria, UK
Printed and bound in the EU by Cox & Wyman, Reading

Distributed in the USA exclusively by Palgrave, a division of
St Martin's Press, LLC, 175 Fifth Avenue, New York, NY 10010

A catalogue record for this book is available from the British Library
US CIP data is available from the Library of Congress
Canadian CIP data is available from the National Library of Canada

ISBN 1 55266 112 1 Pb (Canada)
ISBN 81 87380 81 0 Pb (India)
ISBN 0 86486 633 X Pb (Southern Africa)
ISBN 1 84277 112 4 Hb (Zed Books)
ISBN 1 84277 113 2 Pb (Zed Books)

CONTENTS

ABBREVIATIONS

ACP Americans for Computer Privacy
ADL Anti-Defamation League (US)
AF Air Force Intelligence (Syria)
Aman   Agaf ha-Modi'in (Military Intelligence Service, Israel)
ANC African National Congress (South Africa)
ANC–DIS African National Congress Department of Intelligence and Security
APEC Asia Pacific Economic Conference
ASEAN Association of South-East Asian Nations
ASIO Australian Secret Intelligence Organisation
ASIS Australian Secret Intelligence System
ATM Asynchronous Transfer Mode
AWACS Airborne Warning and Control System
BDL Bureau de Liaison (EU)
BfV Bundesamt für Verfassungsschutz (Germany)
BND Bundesnachrichtendienst (Germany)
BNL Banko Nazionale de Lavoro
BOSS Bureau of State Security (South Africa)
BRGE Brigade de Renseignement et de la Guerre Électronique (France)
BSI Bureau of Special Investigations (Burma)
BSPP Burma Socialist Programme Party
CALEA Communications Assistance for Law Enforcement (US)
CASIS Canadian Association for Security and Intelligence Studies
CBW Chemical and biological warfare
CCB Civil Cooperation Bureau (South Africa)
CCSE Comité Pour la Compétitivité et la Sécurite Economique (France)
CFSP Common Foreign and Security Policy (EU)
CIA Central Intelligence Agency (US)
CIG Current Intelligence Group (UK)
CIO Central Imagery Office (US)
CIS Commonwealth of Independent States
Comint   Communications intelligence
Comsat   Communication satellite
CRD Communications Research Division (US)
CSE Communications Security Establishment (Canada)
CSIS Canadian Security Intelligence Service
CTC Counter-Terrorist Center (US)
DARPA Defense Advanced Research Projects Agency (US)
DCC Directorate of Covert Collection (South Africa)

DCI Director of Central Intelligence (US)
DDSI Directorate of Defence Services Intelligence (Burma)
DEA Drug Enforcement Administration (US)
DES Data Encryption Standard
DFLP Democratic Front for the Liberation of Palestine
DGMI Directorate of Military Intelligence (India)
DGSE Direction Générale de la Sécurité Extérieure (France)
DIA Defence Intelligence Agency (India)
DIA Defense Intelligence Agency (US)
DINA Dirección de Inteligencia Nacional (Chile)
DIS Defence Intelligence Staff (UK)
DRM Direction du Renseignement Militaire (France)
DSD Defence Signals Directorate (Australia)
DST Direction de la Surveillance du Territoire (France)
DTI Department of Trade and Industry (UK)
ECHR European Convention on Human Rights
Elint   Electronic intelligence
ELN National Liberation Army (Colombia)
ENFOPOL Law Enforcement Police Matters (EU)
EP European Parliament
EU European Union
EUROPOL European Police Agency
FAPSI Federal'noye Agentsvo Paravitel'stvennykh Svyazi i Informatsii (Federal Agency for Government Communications and Information, Russia)
FARC Revolutionary Armed Forces of Colombia
FBI Federal Bureau of Investigation (US)
FEMA Federal Emergency Management Agency (US)
FIC Free Iraqi Council
FIS Front for Islamic Salvation (Algeria)
FISA Foreign Intelligence Surveillance Act (US)
FMF Foreign Military Financing (US)
FOI Freedom of information
FRU Force Research Unit (UK)
FSB Federal'naya Sluzhba Bezopasnosti (Federal Security Service, Russia)
FSK Federal Counter-Intelligence Service (Russia)

FSO Federalnaya Sluzhba Okrhrany (Federal
    Protection Service, Russia)
FTO Foreign terrorist organisation
GAO General Accounting Office (US)
GATT General Agreement on Tariffs and Trade
GCHQ Government Communications
    Headquarters (UK)
GCSB Government Communications Security
    Bureau (New Zealand)
GIA Armed Islamic Groups (Algeria)
GILC Global Internet Liberty Campaign
GIS General Intelligence Service (Palestine)
GRU Glavnoye Razvedyvatelnoye Upravleniye
    (Russian Military Intelligence)
GTAC Government Technical Assistance
    Centre (UK)
GUO Main Protection Directorate (Russia)
GUSP (Glavnoye Upravelenniye Spetsyalnykh
    Program – Main Directorate of Special
    Programmes, Russia)
HSC Homeland Security Council (US)
Humint   Human intelligence
I/OPS Information Operations (UK)
IAO Information Awareness Office (US)
IB Intelligence Bureau (India)
IB Intelligence Bureau (Pakistan)
IDF Israeli Defence Force
IEO Information Exploitation Office (US)
IFP Inkatha Freedom Party (South Africa)
IGIS Inspector General of Intelligence and
    Security (Australia)
IIS Iraqi Intelligence Service
ILC International leased carrier
ILETS International Law Enforcement
    Telecommunications Seminar (EU–US)
IMET International Military Education and
    Training (US)
IMF International Monetary Fund
Imint   Imagery intelligence
INA Iraq National Accord
INC Iraq National Congress
Intelsat   Intelligence satellite
IOSA Integrated Overhead Sigint Architecture
IP Internet Protocol
IPA International Police Academy
IRD Information Research Department (UK)
ISC Intelligence and Security Committee (UK)
ISI Inter-Services Intelligence (Pakistan)
ISP Internet service provider
IT Information technology
IXP Internet exchange point
JCET Joint Combined Exchange Training
    Program (US)
JCIB Joint Counter-Intelligence Bureau (ISI,
    Pakistan)
JCIC Joint Coordinating Intelligence
    Committee (South Africa)

JIB Joint Intelligence Bureau (ISI, Pakistan)
JIC Joint Intelligence Committee (UK Cabinet
    Office)
JIC Joint Intelligence Committee (Indian
    Cabinet Office)
JIE Jama'at-e-Islami movement (Pakistan)
JIM Joint Intelligence Miscellaneous (ISI,
    Pakistan)
JIN Joint Intelligence North (ISI, Pakistan)
JIT Joint Intelligence technical research bureau
    (ISI, Pakistan)
JIX Joint Intelligence administration (ISI,
    Pakistan)
JKLF Jammu and Kashmir Liberation Front
JMIP Joint Military Intelligence Program (US)
JSIB Joint Signals and Elint Bureau (ISI,
    Pakistan)
JUI Jamiat-e-Ulema Islam (Pakistan)
KDP Kurdish Democratic Party
KGB Komitet Gosudarstvennoy Bezopasnosti
    (Committee for State Security, Soviet
    Union)
LAN Local area network
Lekem   Leshkat Kesher Madao (Bureau of
    Scientific Relations, Israel)
MEP Member of the European Parliament
MI 5 Security Service (UK)
MI 6 Secret Intelligence Service (UK)
MI Military Intelligence (South Africa, Syria))
MITS Midland Bank Industrial and Trade
    Services
MKO Mujahidin Kalq (Iran)
MNDAA Myanmar National Democratic
    Alliance Army (Burma)
Mossad   ha-Mossad le-Modi'in ule-Tafkidim
    Meydahadim (Foreign intelligence service,
    Israel)
MPRI Military Professional Resources (US
    company)
MQM Mojahir Quami Movement (Pakistan)
MVD Ministry of Interior Security (Russia)
NAFTA North American Free Trade
    Association
NATO North Atlantic Treaty Organisation
NCIS National Criminal Intelligence Service
    (South Africa)
NCIS National Criminal Intelligence Service
    (UK)
NIA National Intelligence Agency (South
    Africa)
NIB National Intelligence Bureau (Burma)
NICOC National Intelligence Coordinating
    Committee (South Africa)
NIF National Islamic Front (Sudan)
NIMA National Imagery and Mapping Agency
    (US)
NIS National Intelligence Service (South Africa)

NLD National League for Democracy (Burma)
NRO National Reconnaissance Office (US)
NSA National Security Agency (US)
NSC National Security Council (US)
NSD National Security Directive (US)
NSR National Security Review (US)
NWFP North West Frontier Province (Pakistan)
OHS Office of Homeland Security (US)
OSC Office of Surveillance Commissioners (UK)
OSS Office of Strategic Studies (Burma)
PA Palestine Authority
PAC Pan-Africanist Congress (South Africa)
PAR Performance Appraisal Report
PDD Presidential decision directive (US)
PFLP Popular Front for the Liberation of Palestine
PFLP–GC Popular Front for the Liberation of Palestine–General Command
PGP Pretty Good Privacy (encryption software)
PGU First Chief Directorate (of the KGB)
PKK Kurdish Workers Party
PLO Palestine Liberation Organisation
PNA Palestine National Authority
PPP Pakistan Peoples Party
PSS Preventive Security Service (Palestine)
PUK Patriotic Union of Kurdistan
RAW Research and Analysis Wing (India)
RISS Regional Information Sharing System (US)
RPF Rwandan Patriotic Front
RSOC Regional Sigint Operations Centre
RTZ Rio Tinto Zinc
RUC Royal Ulster Constabulary
SACP South African Communist Party
SAIRI Supreme Assembly of the Islamic Revolution (Iraq)
SANDF South African National Defence Force
SAPS South African Police Service
SAS Special Air Service (UK)
SASS South African Secret Service
SBIRS Space Based Infra-Red System
SBP Sluzhba Bezopasnosti Prezidenta (Presidential Security Service, Russia)
SBS Special Boat Service (UK)
Shin Bet   Sherut ha-Bitachon ha-Klali (Domestic intelligence service, Israel)
SID Special Investigation Department (Burma)
Sigint   Signals intelligence
SIN Servicio de Inteligencia Nacional (Peru)
SIRC Security Intelligence Review Committee (Canada)

SIS Secret Intelligence Service (UK)
SLORC State Law and Order Restoration Council (Burma)
SMO Support for Military Operations (US)
SORM System for Ensuring Investigated Activity (Russia)
SOVAM Bureau of Soviet Analysis (CIA)
SPCS Satellite personal communications system
SPDC State Peace and Development Council (Burma)
SPLA Sudan Popular Liberation Army
SRC Supercomputer Research Center
SSF Special Security Force (Palestine)
START Strategic Arms Reduction Treaty
STOA Scientific and Technological Options Assessment (EU)
STRATCOM Strategic Communications (South Africa)
SVR Sluzhba Vnesheny Razvedki (Foreign Intelligence Service, Russia)
TEC Transitional Executive Council (South Africa)
TES Technology Experimental Satellite (India)
TIARA Tactical Intelligence and Related Activities (US)
UAV Unmanned aerial vehicle
UHF Ultra high frequency
UK United Kingdom
UK/USA Global Sigint system of US, UK, Australia, Canada and New Zealand
UN United Nations
UMEH Union of Myanmar Economic Holdings (Burma)
UNITA National Union for the Total Independence of Angola
URNG Guatemalan National Revolutionary Unity
URPO Directorate of Analysis and Suppression of the Activity of Criminal Organisations (Russia)
US United States
USDA Union Solidarity and Development Association (Burma)
UWSA United Wa State Army (Burma)
VEVAK Ministry of Intelligence and Security (Iran)
VHF Very high frequency
WAN Wide area network
WDM Wavelength division multiplying
WEU Western European Union
WMD Weapons of mass destruction
WTC World Trade Centre

INTRODUCTION

INTELLIGENCE
AFTER
9/11

A New Internationalism?

'Coming events,' as Goethe knew, can sometimes 'cast a long shadow.' Clearly, the events of 11 September 2001 and after – spectacular public destruction, the prospect of truly catastrophic biological or nuclear strikes – had long been prefigured in intelligence threat assessments, civil contingencies planning and, indeed, popular film and fiction. But for those professionally charged with defining their likelihood – the intelligence services – the grimly effective simplicity of the September hijackings hit with a shocking abruptness. Since then, with the covert world under unprecedented public scrutiny, the 11 September ground zero has been cast as only part of a coming global struggle. However, if the concept of war on (or by) terrorism is one now shared by all its protagonists, then we may plausibly ask why and how the phenomenon it describes has come about, and – above all – also seek its origins. For unlike the doomed US airliners, these deeper currents of global conflict have not come out of the blue.

In this short book we hope to shed some light on the nexus between conventional, overt politics and the more covert, clandestine activities of states. But our book is not about foreign policy as such, or even about defence and security policy; instead, its focus is the perspectives and aims of world intelligence agencies. Historically, such agencies have served a dual function – predicting and countering military/ security threats, on the one hand, and a wider agenda of social control on the other. The advent of globalisation – or of liberal capitalism on a global scale – and the accompanying revolution in world communications have both enabled these tasks and made them more difficult. We aim to chart how intelligence is adapting to the new world that emerged with the end of the Cold War and the uncertain beginnings of an era of (involuntary) interdependency.

For what clearly emerges from the disaster at the World Trade Center is a pointer to the obsolescence of existing, firmly held conceptions about the nature of world politics and the abilities of states, and the remaining superpower in particular, to contain and compartmentalise their relations with the world at large in the face of emergent global networks and social forces. It is also apparent that the explicit assumption underlying Western, and certainly US, conceptions of their role in the world – that globalisation is an inherent force for good, a 'default setting for the universe' – is strongly contested, and not solely by those obviously dispossessed and marginalised by the much-heralded 'end of history'.

But what has actually changed? Air hijackings originated in the Middle East in the 1970s, attacks on high-profile economic targets – prestige buildings, infrastructure – have been carried out with formidable success in Britain. The US, too, has struggled for years to find an appropriate strategy to deal with Al–Qaida and similar groups – veering between ineffectual cruise missile attacks and awkward efforts by the Federal Bureau of Investigation (FBI) to mount overseas prosecutions. These efforts have been characterised by a lack of the clear institutional focus provided by the Cold War. A concentration on technical means of intelligence gathering and a reluctance to commit or even train human assets has led intelligence – certainly in the US – to an equivalent of the 'Powell Doctrine' of warfare by overwhelming technological means. In coming chapters, we look at the extent to which the focus has shifted from conventional, state-oriented counter-espionage and agent running to countering non-state threats. We discuss the exponential changes in technical capability that have taken place, but our emphasis is on issues of redefined mandates, new roles and the somewhat neglected areas of democratic accountability and public control.

Defining the threat

Although the scope of this study necessarily reflects an age of globalisation, the increasing interconnectedness of world polity continues to be dominated by a balance of power overwhelmingly weighted in favour of the industrialised nations of the West, and the US in particular. Accordingly, much attention will focus on the internal debates, organisational transformation and mission parameters of the US Central Intelligence Agency (CIA) and its principal junior ally, Britain's MI 6. As we chart this process, from the fall of the Berlin Wall in September 1989 and through the Gulf War, the Moscow coups and the slide into anarchy in the Balkans, a common thread emerges – in none of these instances was timely intelligence provided to policy makers in order to effect any pre-emptive leverage on events.

Meanwhile, such transformations as were coming on stream reflected what were perceived as more general post-Cold War changes in world affairs. With the collapse of the Warsaw Pact came the ending of the need for comprehensive intelligence on Soviet troop movements, missile deployments and 'order of battle' requirements in general by the Western powers. To be sure, the emergent Russian Federation was still ranked as the world's second most formidable military player in its own right, but intelligence efforts were now marked by a major shift towards monitoring technology exports, overseeing arms reductions in accordance with the Strategic Arms Reduction Treaty (START) arrangements on nuclear weapons, and charting the general proliferation dangers stemming from ongoing social and state instability – as the Moscow regime sought to adapt to the 'shock therapy' of successive prescriptions from the World Bank and the International Monetary Fund (IMF). Here, the inherent double dealing of intelligence activity was attended by a sometimes uneasy cooperation with the Kremlin successors to the collapsed Soviet empire.

The ending of the enduring threat from Soviet power was reflected in major structural changes in the US intelligence effort. The CIA's Directorate of Plans, the focus of its human intelligence (Humint) and covert operations, was run down in favour of technological means of intelligence gathering. Fresh emphasis was placed on the National Security Agency (NSA) as the favoured instrument. This also reflected shifting perceptions of the need to emphasise economic intelligence issues apparent in the growth of Echelon – the US/UK/Australia/ Canada/New Zealand eavesdropping network alleged to gather commercial intelligence for US corporations. By the end of the 1990s, a 'peace dividend' – a reduction of some 30 per cent in the intelligence budget – had been implemented, based on explicitly optimistic assumptions about a new and inherently benign chapter in world affairs.[1]

After the Berlin Wall

The end of the Cold War took most observers completely by surprise – not least those professionally charged with predictions in precisely this area. In the post-Cold War world, prognosis did not get any easier. For some, the coming age would be characterised by unrivalled peace and prosperity, as liberal capitalism completed its historical destiny as the motor of human progress. The end of history would mean greater world order and the progressive marginalisation of the nation state as the natural problem-solving unit.[2] For others, a more traditional era of great power hegemony loomed – the 'unipolar moment' dominated by the remaining superpower, the United States.[3] Others, again, saw a new era of chaos and international anarchy, as world polity slipped inexorably 'back to the future'.[4]

For the world's intelligence services – and the standard bearers in London and Washington in particular – 'victory' over the evil empire presented an ironic challenge. With the demise of the Warsaw Pact and its awesome military apparatus, where would the continuing rationale lie? Of course, existing other threats – drugs, money laundering, nationalist/fundamentalist terrorism – had not only not gone away but had taken fresh impetus from the ending of such restraint as Moscow had sometimes imposed on its global demesne. And, indeed, the erosion of what even the West recognised as fairly rigorous centralised control over such matters as nuclear/chemical/biological weapons in the old Soviet Union had, in many ways, compounded the dangers of random proliferation in these areas.

The growth of the Internet provided another dilemma for intelligence. Whilst in some ways providing a 'fabulous instrument for surveillance', the interconnection of data on a world scale also provided unparalleled opportunities for terrorist and criminal networks – as well as civil libertarians – and opened up new horizons for cyberwarfare. To be sure, the response from Langley and Whitehall was, at the least, creative. The NSA invested massively in new eavesdropping and satellite technology, whilst Britain's MI 5 accomplished a shift from counter-espionage to counter-terror with impressive mandarin aplomb.

Intelligence agencies today

In the light of the above, we take up the following perspectives:

- *Old-style repressive agencies continue to exist* – in countries like China, Cuba, Burma, Zimbabwe and throughout the Middle East. Israel's Mossad and Shin Bet retain essentially the same mission as at their inception.

- *Some formerly repressive agencies either have been abolished or have changed their briefs fundamentally*, and may no longer engage significantly in extra-territorial activities. The East German Stasi is a clear example of the former. The Bureau of State Security (BOSS) in South Africa and some of the Latin American agencies – notably Dirección de Inteligencia Nacional (DINA) in Chile – are examples of the latter. Perhaps somewhere in between is the case of the FSB in Russia.

- *Old Cold War agencies are finding new rationales* in order to preserve their institutional existence and budgetary resources. The CIA and MI 5 are leading examples. New, partly self-assumed roles include the 'war on drugs', the notion of 'rogue states' and the idea that state agencies have a legitimate role in supporting national companies by monitoring the commercial activities of rivals. Here, though, the continuing spread of globalisation and transnational conglomerates has made that role an increasingly problematic one. Another possible target, with the rise of ultra-nationalist and ethnic terrorist groups in many countries in Europe, is the monitoring of the extreme right – although here we may question how effectively agencies which have demonised the left for decades can change their mentality.

As they redefine their missions they pose new dangers to civil rights. The growing media currency – particularly in the US – of such notions as 'ecoterrorism' serves to legitimise state surveillance of a potentially open-ended range of environmentalist groups and non-governmental organisations (NGOs). The rise of counter-globalisation coalitions that include such groups alongside more traditional trade union and worker organisations has been eagerly grasped in some intelligence circles as a working substitute for the vanished spectre of world communism. And, as we shall see, the always close-knit relationship between intelligence agencies and big corporations has led surveillance to slip imperceptibly into covert action. Another growth area for intelligence agencies is the world of private security 'consultancy'. Here, the glut of laid-off Cold War personnel and the current international business fad for 'outsourcing' have combined to produce a new Iron Triangle – where corporations, particularly in the sensitive oil and mineral sectors, combine with government agencies via the convenient cut-off of risk consultancies staffed largely by ex-intelligence personnel. Although, as a leading John Le Carré character once observed, 'no one is really "ex" in this game, old boy'.

So, why is the issue of intelligence and security agencies still important?

Because:

- Some of the old agencies continue in their old ways. The Israeli agencies' activities in the West Bank and Lebanon are a classic example. The Syrian Mukhabarat are another.

- The Western democracies' agencies have redefined their mandates without proper public debate, and this redefinition of targets already contains the seeds of future abuses.

- The huge changes in technology have vastly increased the potential for totalitarian monitoring and manipulation of public understanding.

- The fundamental democratic question of effective accountability, transparency and control remains acute – certainly in the UK, but it is of growing concern in the US case, too.

For all these reasons, an elucidation of these agencies and their changing role has become increasingly important. Certainly this is an issue that transcends old North–South divisions. Chapter 1 opens with an examination of how intelligence has defined, combated and sometimes collaborated with 'terrorism'. With the balance of conventional military power ever more decisively favouring global great powers, terrorism has been the traditional weapon of the dispossessed and of would-be insurgents. But it has also been the weapon of choice of unstable and authoritarian states – particularly in the Middle East – and, of course, of intelligence agencies in general. With threats from various forms of terrorism elevated to become the central concern of intelligence work, questions of its definition have become ever more loaded. We consider the methods governments have used to push their preferred candidates – India in Kashmir, Putin in Chechnya, Israel with the PLO, the US with just about anyone – and ask how the prospects of intelligence-led victory stand in relation to the costs imposed on civil society.

In Chapter 2, we chart the rise of new intelligence technologies. In providing an overview of technological growth areas, we consider how agency capacity is enhanced by them and report on the great effort put into research and development. Specifically, we consider the expansion of the already vast US effort – and its related activities in the UK – via the global Echelon surveillance system. The diffusion of IT worldwide is also brought into focus. Clearly a two-edged sword for intelligence agencies, it has not only transformed surveillance and intelligence gathering, but brought hitherto unimagined resources to the fingertips of ordinary people. We look at how agencies are coping with the information paradox and at attempts to control IT and the Internet in 'emerging markets' – Russia, China and throughout the South in general.

Chapter 3 is devoted to the major US agencies – the world's largest intelligence community by far. We consider how the CIA had been adapting to the post-Cold War era – notably, the fundamental shift towards business intelligence pursued under the Clinton administration and the equally dramatic about-face to more traditional targeting after 9/11. Two case studies are highly relevant here – Iraq and Afghanistan. Both concern the effects of 'blowback' on US policies, where an almost casual support has been showered on tyrannical movements and regimes in the name of an unthinking 'my enemies' enemy' expediency. The focus is also on the Agency in the context of the (somewhat involuntary) new internationalism in US foreign and security policy. This trend clearly predates the 2001 WTC attack – the efforts at cooperation with the Palestine Authority and the further integration of Echelon, for example – but it has been given a dramatic boost. We look at the return to covert operations and the drive for a multitude of new trade-offs with new allies.

Chapter 4 assesses agencies in the European Union – principally France, Germany and the UK. We look at the expansion of transnational roles and pan-European cooperation – notably in the context of the putative Common Foreign and Security Policy (CFSP). The aftermath of 9/11 has given a boost to an already massive security bandwagon, and a shared European space for the pooling of data and common policies is being cleared. We also focus on the often uneasy prior history of partnership with the US and the rise of a new Atlanticism in intelligence affairs. Chapter 5 looks at the ex-KGB. The Russian intelligence services have found new bosses, a new sponsor (Putin) and a new role in the former Soviet 'near abroad'. We chart the sometimes chaotic ups and downs of the Yeltsin period and how the Internet has helped produce the greatest security outsourcing conglomerate of all out of the Russian secret state. We consider moves afoot to resurrect the old KGB and the erosion of many of the

Yeltsin-era legal restrictions on surveillance, seizure of suspects and civil rights in general.

In Chapter 6 we look at the one country where the security services have remained unchanged since the end of the Cold War – as has the security problem. The Israeli services – Aman, Mossad and Shin Bet – are a special case in the sense that, more than any others elsewhere, they continue to operate in the old manner. Prosecuting what they see as a life-and-death struggle for the state's existence, they also maintain a global capability possibly unmatched outside the CIA. We consider the unique relationship with the US and how the cushion of unreserved US backing has allowed almost unlimited licence to Israeli agencies – not least in the US itself.

In the South, the Middle East–Central Asia region will inevitably become the hub of intelligence activities. In Chapter 7 we consider how agencies have fared since the Cold War gravy train stopped running, and how in the service of unstable and unrepresentative regimes they will take the opportunity of a 'war against terrorism' to crack down on opposition in general. We assess the transformation of intelligence in South Africa and the growing 'hired gun' role of private companies in kitting out Third World governments with security and intelligence capabilities, and the enduring role of intelligence in the governance of Burma, India and Pakistan.

Finally, in Chapter 8 we sum up developments to date and consider some pointers to a less dystopian future. We highlight the question of democratic control and try to establish its critical importance. We see what measures democratic countries, notably the US, have taken to institutionalise accountability more effectively – including the Freedom of Information Act, Congressional oversight and the role of media. And we survey current and pending European legislation and the present drive to sideline civil liberties in favour of ill-defined social control.

Notes

1 See Richard A. Best Jr for the US Congressional Research Service, *Intelligence Issues for Congress*, Washington: IB 10012 (16 August 2001) – hereafter *CRS/Intelligence*.

2 See Nicholas Guyatt, *Another American Century?* London: Zed Books, 2000, pp. 183–4.

3 See Charles Krauthammer, 'The Unipolar Moment', *Foreign Affairs*, 70, 1 (1990/1991).

4 See John J. Mearsheimer, 'Back to the Future? – Instability in Europe after the Cold War', *Atlantic*, August 1990.

CHAPTER 1

'TERRORISM'

The Dark Side of Globalisation

'The sword is the key to Paradise.' – Ruhollah Khomeini
'… dead or alive.' – George W. Bush

'Terrorism' has coexisted with intelligence services throughout their modern phase, serving not only as a principal *raison d'être* but also as a covert methodology. The concept was well established long before the current preoccupation with radical Islam as its supposedly foundational driving force. The British Special Branch owes its inception to Irish Fenian bomb outrages of the 1870s, for example, while the Russian secret service – the Okhrana – targeted the anarchist and nihilist bombers of the same era. With the 'war on terrorism' proclaimed as the guiding aim of present-day security policy by the United States and more or less every major country, it is useful to consider the current phenomenon in the light of the social stresses and ruptures accompanying the other central feature of our age – globalisation. Here, the declining autonomy of nation states and the rise of shifting non-state coalitions have provided a new terrain of opportunity not only for the disaffected but also for opportunist use and sponsorship of terrorism by states themselves.

Inevitably, given so pejorative a term, the definition of the terrorist enemy is strongly contested. Each government has its preferred candidates, but the catch-all becomes more elastic in the scramble to board what is, for some, a very timely politico-military bandwagon. Whether adopted by the dispossessed and would-be revolutionaries, by unstable and authoritarian states – in the Middle East, but also in Africa, South Asia and Latin America – or (as a matter of course) by Western agencies, the advantage of terrorism lies in degrees of deniability. While we should avoid identifying the terrorism phenomenon exclusively with Islamist fundamentalism, special attention must be paid to the unique politico-cultural milieu of the Middle East, where there is both a unifying discourse of opposition to globalisation (albeit internally fractured) and a region-wide pattern of authoritarian government and external dependency. This chapter will raise three related issues: What of state terrorism? What are the prospects of 'winning' the anti-terrorist war? And will the victory prove elusive, its aims diffused in ever more open-ended licence to pursue the struggle?

Terrorism and intelligence – Siamese twins?

After the end of the Cold War, intelligence agencies in the West moved swiftly to promote counter-terrorism – together with transnational crime – as the new target area for operations. To be sure, special pleading aside, this had some empirical justification. There was an undoubted growth in sophisticated global criminal networks and the diffusion of technology gave hitherto insignificant radical groups – some clearly 'terrorist' by any definition – a massive increase in striking power. Relations, though, between the latter and supposedly legitimate state agencies have always been clouded by a certain ambiguity.

At first sight, there is an identifiable distinction between intelligence operations, by definition conducted by states, and terrorist actions, which can be completely autonomous. In practice, however, this dichotomy tends to break down. Clearly, the whole point of covert action is deniability – the more plausible the better – and the perceived need to take effective action in the absence of a comprehensive framework of international law. As one US Congressional report put it, 'while such covert initiatives will be endorsed by few countries, they will be understood and tolerated by most'.[1] This, however, begs the question of rogue elements within intelligence services or shifting *ad hoc* alliances between state intelligence agencies, or between agencies and terrorist groups – and the uncomfortable fact that, in terms of methodology and lack of accountability, the two are close, or in some cases identical.

The emerging breed of terrorists' favoured mode, adopted by such groups as Al-Qaida, is what social scientists term 'heterarchy'[2] – that is, authority determined by knowledge or function rather than position. Within a loose framework of agreed common goals – largely, in this case, hostility to US policies – otherwise disparate groups and organisations can develop a shared field of action. This approach has flourished particularly in the Middle East, where aiding the 'enemy's enemy' has long been recognised as overriding the need for more tightly defined common purpose. Moreover, the close-knit clan and tribal linkages that do exist are suited to the use of open codes – words or phrases agreed beforehand – over the Internet and other public communications media, rather than encryption, making them, as we shall see, less vulnerable to traffic analysis. Perhaps significantly for those considering themselves as *Jihadis* or holy warriors, the heterarchical structures encouraged by the Internet are also those typical of armies in combat situations, and especially of élite forces such as the SAS. Here, a historical weakness of conventional political structures in the Middle East – their fissiparous nature – has been turned into a source of strength.

Islam and the myth of confrontation

The spread of globalisation has offered hitherto unheard-of capabilities to oppositional movements and individuals, even while it has provided, in the Islamist case, a declared primary rationale. Here, though, the ostensibly global yet anti-globalist aims of Islamists are generally linked to localised sectarian conflict and specific regional power struggles – often in close association with state agencies. The Saudi example is particularly instructive. The Saudi monarchy is a somewhat *arriviste* dynasty – finally installed as late as 1926 – and the major al-Saud claim to legitimacy stems from their role as Guardians of the Two Holy Places – Mecca and Medina. Brought to power in alliance with the puritanical Wahabi sect – the founders of modern Islamist fundamentalism – the Saudi monarchy has sought to maintain its autocratic rule by channelling internal dissatisfaction into the vigorous promotion of Wahabism internationally.

The official Saudi government English-language weekly *Ain al-Yaqeen* records that

> The cost of King Fahd's efforts in this field has been astronomical, amounting to many billions of Saudi Riyals. In terms of Islamic institutions, the result is some 210 Islamic centres wholly or partly financed by Saudi Arabia, more than 1,500 mosques and 202 colleges and almost 2,000 schools ... in Europe, North and South America, Australia and Asia. All over the world the Kingdom of Saudi Arabia has supported and contributed in the establishment of mosques and Islamic centres.[3]

Whilst the stated rationale is to 'challenge ... the bias against Islam, the tendency, in some quarters, to identify Islam with fanaticism or even terrorism', for many non-Wahabi Muslims it is the sectarian bias within the Islam promoted by the Saudi-financed mosques and *madrassas* (religious schools) that is the issue. In the US, an estimated 80 per cent of mosques catering to the Muslim community of ten million are Wahabi.[4] As one concerned Muslim observer points out, 'children of the immigrants ... get exposed only to this one-sided version of Islam, and are led to think this is the only Islam'.[5] And in the view of senior University of California academic and author Seyyed Nasr,

> The 'rogue states' are less important in the radicalisation of Islam than Saudi Arabia. Saudi Arabia is the single most important cause and supporter of radicalisation, ideologisation, and general fanaticism of Islam ... if the United States wants to do something about radical Islam, it has to deal with Saudi Arabia.[6]

The official figures, vast as they are, are matched by the many private donations to Islamic charities and from wealthy individuals to a variety of Islamist causes – notably, militant groups throughout the Middle East. This largesse has the multi-purpose agenda of establishing a measure of radical credibility, trading intelligence and bringing potentially hostile or threatening radical groups onside. The former head of Saudi Intelligence – Prince Turki al-Faisal – played this role in Afghanistan, albeit in rivalry with the Interior Ministry Intelligence of Prince Nayef, which had been energetically trying to extend its reach both inside the country and abroad.[7]

The Taliban were long-term beneficiaries of Saudi largesse – private and public – as were their sponsors in Pakistan. For decades, Pakistan has enjoyed a close security and intelligence relationship with Saudi Arabia, which has bankrolled Pakistani Islamist parties such as Jama'at-e-Islami and a large number of *madrassas* – effectively replacing the state education system in areas like the North West Frontier. Also in receipt of Saudi funding are the FIS (Front for Islamic Salvation) in Algeria, many Egyptian organisations such as the Muslim Brotherhood and Gama'at al-Islami, and the People's National Front in Sudan, headed by the would-be Lenin of East African Islam, Hassan al-Turabi.[8]

The former Soviet territories of Central Asia are a further focus of Saudi efforts, where Islamist charities and Tadjik and Turkic translations of the Koran have been massively promoted in fierce competition with the *mullahs* of Tehran – which formed an important subtext in the Rushdie affair. A graphic manifestation of the religious tensions coursing beneath the surface of Saudi society erupted in the attempted takeover of the grand mosque in Mecca in 1979. The coup leader, Jouhaiman al-Utaibi, was a protégé of senior Saudi *mufti* Muhammed al-Baz.[9] Whilst Jouhaiman and some 68 followers were publicly beheaded in the coup's bloody aftermath, another favoured pupil of al-Baz has remained in public prominence – Osama bin Laden.

A new internationalism?
The US experience before and after 9/11

Given that a widespread perception of US unilateralism has been an avowed *casus belli* for terrorists – certainly of the Islamist variety – much would seem to hang on Washington's post-9/11 international response.

President Bush's State of the Union speech of 29 January 2002 took up the threat to the US from regimes that 'sponsor terror' and are pursuing weapons of mass destruction. Declaring that 'states like' Iran, Iraq and North Korea 'and their terrorist allies constitute an axis of evil, arming to threaten the peace of the world', Bush promised military aid to 'governments everywhere' in the fight against terrorism. Students of US foreign policy will recognise clear parallels with the 'free peoples everywhere' universalism of the March 1947 Truman Doctrine and the 'pay any price' rhetoric of the Kennedys. The State Department has claimed, in its April 2001 report on *Patterns of Global Terrorism*, that approximately 47 per cent of all terrorist incidents worldwide were committed against US citizens or property.[10] Leaving aside the highly contested definition of the term itself, it is easy to see how terrorism has seamlessly replaced communism as the mobilising logic of US internationalism in the face of a self-proclaimed rival universal creed – fundamentalist Islam. It is the frame for a very big tent of US concerns embracing oil, the Arab–Israeli conflict, potential mass destruction and a more inchoate, visceral challenge to the wholesale identification of US policies with global capitalist values, embodied in the now famous formulary of the 'clash of civilisations'.[11]

Notwithstanding the evident self-serving and agenda packing of the above, the sheer cinematic horror of 9/11 and a more pragmatic recognition of mutual interest have lent the administration much international support. By late November 2001, agencies in some 50 countries had arrested over 360 suspects with alleged connections to Al-Qaida, mirroring the massive 1,200-person round-up of suspects in the US itself. And a total of 136 countries offered varying degrees of support for Operation Enduring Freedom. By March 2002, US special forces and CIA anti-terrorist personnel were deployed in the Philippines (650), Yemen (100) and the former Soviet republic of Georgia (180)[12] as well as the large regular contingent in the military front line in Afghanistan and former Soviet territories in Central Asia.

From the perspective of some in the US intelligence community, such moves are long overdue. In a widely cited – and highly prescient – article of July 2001, ex-CIA operative Reuel Marc Gerecht noted the reluctance of the Agency to conduct clandestine operations under 'non-official cover', the refusal to engage in local milieux away from the business/embassy circuit and the total absence of staff trained in local languages. 'America's counter-terrorism programme in the Middle East and its environs,' declared Gerecht, a former Directorate of Operations chief, 'is a myth.'[13] Scrambling to make up for lost time, the Agency was to massively expand its Humint capabilities, including the stationing of operatives in various combat support roles. The Special Activities Division, responsible for covert actions, and the paramilitary Special Operations Group were amongst the first US personnel to deploy in Afghanistan after 11 September. Operating in conjunction with technological aids such as the Predator and Global Hawk unmanned aerial vehicles (UAVs),[14] the CIA was to mount a covert warfare effort unseen since Vietnam.[15] The FBI's more prominent anti-terrorist role was reflected in the stationing of officers in some 44 countries and expanded training of allied personnel.[16]

The economic taproot of terrorism has also come in for sustained attention. Within the US, the Treasury Department's Financial Crime Enforcement Network – FinCen – uses the increasingly widespread data-mining techniques to identify 'suspicious' bank transactions of $5,000 or more,[17] and efforts are being made to spread the technology internationally. It remains a major problem, however, that much financial traffic in the Middle East and throughout the Islamic world generally is carried by shadowy *hawala* chains of money brokers, whose clan-based relationships are virtually untraceable. On 25 September 2001, President Bush signed executive order 13324 freezing the assets of 27 organisations believed to be affiliated with Al-Qaida and giving the US Treasury broad powers to impose sanctions around the world on banks viewed as not cooperating. From January 2002, 168 groups, entities and individuals were covered by the order. For this initiative, too, Washington was able to secure widespread international support. UN Resolution 1373 of 28 September 2001 required UN member states to deny money, support and sanctuary to terrorists. As of April 2002 some $104 million in suspected terrorist assets had been blocked in more than 140 countries.[18]

In addition to seeking broad diplomatic support and strengthening ties with its established allies, the US administration has looked to rapprochement with hitherto suspect regimes. Pakistan provides a prominent example, with the US reversing previous strictures on categories of dual-use exports and muting its opposition to Islamabad's nuclear weapons programme. The CIA was close to Pakistan's intelligence service, the Inter-Services Intelligence (ISI), during the Cold War, and this relationship has been rekindled. Agents of the recently purged ISI were quick to seize suspected killers of US journalist Daniel Pearl – one of the few known cases where suspected terrorists have been traced through e-mail. (The abductors used Hotmail, Microsoft's Web-based e-mail service, to announce their deed.) And in early April 2002 more than 60 Al-Qaida operatives were arrested in Faisalabad, along with Abu Zubayda, the organisation's third-highest-ranking member. Pakistani federal police agents, accompanied by FBI agents from the US, were said to be acting on an overheard telephone conversation between Zubayda and Osama bin Laden. Yet the extent of a genuine desire for cooperation with the US on the part of even a reformed ISI is uncertain. The leading figure in the Pearl investigation, former British public schoolboy Ahmad Sheikh, had surrendered voluntarily to a retired ISI officer under circumstances which remain unclear. And a great many Taliban and 'Arab Afghans' found ready sanctuary in Pakistan's North West Frontier Province after the start of US military operations.

Also responsive to US attention are Yemen – which is hosting US personnel – and terrorist-list countries Libya and Sudan, who have come forward with condemnations of the WTC bombing and offers of some level of intelligence pooling. Sudan, in particular, is hoping for a period of normalisation in its relations with Washington and removal from the State Department's blacklist. A US Special Envoy, former Senator John Danforth, was appointed on 6 September 2001 and met with the ruling National Islamic Front (NIF) in late November that year. Sudan's recent harbouring of a range of Islamist militant organisations – including Hizbollah, Palestinian Islamic Jihad, Hamas, Egyptian Gama'at al-Islami and, most famously, Al-Qaida itself (1991–6) – is of great interest to US intelligence. And according to Secretary of State Colin Powell, the Khartoum regime has indeed 'been rather forthcoming in giving us access to certain individuals within the country and taking other actions which demonstrate to us a change of attitude'.[19]

As for the 'axis' countries themselves, whilst Iraq is clearly *sui generis*, North Korea signed two international anti-terrorism conventions in November 2001 (albeit with some reservations); Iran has been 'in discussion' with US officials on the Afghan situation and received a visit from the British Foreign Secretary. For both the US and UK, past diplomatic effort has proved at least partially effective in modifying policy. By focusing on individual issues, they can cultivate trade-offs with the shifting and volatile internal ruling élites. Iran is a particular case in point, with the President and a probable majority of the population seeking better relations with the West in fierce opposition to the clerics and security establishment.

For both, foreign policy is viewed overwhelmingly as an index of commitment to be manipulated in the domestic power struggle. And as many in Europe have been observing, the Bush hard line will have the same effect as previous US policy, notably the failed (Iran–Iraq) 'dual containment' of the Clinton years: reinventing the Great Satan. From an intelligence point of view, this could have unfortunate consequences for US efforts. Iran's Ministry of Intelligence and Security (VEVAK) runs an extensive network internationally, in competition with Military Intelligence and the Pasdaran Revolutionary Guards. There is potentially a fertile field for cooperation *vis-à-vis* the Sunni Muslim – and particularly, Wahabi – networks in the Middle East. Whether such pragmatism will obtain in Washington in the light of Iran/Contra – still a sore point for the Bush administration – and memories of the 1979 hostage affair, remains to be seen.

Despite some tensions over US troop deployments in Central Asia, Russian President Vladimir Putin was quick to link the US war on terrorism with the Kremlin's own long-running conflict in Chechnya. Stressing the established links between bin Laden and Chechen Islamist fighters, the Russian intelligence agency FSB, now in overall charge of the war, was to provide details of some 55 Al-Qaida camps and bases in Afghanistan and much detail of the network's infrastructure.[20]

The new Russia–US rapprochement in intelligence matters reflects, perhaps, the re-emergence of a more pragmatic cast of US official mind, as opposed to the residual Cold War reflexes of the early Bush presidency. Generally, US anti-terrorism policy from the late 1970s to the mid-1990s focused on state sponsors rather than the groups themselves. Whilst there were many high-profile and undoubtedly terrorist actions against the US in the 1980s – Beirut (1983), West Berlin (1985), Lockerbie (1988) – the inclination in the Bush senior and Reagan administrations was to link these, however indirectly, to the Soviet Union. However, following the end of the Cold War and, in particular, the close intelligence cooperation between the US and Moscow during the Gulf War (1990-1), the changed international realities dictated a shift of focus. By 1993, only 13 per cent of the intelligence budget was aimed at Russia,[21] and international narcotics, organised crime and a then somewhat amorphous 'international terrorism' became the buzzwords of the day.

Anti-terrorism – the legislative background

Although historically the FBI has been charged with the counter-espionage and, by extension, counter-terrorist mission within the metropolitan US, it was the CIA that made an early move to adapt to the new climate when it established a Counter-Terrorist Center (CTC) at its Langley headquarters in 1986. Claiming a range of successful operations from 'the uncovering of Libya's role in the bombing of Pan Am 103 to the thwarting of Ramzi Yousef's attempts to blow a dozen United States airliners out of the sky in 1995', the CTC has had an equally important quasi-diplomatic role in the training of personnel from allied and client countries in a similar fashion to the Army's Fort Benning, Georgia, and the controversial International Police Academy (IPA), closed down in 1975. In 1998 Senate testimony, CIA Director George Tenet was to state that, 'over 18,000 individuals in 50 nations have been trained in counter-terrorism in the past decade'.[22]

The Clinton administration was to see the shape of things to come. It was the (at the time) scarcely credible attempt by the same Ramzi Yousef to blow up the World Trade Center on 26 February 1993, followed by attempted bombings of the UN building, the FBI New

York office and Lincoln and Holland road tunnels by Egyptian Islamist Sheikh Omar Abdel Rahman which cast existing 'anti-terrorist ' efforts in an entirely new light. Little noticed at the time of general media condescension to the WTC bombers' somewhat rustic methodology – they had returned to claim a deposit from the truck hire company – was trial technical evidence that, with two or three times the explosive, the plot could have been all too successful.[23]

The Antiterrorism and Effective Death Penalty Act (1996) signalled an important shift in US policy, away from state sponsors to independent groups and non-state actors. It created a new legal category of 'foreign terrorist organisations' (FTOs) and banned funding, visas and other material support. The Act also established guidelines for the seizure or 'rendering' of terrorist suspects from abroad and authorised the Secretary of State to designate terrorist organisations and states deemed to be sponsoring terror, which are published in an annual report on *Patterns of Global Terrorism*.

Further moves included the establishment of a Committee on Transnational Threats within the National Security Council (NSC) – aiming to 'enhance ... the coordination of ... Federal Law Enforcement and elements of the intelligence community outside the United States with respect to transnational threats'. The Bush administration subsequently transferred these responsibilities to the NSC Policy Coordinating Committee on Counter Terrorism and National Preparedness.[24] In 1998, two presidential decision directives (PDDs 62/3) created a National Coordinator for Security, Infrastructure Protection and Counter-Terrorism within the NSC and set up a National Infrastructure Protection Agency under the aegis of the FBI, bringing together Intelligence and Defense Department personnel.

Finally, in the charged aftermath of 11 September, the Bush administration moved to coordinate international and domestic anti-terrorist efforts in a new Office of Homeland Security. Set up by executive order 13228 on 8 October 2001, the OHS combines intelligence and law enforcement agencies under the aegis of a Homeland Security Council (HSC) similar in structure and function to the NSC. The HSC was designated as the 'principal forum for consideration of policy', amending a previous 1988 executive order assigning such responsibility to the NSC. However, as the (presidentially appointed) HSC National Director, General Wayne Downing, is also Deputy National Security Advisor for Combating Terrorism, the chain of command goes directly to the National Security Advisor. Since NSC members do not generally appear before Congress, this effectively rests the whole area of anti-terrorism strategy in the hands of presidential appointees and the White House itself – particularly under conditions of (presidentially declared) 'national emergency'.

The enactment of the Uniting and Strengthening of America to Provide Tools Required to Intercept and Obstruct Terrorism Act – 'USA-Patriot' – on 26 October, after a hectic 24-day passage, may also give more reflectively minded Congress members pause to repent at leisure. Forming a legislative counterpoint to OHS provisions, it gave increased authority to investigate suspected terrorists and authorised 'roving' (or practically unlimited) wiretaps and disclosure of foreign intelligence information obtained in criminal investigations to intelligence and national security officials – breaking down the long-established 'firewall' on such inter-agency information pooling.

Also included in the rush of legislation were revisions to 1995 guidelines restricting CIA recruitment of contract staff with 'unsavoury backgrounds', introduced after a slew of damaging revelations of CIA human rights abuses in Guatemala and elsewhere. Section 403 of the Foreign Intelligence Authorisation Act (2002) instructs the CIA's Director to rescind ordinances involving 'foreign assets or sources with known human rights violations'. And section 903 of USA-Patriot expressed the 'sense of the Congress' that US agents 'should make every effort to establish and maintain intelligence relationships with any person, entity or group' with possible information on terrorism.[25] With oversight responsibility spread between as many as ten Congressional (House/Senate) committees and numerous sub-committees, the ultimate scope for initiative and chain of command accountability is far from clear. There is still, in the US, widespread opposition both to altering the proscriptions in the 1947 National Security Act on the CIA gaining law enforcement powers and to wholesale revision of the 1879 *Posse Comitatus* statutes that regulate any involvement in law enforcement by the military. It is, however, worth stepping back from the current atmosphere of crisis to review some recent antecedents.

Terrorism redux – the Reagan–Bush years

'Terrorism' as a stand-alone term first came into widespread circulation in the US political discourse at the end of the 1970s. It was, as a Marxist might say, no accident. The resurgent US right was searching for a suitably unifying global issue to counterpose to the human rights agenda promoted by the Carter administration. However dilatory the actual pursuit of human rights became under the man from Plains, Georgia, the threat to numerous unsavoury US client regimes in the Third World and, above all, to the occupation policies of the greatest client of them all – Israel – was all too clear.

The election of Ronald Reagan in 1980 saw two initiatives come to fruition in this field. The first policy shift was enacted through a series of directives on expanding the Federal Emergency Management Agency (FEMA). The latter body took on sweeping powers for the suspension of civil liberties and military rule under somewhat vaguely specified conditions of 'national emergency'. Like its direct offspring, the OHS, FEMA was based in the NSC and designed to 'provide maximum flexibility to the President for his [sic] implementation of emergency actions'.[26] Closely related, but perhaps even more directly relevant both conceptually and dynastically to post 9/11 planning, was the 1985 creation of the Vice-President's Task Force on Combating Terrorism, under then Vice-President and former CIA Director, George Bush senior. The task force – its profile was eclipsed somewhat after revelations of its central role in Iran/Contra – was also concerned with contingency planning for the large-scale internment of domestic dissidents and 'terrorist aliens'. More recently, the 31 January 2001 report of the bi-partisan Commission on National Security recommended merging the Coast Guard, Border Guard and Customs Service with FEMA as 'in effect, a national homeland security agency'.[27] Another proposal is that the National Guard be given domestic security as a primary mission.

The plans, frustrated in the past by bureaucratic infighting, surfaced again in a massively expanded form in the Office of Homeland

Security. And in a further recrudescence of 1980s-style White House security activism, the administration set up two new agencies – the Information Awareness Office (IAO) and its associated Information Exploitation Office (IEO). Both are offshoots of the Pentagon's Defense Advanced Projects Agency (DARPA) and aim to provide coordinated intelligence on both domestic and overseas phone and e-mail traffic, with the IEO tasked to provide targeting information for an 'instant' response. The new head of the IAO, recruited from DARPA associate, Synteck Technologies, is a leading Iran-Contra veteran and former National Security Advisor, John M. Poindexter.[28]

Western Europe – rolling the new bandwagon

The expanding boundaries of the EU are no stranger to terrorism, however defined. In the past, this has stemmed largely from nationalist breakaway movements such as the Irish Republican Army (IRA), the Basque ETA and the Corsican FNLC. This has led to highly organised counter-terror campaigns run by the UK and Spain, for example, conducted with various degrees of legality. Neither is Islamist terror-ism a new phenomenon in Europe. These cells have often been tolerated, however, for intelligence-gathering purposes and reasons of national advantage. Iran, for example, maintains a large intelligence operation in Germany with considerable terrorist crossover, tolerated in some measure by the Bundesnachrichtendienst (BND).[29]

The World Trade Center bombing and frustrated attempts by the same network to blow up the US Paris embassy have prompted a rethink on some of these policies – along with much international mudslinging. Leading Islamist cleric Abu Qatada – wanted on terrorist charges by eight police forces internationally – was living openly in Acton, West London, from 1993 to December 2001, prompting spec-ulation of incompetence, if not out-and-out collusion, by the UK intelligence services.[30]

Overall, though, the surge in terrorism has strengthened the case of those urging a greater integration and expansion of the EU's collective intelligence and law enforcement powers. The integrationists received a powerful boost with moves to set up a Common Foreign and

Security Policy (CFSP), agreed in principle at the Treaty of Maastricht (1991) and given institutional form at the Treaty of Amsterdam (1997). EU efforts to coordinate 'sources of intelligence' first received specific mention in the Anglo-French Declaration of St-Malo (December 1998) and was given further impetus by the Kosovo conflict and the Cologne Summit (June 1999) which called for 'the reinforcement of our capabilities in the field of Intelligence'.[31]

Whilst efforts to coordinate law enforcement and intelligence have long been in train under the auspices of the transatlantic ILETS (International Law Enforcement Telecommunications Seminar) and the EU-wide ENFOPOL (Law Enforcement Police Matters), these have focused mainly on football hooligans and anti-globalisation protesters, with the former providing a convenient rationale for the much greater importance placed on combating the latter. These efforts have focused on creating pan-European data sharing on 'troublemakers' coordinated by the established Schengen protocols on cross-border intelligence cooperation.[32]

With a rising tide of increasingly massive and well-organised protests at major EU summits, notably the EU Gothenburg Summit (July 2001), the EU Justice and Home Affairs Council, at a special meeting on 13 July, agreed a raft of measures restricting the right of free movement and the right to protest, and providing for general surveillance of political activity. Whilst not legally binding at the time, these included the expansion of national databases on, 'persons or groups likely to pose a threat to public order and security', and 'more structured exchanges of data on violent troublemakers on the basis of national files'.[33] The council agreed that all legal instruments should be used 'to prevent such individuals' from crossing national borders where it is believed they are 'travelling with the intention of ... participating in serious disturbances'. Following the mayhem at the 2001 Genoa G8 Summit – provoked, in the eyes of most observers, by unrestrained Italian police violence – EU interior ministers agreed to set up permanent mechanisms for exchanging information on protesters and to establish a pool of police/intelligence liaison staff before each future summit, staffed by officers from countries where the perceived main 'risk groups' originated. Whilst German calls for a pan-European, FBI–style, international force were rejected, the extended cooperation undertaken within the Schengen system is viewed as preparing the way for extending the international competence of the European police force Europol, at present limited in scope to international crime and drug trafficking. Finally, in the aftermath of 11 September, the Council of the EU began debating the creation of two new EU-wide databases, the first to target 'potentially dangerous persons' under the Schengen system to restrict cross-border travel, and the second to establish a register of all third-party nationals in the EU on the model of the German Central Foreigners Register.

The EU's 'Anti-terrorism roadmap' will advance intelligence integration further under moves urged by the 2002 Spanish Presidency. EU justice and interior ministers agreed a doubling of the Europol budget at a meeting on 28 February 2002 to enable expansion of its anti-terrorism remit; under further proposals a new intelligence services office will be created under the EU's foreign affairs chief, Javier Solana. Viewed as complementary to the expanding CFSP platform, the moves are still couched in such a way as to avoid infringing sovereignty considerations, especially amongst non-NATO EU states. As tabled by the Spanish Defence Minister, Frederico Trillo, the proposals stress that, 'This is not a new intelligence service, nor a joint intelligence service. It is a question of coordinating the efforts of the different services relative to information on terrorism from the outside.'[34]

In the UK, both the Secret Intelligence Service (SIS–MI 6) and the Security Service (MI 5) had repositioned themselves energetically to take on expanded anti-terrorism missions after the end of the Cold War. For SIS, the advent of David Spedding as Director in 1994 had seen the setting up of the Global Tasks Controllerate, which merged some of the existing six geographical controllerates (London, Middle East, Far East, Western Hemisphere, Western/Eastern Europe and Africa). Africa and the Middle East were merged, as were the Far East and the Western Hemisphere. Also elevated was operational support for the assistance of deep cover operations overseas.[35] With counter-espionage and subversion clearly looking threadbare to an increasingly cash-strapped Treasury in the early 1990s, incoming MI 5 head Stella

Rimington seized upon counter-terrorism as the principal new rationale for the agency.[36] New roles were also eagerly sought in the expanding Europol, with which MI 5 has been maintaining a permanent liaison since the early 1990s.

Despite much stress on the terrorism threat in the mid-1990s, the reality for both intelligence services was the threat of budget cuts and increasing opening to 'market discipline' from the Treasury.[37] The enduring IRA ceasefire after the exemplary bombings of 1996 seemed also to give fresh scope for Treasury cost-cutters. The advent of a palpable terrorist campaign in the aftermath of 9/11, however, was to herald a new era of activism and budget loosening unseen since the height of the Cold War. MI 5, MI 6 and Government Communications Headquarters (GCHQ) are believed to have put in separate bids for more than £2.4 billion to cover expansion in 2001–4. MI 6 made particular gains, receiving an immediate £15 million extra funding on top of its acknowledged £200 million annual budget, with a view to eventually doubling in size to some 3,000 personnel. MI 5 was to seek an extra £30 million to fund a 20 per cent staff increase above the existing 1,750 to an estimated 2,300. For both agencies, recruitment of Muslim and ethnic minority personnel is a priority. Public advertising – cautiously introduced by Century House in the early 1990s – is being specifically targeted at the ethnic press, with a new MI 5 logo and an appeal to 'make the world a safer place'. In MI 6, the established Oxbridge nod-and-wink procedure is being succeeded by the 'need to be in the back streets of Bradford, looking for bright young people'.[38]

These strands came together in the Anti-terrorism, Crime, and Security Bill (November 2001). David Blunkett, the Home Secretary, sought a wide-ranging package of measures on detention, surveillance and expanded scope for prosecution. The 125 clauses also extended the powers of the Ministry of Defence Police to operate outside MOD property and, controversially, included a raft of EU criminal law – the 1997 harmonisation measures – as 'secondary legislation' not subject to full parliamentary debate. If these new laws on surveillance and internment without trial were pleasing to some sections of the intelligence establishment, the provisions for confidential information to be available from 81 government agencies, from the BBC to the NHS, caused widespread concern even from the opposition Conservative Party. Shadow Home Secretary Oliver Letwin observed that the Bill would allow generalised access to 'somebody's records, even if they were being investigated for a traffic offence in the US'.[39]

Israel – 'manipulating the Bush doctrine'

If security agencies worldwide have scrambled to jump aboard the Bush administration's war on terrorism, nowhere has the opportunity been seized more avidly than in Israel. For the embattled Sharon government in particular, the chance to identify US efforts with its own long-sought ambition to dismantle the Palestine Authority (PA), established in 1994, and the overall framework of the Oslo peace accords in general, was one to be taken with alacrity.

While initially Sharon was wrongfooted by adroit Palestinian diplomacy in the immediate aftermath of 9/11 – including an early meeting by Yasser Arafat with Tony Blair and an unequivocal condemnation of the bombing by the PLO Chairman – the heightened tempo of Israeli Defence Force (IDF) and Shin Bet (Sherut ha-Bitachon ha-Klali – Internal Security Service) assassinations, and the increasing use of air strikes and heavy armour, was to draw the always loosely controlled Palestinian armed factions into a deadly spiral of response. Aided by a vociferous media campaign in the US, Israel was able to secure the almost complete dismantling of the PA security apparatus – whose cooperation with Israel and the CIA had been 'widely credited with keeping terrorist attacks to a minimum' in one US report[40] – and the arrest of senior officials such as West Bank security chief Marwan Barghouti[41] rendered the prospect of maintaining peace physically impossible, even given support for this objective within the PLO ruling councils.

Indeed, Israel's longstanding policy of 'targeted killings' of suspected Palestinian militants – from a reported shortlist[42] of 453 – and its Spring 2002 round-up of an admitted 1,200 civilians and security personnel have caused even its close ally and patron some unease. Israel's covert Mista'averim (Marauder) Squads, operating deep in the

Palestinian territories, had claimed over 60 killings before 9/11, and were to expand their operations massively with the reoccupation in Spring 2002. In the view of one prominent former CIA anti-terrorist official, 'the Israeli policy of targeted killings has simply legitimised extremism. The result is that Arafat has less and less influence to exert as the Islamic terrorists gain more prestige.'[43] Amongst the targets were many from the PA's Preventive Security Service (PSS), whose headquarters was destroyed in shelling. Standing outside the gutted building, the head of the unit stated that it is 'not my priority' to stop attacks on Israel. 'I don't think it's possible for us, after this sea of blood, to talk about security coordination or any kind of coordination with Israel. It's over.'[44] The PSS and its leader, Jibril Rajoub, were long-term associates of the CIA and regarded as 'the only Palestinian security service with the potential to enforce a ceasefire'.[45] Their continuing viability was regarded as critical in ensuring the previously agreed Tenet Plan for Israeli–Palestinian security cooperation, underpinning the US-brokered Mitchell ceasefire proposals of April 2001.[46] The unusually high-profile role assumed by the Agency in mediating between Israeli and Palestinian security forces had been strongly criticised in both the US and Israel, with the Netanyahu government in particular taking exception to this latest undermining of its stonewalling tactics on the security issue.

President Bush felt compelled to offer a clarification of his doctrine on terrorism on 1 April 2002, stating that Arafat's past as a peace negotiator exempts the Palestinian leader from the post-9/11 US policy that a country or entity harbouring terrorists will be dealt with as terrorists. The administration's recognition that 'It would not serve our purpose right now to brand him individually as a terrorist,' as Secretary of State Colin Powell put it,[47] met with widespread condemnation from Israeli public figures, notably former Prime Minister Ehud Barak. But the White House was careful to maintain the distinction between approaches to Arafat (and the mainstream PLO) and named 'foreign terrorist organisations' such as Al-Qaida. 'The situation in the Middle East is, indeed, different,' said White House spokesman Ari Fleischer, who noted that Arafat signed the 1993 Oslo accords, under which the Palestinian movement for the first time recognised Israel's right to exist. 'That was not, is not, the case with Al-Qaida. And I understand you (reporters) want to compare them, but that's not a comparison that the President accepts.' In the view of senior US analyst Joe Montville, director of the preventive diplomacy programme at the Georgetown Center for Strategic and International Studies, by exempting Arafat, Bush also made it clear to Israeli Prime Minister Ariel Sharon that he will not allow Israel to manipulate the Bush doctrine at will. 'He implies that Arafat is not running the terrorist initiatives like a guy sitting at the Wurlitzer, controlling the movements,' Montville said. 'He is telling Sharon … for better or worse, Yasser Arafat is the symbol of the Palestinian nation, and we have to deal with him. Sharon can call Arafat the enemy of all mankind. And it simply won't work.'[48]

However, in the light of likely PLO complicity in the import of some 50 tonnes of arms, traced and seized from Washington's *bête noire*, Iran, and more sharply contested Israeli evidence of direct PLO funding for suicide bombers,[49] the administration would seem to be in danger of being dragged willy-nilly on a course set by Israel's agenda. Not the least of White House worries is the trenchant US Israeli lobby – exemplified by the 'banish Arafat' rhetoric of columnist Charles Krauthammer[50] and calls from Dick Armey, Republican House leader, to expel the Palestinian population from the West Bank altogether. The President, in the view of one *Wall Street Journal* editorial, has 'lost his foreign policy bearings' in calling for Israeli withdrawal from the occupied territories, and the President himself will be acutely aware of the fate meted out to Bush senior on the much less contentious issue of withholding Israeli loan guarantees.

In the eyes of some analysts there has indeed been a strengthening of intelligence and military links between elements of Iran's Pasdaran and the Shi'ite Lebanese Hizbollah guerrilla organisation – increasingly allied to more militant PLO factions such as Palestinian Islamic Jihad. In some reports, the linkage was strengthened in a clandestine meeting in Moscow in May 2001 between two top Yasser Arafat aides and Iranian government officials. The meeting allegedly took place while Arafat was visiting President Putin and led directly to the seized arms shipment mentioned above. Denial and counter-claim notwithstanding, there is at least circumstantial evidence for inter-agency collusion at some level.[51] And whilst Israel's Mossad was quick to claim another intelligence coup, more thoughtful observers within the US intelligence community were pointing to the impact of Israeli occupation policies on the fostering of extremism throughout the region. CIA Director George Tenet told Congress that Iran's political reformers were losing momentum in the long-running battle for power with the conservative clerics who control the Iranian intelligence and security agencies and warned that, in true 'enemy's enemy' Middle East fashion, alliances were being forged between Tehran and its hitherto deadly rival, Al-Qaida.[52]

The emergence of a composite Islamic terrorist demon, opposed to Israel and the US alike, has clearly become the conventional line in Israeli pronouncements, even if a significant part of the spin is imparted in the intelligence domain. Repeated claims of a direct Arafat role in promoting terrorism have been at issue here, partly, some in the CIA believe, as the by-product of an ongoing turf war between the more sceptical Shin Bet and Israeli Military Intelligence – Aman – who push for a 'worst-case scenario'. On more than one occasion, Israeli agencies have foisted inaccurate reports of Iranian and other external involvement in the Intifada on their US counterparts.[53] And Israeli intelligence activities closer to home may also give the US pause for reflection. Largely unnoticed in the mass arrests and detentions in the US following 9/11 was the presence among the arrestees of some 200 Israeli citizens. In a report leaked by the US Drug Enforcement Administration (DEA), these arrestees 'may well be an organised intelligence gathering activity'.[54] Although no allegation of espionage has been made, the arrest of staff of the two Israeli-owned companies currently performing wiretaps for local and Federal law enforcement[55] led to handwritten warnings delivered to FBI Director Mueller and Attorney General Ashcroft that 'law enforcement's current electronic surveillance capabilities' were at risk of compromise.

A clash of bandwagons?

Former US National Security Council consultant Samuel Huntington – who coined the 'clash of civilisations' concept in a widely cited

Foreign Affairs article of 1993 – has been quick, in the current crisis, to add some qualification to his prognosis. 'I don't think Islam is any more violent than any other religions,' Huntington observed. 'Islam, like any great religion, can be interpreted in a variety of ways.'[56] As indeed, can readings of his own text. Certainly, it has been seized upon by sections of the Islamist movement. As Huntington admits, 'Osama bin-Laden wants it to be a clash of civilisations between Islam and the West.' And, as we have seen, the concept has provided a ready template to advance the often longstanding legislative and policy agendas of state security services, catapulted to the front line in the 'war against terror'. Across the board, budgetary purse strings are loosening and career prospects blooming as never before. But just as the Cold War provided a legitimising framework for the unprincipled and frequently counterproductive waging of covert warfare, so the dangers of a new era of intelligence 'blowback' are all too clear. If Israel provides the most blatant example of such bandwagoning, the shadow of a vast new framework of surveillance and control is looming globally, providing the terrain for what may turn out to be the real clash – between unaccountable power and civilisation itself.

Notes

1 Richard A. Best for the US Congressional Research Service (hereafter CRS), *Intelligence and Law Enforcement: Countering Transnational Threats to the US*, RL30252: 16 January 2001 (hereafter CRS/Threats), p. 27.

2 See Michael Wilson, *Considering the Net as an Intelligence Tool*, Decision Support Systems/INFO@METATEMPO.COM, 1996–2002, p. 6.

3 See *Ain al-Yaqeen*, 1 March 2002, cited in Middle East Monitoring and Research Institute (MEMRI), *Special Dispatch Series No. 360*, 27 March 2002.

4 Cited in Stephen Schwarz, 'This Business All Began in Saudi Arabia', *Sunday Telegraph*, 23 September 2001.

5 Bengali writer Zeeshan Ali, cited in *ibid*.

6 Ibid.

7 Richard Norton-Taylor, 'Dirty War That Could Prove Decisive', *Guardian*, 2 October 2001.

8 See Al Venter, 'Sudan's Spymaster: Hassan al-Turabi', *Pointer*, July 1998.

9 See Amir Taheri, *Holy Terror*, London: Sphere, 1987, pp. 159–63.

10 See Rensselaer Lee and Raphael Perl for CRS, *Terrorism, the Future and US Foreign Policy* (hereafter CRS/Terrorism), IB95112: 18 April 2002, p. 5.

11 See Samuel P. Huntington, 'A Clash of Civilisations?', *Foreign Affairs*, Summer 1993.

12 See Bob Woodward, 'CIA Plays Key Role in War on Terror', *Washington Post*, 22 November 2001; see also, CRS/Terrorism, p. 2.

13 See Reuel Marc Gerecht, 'The Counterterrorist Myth', *Atlantic Monthly*, July/ August 2001.

14 Richard Best for CRS, *Intelligence Issues for Congress* (hereafter CRS/Issues), IB10012: 7 December 2001, p. 13.

15 See 'CIA Has Special Paramilitary Force', *Guardian*, 2 December 2001.

16 CRS/Terrorism, p. 16.

17 See Eric Chabrow, 'Tracking the Terrorists', *Information Week*, 10 January 2002.

18 CRS/Terrorism, p. 4.

19 Ted Dagne for CRS, *Sudan: Humanitarian Crisis, Peace Talks, Terrorism and US Policy* (hereafter CRS/Sudan), p. 2.

20 See Norton-Taylor, 'Dirty War'.

21 As opposed to 53 per cent in 1980. See James Bamford, *Body of Secrets: How America's NSA and Britain's GCHQ Eavesdrop upon the World*, London: Century, 2001, p. 553.

22 CRS/Threats, p. 19.

23 Barton Gellman, 'From Third Tier to Top Gear: How the US Anti-Terror Fight Evolved', *International Herald Tribune*, 21 December 2001.

24 CRS/Threats, p. 20.

25 CRS/Issues, p. 5.

26 See Diana Reynolds, 'The Rise of the National Security State', *Covert Action Information Bulletin*, 33 (Winter 1990): 54–9.

27 CRS/Terrorism, pp. 14–15.

28 *Guardian*, 18 February 2002.

29 See, for example, Olivier Schmidt (ed.), 'Germany: Iranian Leaks Make It to Israel', *Intelligence*, 36 (April 1996): 58; 'Open House, but Low Morale at the BND', *Intelligence*, 39 (June 1996): 44–5.

30 See Barnet *et al.*, 'Britain's Most Wanted', *Observer*, 5 May 2002.

31 See Ole R.Villadsen, 'Prospects for a Common European Intelligence Policy', http://www.cia.gov/csi/studies/summer00/art07.html), pp. 2–3.

32 Schengen is a small town in Luxembourg where (in March 1995) seven EU countries signed a treaty to end internal border checkpoints and controls. By 2003 there were 15 Schengen countries, all in Europe.

33 See 'The Enemy Within', *Statewatch Report 1*, August 2001, p. 1.

34 See Ian Black, 'EU Plan to Pool Anti-terrorism Intelligence', *Guardian*, 2 March 2002.

35 See Mark Urban, *UK Eyes Alpha*, London: Faber, 1996, p. 262.

36 *Ibid.*, pp. 207, 224.

37 See Richard Tomlinson, *The Big Breach*, Edinburgh: Cutting Edge, 2000, pp. 169–70.

38 *Observer*, 7 October 2000; see also *Financial Times*, 12 April 2002.

39 *Guardian*, 10 December 2001.

40 See Kenneth Katzman for CRS, *Terrorism: Near Eastern Groups and State Sponsors, 2001*, RL31119: 10 September 2001, p. 6.

41 The alleged *de facto* leader of the Al-Aqsa Martyrs Brigades.

42 Former CIA counter-terrorism official Victor Cannistraro, cited in 'Arafat Ignored CIA Warning', UPI, 17 August 2001.

43 *Ibid.*

44 See Doug Struck and Craig Whitlock, 'Palestinian Vows End to Cooperation', *Washington Post* Foreign Service, 23 April 2002.

45 Palestinian analyst Khalil Shikaki, cited in Suzanne Goldenberg, 'Sharon Tries to Destroy All Traces of Arafat Rule', *Guardian*, 6 April 2002.

46 For full text, see *Ha'aretz*, 15 June 2001.

47 CBS News, *The Early Show*, 26 March 2003.

48 Sonya Ross, 'Bush Clarifies "Terror Doctrine"', Associated Press, 2 April 2002.

49 Lee Hockstader, 'Israel Says Documents Link Arafat, Terrorism', *Washington Post* Foreign Service, 3 April 2002 .

50 For a sampling, see Charles Krauthammer, 'Banish Arafat Now', 'Arafat Harvest of Hate', *Washington Post*, 5 April, 26 March 2002.

51 Douglas Frantz and James Risen, 'A Secret Iran–Arafat Connection Is Seen Fuelling the Mideast Fire', *New York Times*, 23 March 2002.

52 *Ibid.*

53 UPI, 'Arafat Ignores CIA Warning', 17 August 2001.

54 Ben Fenton, 'US Arrests 200 Young Israelis in Spying Investigation', *The Times,* 7 March 2002.

55 Charles R. Smith, 'US Police and Intelligence Hit by Spy Network', *Yahoo Groups*, 19 December 2001.

56 Samuel P. Huntington, interview by Michael Steinberger, *The Observer,* 21 October 2001.

CHAPTER 2

TECHNOLOGIES
OF
SURVEILLANCE

*'One of the first things we noticed when we got on the Internet was that it's
one of the most fabulous surveillance systems ever invented.'*
– John Young, *Cryptome* public information website

Overview

Successful intelligence has always depended on the collection of
information. Of the four stages in the classic 'intelligence cycle'
(collection, analysis, dissemination, action),[1] it is perhaps here that the
changes in the environment are at their most profound. In what
follows, we consider the intelligence implications of the technological
revolution in three main aspects. First, we assess the technologies
themselves: what they consist of, how they have evolved, and what
their driving forces are. Second, we review the applications of information technology (IT) in the intelligence process – the 'independent
variable' which threatens to elude state control. Third, we examine
the implications for a civil society both threatened and empowered by
the information revolution.

For the populations of advanced industrialised countries in particular, the twenty-first century is an age of surveillance unparalleled in
history. Possessing a credit card will yield details of a person's address,
employer, bank, salary and spending patterns. E-mail, fax, telex and
telephone calls are routinely recorded and monitored. Closed circuit
TV is increasingly all-pervasive, whilst satellite imagery can detect

ever more details and download in real time at 10 frames per second. A mobile phone can become a tracking device and, likewise, surfing the web will leave an indelible trail. At a more advanced, proactive level, there are the means to remotely read the contents of computer screens, scan the content of sealed letters and detect conversation through the vibration effects on glass windows.

Privacy

Despite guarantees under the UN Universal Declaration of Human Rights (Article 12 – 'No one shall be subjected to arbitrary interference with [his/her/their] privacy') and the European Convention on Human Rights (ECHR) (Article 8 – 'the right to respect for [his/her/their] correspondence'),[2] in practice there has been no real defence against a determined effort at in-depth surveillance of virtually every aspect of an individual's or organisation's affairs. Even where national legislation provides for extensive safeguards on individual privacy – as in the US and the UK – a determined agency can, as we shall see, simply call upon its allies. To the discomfiture of many in the intelligence world, however, this situation is changing.

The independent variable

For the specialised purposes of state intelligence services, the revolution in technology is turning into a sharply two-edged sword. Initial bedazzlement by the vast prospects for intelligence gathering offered in the information age, described below, is in some quarters turning to foreboding. For the US, it was the unmatched technical capability of the National Security Agency (NSA) in particular which gave it an acknowledged edge in triumphing in the Cold War.[3] It should also be recalled, however, that it was this very independent variable – understood now as Soviet inability to get to grips with the 'scientific and technical revolution' – that led to the communist empire's ultimate downfall.

There are perhaps three major areas where technology is running ahead of the state – fibre optics, encryption and overall technological literacy. Here, skills and abilities hitherto the preserve of the highly trained techno-professional are ever more widely dispersed and available. For intelligence agencies, the process and product of their work is conventionally divided into three '-ints' covering the major intelligence disciplines: signals intelligence (Sigint), covering the collection of electronic signals traffic (known as Elint); imagery intelligence (Imint), the recording and observation of physical objects (installations, military deployments); and human intelligence (Humint), the classical craft of espionage derived from human sources. For this chapter, we will be focusing on the first of these – Sigint – and its subfield of specific application to communications (Comint).

The panoptic view – satellite surveillance on a global scale

For military purposes, electromagnetic signals such as radar emissions can provide valuable order-of-battle information about the disposition of air defences, troops, aircraft, ships or submarines. Electronic intelligence – monitoring other states' spy satellites, and recording and decoding photographs and other signals from such satellites – is also useful. The signals are recorded by ground stations, low-orbit satellites or from quasi-geostationary (see next paragraph) Sigint satellites.

Although Sigint surveillance dates back to the beginning of international communications, and reached a particular level of sophistication during the Second World War, it was advances in computing power and the launch of satellite communications on a world scale from 1967 onwards that drove intelligence gathering in its current direction. By using appropriate antennae, microwaves can be focused effectively, allowing microwave radio links to replace cables. To avoid the line-of-sight limitations imposed by the earth's curvature, satellites can act as mirrors that bounce signals to any part of the globe. If a satellite is placed in a circular, 24-hour orbit parallel to the equator, it will follow the rotation of the earth exactly at a height of 36,000 kilometres – in other words, it will hold a particular geostationary position. Most communications and television satellites are of this type – including global systems (Intelsat, for example), regional (continental) systems (Arabsat, Eutelsat), or national systems (Italsat). Today, 120 private companies throughout the world operate some 1,000 satellites.

As geostationary satellites and the attendant commercial earth stations – largely run by the Washington-based International Tele-communications Satellite Organisation – began taking over the world's communications, intelligence organisations began building mirror sites nearby. The world leaders in this field – by a formidable margin – are the NSA and its partners in the UK/USA Agreement ('Yookusa'): Britain, Australia, Canada and New Zealand – of which more below.

The rise in the perceived importance of Sigint is clear from the change in the respective positions of the NSA and the CIA. During the 1990s, the CIA's staff was slashed by 23 per cent and its slice of the funding pie diminished correspondingly. In the $27 billion Federal Intelligence budget of 1999, Congress gave the NSA a 'huge increase' and $1.5 billion in supplementary emergency spending, whilst leaving the CIA level, with less than 20 per cent of funding for human assets.[4]

Besides UK/USA there are at least 30 other major state-run Sigint operations, the largest being the Russian FAPSI (Federal Agency for Government Communications and Information) with some 54,000 staff. For nearly 40 years, FAPSI has operated large ground collection sites at Lourdes, Cuba and at Cam Ranh Bay, Vietnam,[5] although these finally closed in January 2002 on economic grounds. France runs a potentially globe-straddling system with bases in Mayotte (Indian Ocean), and the former Pacific colony of New Caledonia.[6] Germany's BND and France's Direction Générale de la Sécurité Extérieure (DGSE) have collaborated in the operation of a Comsat collection site at Kourou, French Guyana, targeted on 'American and South American satellite communications'. DGSE has also operated collection sites at Domme (Dordogne, France), and in the United Arab Emirates. The Swiss intelligence service has recently announced a plan for two Comsat interception stations.[7] China also maintains a substantial system, including two bases directed at Russia run in collaboration with the US and the German BND. Many Middle Eastern and Asian states have invested in Sigint, notably, Israel, India and Pakistan.

Interception from space

Interception depends mainly on the spillage of microwave signals as they are relayed between numerous intermediate ground stations. In the US programme, satellites are able to collect transmissions that are up to 80 degrees longitude distant from the target area. The first (Canyon) series of satellites targeted the trans-Soviet Union microwave net from a base in Bad Aibling, Germany. Seven Canyon Comint satellites were launched between 1968 and 1977. Their success led to the design and deployment of the new Chalet class, based on a ground station developed from a former RAF facility at Menwith Hill, England. Under NSA project P-285, US companies were contracted to install and assist in operating the satellite control system with its downlinks and ground processing system. The first two Chalet satellites were launched in June 1978 and October 1979. In 1982, the NSA gained funding for expanded mission requirements in the programme and began operating four of the satellites (now renamed Vortex) simultaneously. A new 5,000 square metres operations centre (Steeplebush) was constructed. When the name Vortex was revealed in 1987, the satellites were renamed Mercury.[8]

Menwith Hill's expanded mission after 1985 included Mercury collection from the Middle East. The station received awards for support to US naval operations in the Persian Gulf in 1987–8 and the Gulf War operations Desert Storm and Desert Shield in 1991. The station is now the major US site for Comint collection against its major ally, Israel. Its staff includes linguists trained in Hebrew, Arabic and Farsi as well as European languages. Recently Menwith Hill has been expanded to include ground links for a new network of Sigint satellites (Rutley), launched in 1994 and 1995.[9] New radomes were being constructed to cope with the latest role of the base as the European ground relay station for the Space Based Infra-Red System (SBIRS), an integral part of plans for the new US National Missile Defense.[10] In 1999, a US Air Intelligence Agency report – AIA Mission Directive 1517 – outlined the need to 'collect, process, analyse and disseminate global information around the clock to continuously impact peacetime, crisis and wartime operations'.[11] Besides its headquarters, Fort Meade in Maryland, the other main NSA stations are at Buckley Field, Denver, Colorado and Pine Gap, Australia. There are three large Regional Sigint Operations Centres (RSOCs) within the continental United States. The Median RSOC in Lakeland, Texas, focuses on the

Caribbean and Central/South America. The second, an underground complex in Kunia, Hawaii, focuses on Asia, while at Fort Gordon, Georgia, coverage is provided for Europe and the Middle East.[12]

The US developed a second class of Sigint satellite with complementary capabilities over the period from 1967 to 1985. Initially known as Rhyolite and later Aquacade, these satellites were operated from the remote Pine Gap ground station in central Australia. Using a large parabolic antenna which unfolded in space, Rhyolite intercepted lower-frequency signals in the VHF and UHF bands. The larger, most recent satellites of this type have been named Magnum and then Orion. Targets include telemetry, VHF radio, cellular phones, paging signals, and mobile data links. A third class of satellites, known first as Jumpseat and latterly as Trumpet, operate in highly elliptical near-polar orbits enabling them to 'hover' for long periods. They enable the US to collect signals from high northern latitudes poorly covered by Mercury or Orion, and also to intercept signals sent to Russian communications satellites in the same orbits.[13]

Precise details of US space-based Sigint satellites launched after 1990 remain obscure. What did emerge in the public domain were reports of a fierce bureaucratic funding battle within the NSA when cash was refused for a new generation of billion-dollar satellites designed to be 'survivable' under nuclear wartime conditions. This was deemed inappropriate with the retreat of the Soviet threat and contributed to the dismissal of NSA chief General William Odom.[14] It is admitted, however, that collection systems have expanded rather than contracted as the agency has sought new roles in commercial surveillance and drug enforcement.

In 1998 the US National Reconnaissance Office (NRO) announced plans to combine the three separate classes of Sigint satellites into an Integrated Overhead Sigint Architecture (IOSA) in order to 'improve Sigint performance and avoid costs by consolidating systems, utilising … new satellite and data processing technologies'.[15] The end of the twentieth century thus found the US with the unique ability to intercept mobile communications signals and microwave city-to-city traffic anywhere on the planet. No other nation (including the former Soviet Union) has deployed satellites comparable to Canyon,

Rhyolite, or their successors. Both Britain (project Zircon) and France (project Zenon) have attempted to do so, but neither persevered. After 1988 the British government purchased capacity on the Vortex/Mercury system for a reported £500 million per year.[16] A senior UK Liaison Officer and staff from GCHQ work at Menwith Hill and assist in tasking and operating the satellites.

Communications satellite collection

Systematic collection of what are technically known as 'international leased carrier' (ILC) satellite communications began in 1971. Two ground stations were built for this purpose. The first at Morwenstow, Cornwall, England, was aimed at the Atlantic Ocean and Indian Ocean intelligence satellites (Intelsats). The second Intelsat interception site was at Yakima, Washington State. The NSA's Yakima Research Station intercepted communications passing through the Pacific Ocean Intelsat. In the late 1970s a second US site at Sugar Grove, West Virginia was added to the network. Large-scale expansion of the ILC satellite interception system took place between 1985 and 1995, in conjunction with the enlargement of the UK/USA global Sigint processing system (see page 44 ff). Built on cooperation between the US and Britain, Australia, Canada and New Zealand extending from the 1940s, UK/USA provides a global division of labour for its participants and – of particular interest to the senior partner – a truly global reach.[17] New stations were constructed in the United States (Sabana Seca, Puerto Rico), Canada (Leitrim, Ontario), Australia (Kojarena, Western Australia) and New Zealand (Waihopai, South Island). Capacity at Yakima, Morwenstow and Sugar Grove has witnessed continuous expansion and it now appears that the UK/USA nations are between them operating at least 120 satellite-based collection systems.

Surveillance and the Internet

During the 1980s, NSA and its UK/USA partners operated an international communications network larger than the then Internet but based on the same technology. According to its British partner, 'all GCHQ systems are linked together on the largest LAN (local area network) in Europe, which is connected to other sites around the world via one of the largest WANs (wide area networks) in the world … its main networking protocol is Internet Protocol (IP)'.[18] This global network, developed as Project Embroidery, includes Pathway, the NSA's main computer communications network. Since the early 1990s, the Net itself has become a major focus of Comint collection – particularly as communications from Europe to and from Asia, Oceania, Africa or South America normally travel via the United States.

Internet messages are composed of packets or datagrams that include IP addresses, numbers representing both their origin and their destination. These are unique to each computer connected to the Internet. They are inherently easy to identify as to country and site of origin and destination. Handling, sorting and routing millions of such packets each second is fundamental to the operation of major Internet centres. The same process facilitates extraction of traffic for Comint purposes. Internet traffic can be accessed either from international communications links entering the United States or when it reaches major Internet exchanges. Both methods have advantages. Access to communications systems is likely to be remain clandestine, whereas access to Internet exchanges might be more detectable but provides easier access to more data and simpler sorting methods. Since the passage of the USA-Patriot Act (see above), legal restrictions on the NSA have been eased: hitherto it was only permitted to scrutinise communications that start or finish in a foreign country.

For some sections of the Net – messages sent to Usenet discussion groups, for example – intelligence agencies, like other Internet users, have open source access and can store material for analysis. In the UK, the Defence Evaluation and Research Agency maintains a database containing the previous 90 days of Usenet messages.[19] For open access websites of interest, the NSA employs computer 'bots' (robots) to collect data of interest in a similar fashion to commercial search engines such as Alta Vista. For example, a New York public information web-site – www.jya.com[20] – known for extensive coverage of Sigint, cryptography and related issues, was visited every morning by a 'bot' from NSA's National Computer Security Center, which looked for new files and made copies of any that it found.[21]

Overseas Internet traffic of intelligence interest – consisting of e-mail, file transfers, 'virtual private networks' operated over the Net, and some other messages – will form at best a few per cent of the traffic on most US Internet exchanges or 'backbone links'. In some accounts, this was then fairly accessible to NSA-developed 'sniffer' software, inserted at nine major Internet exchange points (IXPs) after 1995. The first two such sites identified, FIX East and FIX West, are operated by US government agencies. They are closely linked to nearby commercial locations, MAE East and MAE West. Three other sites listed were network access points originally developed by the US National Science Foundation to provide the US Internet with its initial 'backbone'.[22]

New satellite networks

The launch of new mobile phone systems using satellites in low- or medium-level earth orbits raised the prospect of unbroken global coverage – and new challenges for Comint collection. These systems, known as satellite personal communications systems (SPCS), can relay signals directly between satellites or to ground stations. Iridium, the first such system to be completed, uses 66 satellites and started operations in 1998, although fluctuating demand and cost factors leave its future uncertain at the time of writing. Iridium presents particular difficulties for communications interception, since the signal downlink can only be received in a small area, which may be anywhere on the earth's surface.

Although telecommunications satellites remain an essential part of global telecommunication, the proportion accounted for by satellite links has decreased substantially over the past few years in Central Europe. In some regions, it has even fallen below 10 per cent. This decline is due to the advantages offered by fibre-optic cables, which can carry a much greater volume of traffic at a higher connection quality. By turning to fibre optics, the US telephone giant AT&T reportedly was able to double its traffic in 90 days. In development are further advances – known as wavelength division multiplying (WDM) – whereby multiple signals can be sent at different wavelengths down the same cable link. In its developed Ultra Dense format, WDM will have the capability to transmit the equivalent of the entire Internet over a single strand of cable: it had become a £4 billion business by 2001. With the production cost of fibre optics falling by a factor of 200 per cent over the 1990s, global coverage is projected to reach 168,000 kilometres. Customers include the Netherlands, Korea and China's Posts and Telecommunications Administration.[23] In the US, the increase in traffic was such that by 2000 only 2 per cent of AT&T's voice and data communication was taken by satellite and the company was selling off its US domestic satellite coverage completely.

Echelon – who's on the watch list?

Although the technology involved in Sigint collection is generic in many ways, by far the greatest surveillance net – and determined to keep it that way – is operated by the US and its junior partners in Yookusa. Rooted in the trans-Atlantic Sigint cooperation of the Second World War, the UK/USA interception system, commonly known as Echelon, began its current phase of development in 1971, and was 'greatly enlarged between 1975 and 1995'.[24] Designed and coordinated by the NSA, the Echelon system is used to intercept non-encrypted e-mail, fax, and telephone calls carried over the world's telecommunications networks. Different from many other electronic spy systems developed during the Cold War, Echelon is designed primarily for non-military objectives: governments, organisations, businesses and individuals in practically every corner of the Earth. It potentially concerns every person communicating between (and some-times within) countries anywhere in the world. Describing Echelon as 'a software programme whose name has become a generic term for eavesdropping on commercial communication', intelligence analyst James Bamford observes that 'No other intelligence source – human, military, diplomatic, photo … provides the answers produced by the Echelon system'.[25]

Despite being the increasing focus of public comment, particularly in the EU, the network has never been acknowledged officially – although, as Glyn Ford, a British Member of the European Parliament, observes, 'Frankly, the only people who have any doubt about the existence of Echelon are in the United States.'[26] The most comprehensive analysis that has appeared to date is the series of reports commissioned between 1997 and 2000 by the Scientific and Technological Options Assessment programme (STOA) of the European Parliament.[27] These were delivered in conjunction with a European Parliament decision of 5 July 2000 to set up a temporary committee to 'verify the existence of the communications interception system known as Echelon' and to assess whether 'the rights of European citizens [are] protected against activities of secret services'.

'Within Europe,' the STOA's working document stated

> all e-mail, telephone and fax communications are routinely intercepted by the United States National Security Agency, transferring all target information from the European mainland via the strategic hub of London, and then by satellite to Fort Meade in Maryland via the crucial hub at Menwith Hill in the North Yorkshire moors in the UK.[28]

Menwith Hill Station – now renamed RAF Menwith Hill, although the United States flag remains flying there – is the largest station in the network, but there are more spying points inside the European Union. Germany and Denmark collaborated with the UK/USA alliance as 'third party' partners – the first and second partners being the US and UK respectively. The largest mainland Europe base was at Bad Aibling, south-east of Munich, now scheduled for closure. This operated in conjunction with the smaller Sandagergård Station on the Danish island of Amager. There have also been recent moves to bring Spain into the association.[29] Outside Europe, other stations involved in Echelon are Waihopai, New Zealand;[30] Leitrim, Canada; Sabana Seca, Puerto Rico; and Kojarena, Western Australia. Throughout, the NSA's Platform collection system effectively targets all global electronic media (fax, e-mail, voice) in conjunction with a storage system capable of retaining five trillion pages of text. According to former NSA Director William Studeman,

> US intelligence operates what is probably the largest information processing environment in the world … just one intelligence collection system alone can generate a million inputs per half hour. Filters throw away all but 6,500 inputs; only 1,000 inputs meet forwarding criteria. Ten inputs are

normally selected by analysts and one report is produced. These are routine statistics for a number of ... systems which collect technical intelligence.[31]

Echelon is not designed to eavesdrop on a specific individual's e-mail; instead the system operates by searching through millions of messages by means of individual keywords. These can include names, localities, phrases and subjects intercepted whether or not specific telephone numbers or e-mail addresses are on the list.[32] The·'watch list' of keywords is interpreted though a software programme known as Dictionary and can be accessed – with various levels of classification – throughout the UK/USA net by means of the common Echelon gateway.

After the NSA receives the watch lists, analysts assign four-digit numbers to them – search codes – and then pass them on, through the Echelon system, to the various UK/USA listening posts. There, Dictionary searches are conducted using much the same process as commercial search engines.[33] For the NSA, the shareable database concept has resulted in the automated storage and retrieval of masses of multimedia Sigint reports. Known as Oceanarium, these can be accessed not only over its own intranet – Webworld – but throughout the intelligence community via a system known as Intelink.[34]

Methods of processing text rely on a basic technique known as 'data mining'. Software combs through hundreds of millions of inter-cepted e-mails, faxes and phone calls to find a single 'hot-bot' sequence – say, the fax number of a suspected terrorist. A programme from software maker Sybase, for example, can sift though 1,000 cross-database variables simultaneously. The major Internet tracking tool publicly admitted by the FBI is Carnivore, its capabilities described on the FBI website. Whilst similar programmes are available commercially, the full reach of Carnivore has never been disclosed. It could, indeed, simply be a generic name for a software family. Carnivore has attracted much criticism in the past on civil liberties grounds and the FBI claimed that the pre-9/11 version was limited strictly to a relatively small number of targets specifically authorised by court order. The post-9/11 Carnivore is said to have a far wider target range and to receive covert support from Internet service providers (ISPs) that allegedly are far more accommodating than previously – a change due in part to increased penalties under the new US legislation.

Wood from the trees – the NSA's semantic forests

One major problem faced by the NSA since the end of the Cold War is the proliferation of targets in 'exotic' languages – Uzbek, for example, or Ovimbundu. The Agency turned to the University of Pennsylvania to develop an automated system of machine translation involving optical scanning technology able to translate texts using typefaces with non-standard features, such as local Cyrillic newspapers in Central Asia. Across the Potomac, the CIA is rushing into service a recently developed programme known as Fluent. Tasked primarily to monitor Arab sources, the software scours foreign websites and displays information in English back to analysts. The programme apparently already understands at least nine languages, including Russian and Japanese. For more commonplace languages, the NSA uses programmes such as Systran that automatically translate text at up to 750 pages per hour, and can claim a 90 per cent accuracy rate for technical publications. The advantages for a notoriously monolingual organisation are obvious. Analysts with no prior knowledge can quickly search machine-readable foreign language databases for keywords and – at the cutting edge of current research – identify non-linear relationships defined by topics.

A breakthrough in the NSA's ability to pick out the right 'tree' in a vast forest of words came with the development of software appropriately called Semantic Forests. This allows operators to sift through printed transcripts of conversations, faxes or any other written intercepts and locate targeted subjects. The name derives from the ability to create a weighted cluster of meanings for each word in a document. Under test conditions, the programme sifted large volumes of printed matter, including transcripts of speech and data from Internet discussion groups. Sample test questions such as what the results were of Iraqi sanctions produced reported results of increased target location ability from 19 to 27 per cent in just one year.[35]

Of greater difficulty than machine translation of printed texts is the automatic translation and transcription of voice communication, a long-sought goal of the NSA. Recent Pentagon-funded research by bio-medical engineers at the University of Southern California (USC) has claimed a breakthrough in creating the first machine system able to recognise spoken words better than humans can. According to scientists, the system can 'instantly produce clean transcripts of conversations, identifying each of the speakers'. Known at NSA as 'Speaker ID', the USC's Berger-Liaw Neural Network Speaker Independent Recognition System can mimic the way brains process information, giving the ability to conduct word spotting in target communications, regardless of origin. It is claimed to be better than the human ear at recognising words in a welter of noise and can pick out words or conversations from a background clutter of general sounds and conversation. 'The system can identify different speakers of the same word with superhuman acuity,' say USC officials. A related CIA breakthrough is Oasis, able to capture worldwide radio and television broadcasts and transcribe them into readable text.[36] The processing of telephone calls, however, is at present largely limited to identifying call-related information and traffic analysis. In the view of one intelligence analyst and EU Parliament consultant, Duncan Campbell, 'Effective voice word-spotting systems do not exist and are not in use despite reports to the contrary.'[37] But it is generally conceded that 'voiceprint' speaker identification systems have been in use since at least 1995.

Other search tools in use include Pathfinder, sponsored by the US Army Intelligence and Security Command's National Ground Intelligence Centre. In service with over 40 intelligence agencies, the system uses a set of 20 advanced text analysis tools to routinely sift through some 500,000 documents in a few minutes.[38] Major users include Ground Intelligence Support Activities at Fort Bragg, North Carolina, and the US European command, where Pathfinder was recently in service in the Joint Analysis Centre at Molesworth in the UK and with forces deployed in the Balkans. Also in wide use is the CIA's Nethound, which apparently has brought automation to the level of writing the President's Daily Brief.

Despite much effort and investment, however, some analysts believe that comprehensive word spotting capability is most effective on fax messages and modem intercepts. The main method of filtering and analysing non-verbal traffic – the Dictionary computers – still utilises traditional information retrieval techniques. Fast special-purpose chips enable vast quantities of data to be processed in this way. In August 1999 the US Patent Office issued the patent number 5937422, awarded to the National Security Agency. Described as a process of 'automatically generating a topic description for text and searching and sorting text by topic using the same', devices based on this patent eliminate the reliance on the presence of specific keywords of earlier methodology. By enabling thematic linkages across a vast range of raw intelligence data, the patent opens the way for cross-database analysis of discourse.[39]

The race for hardware

Despite the prodigious efforts being put into data filtering software, the sheer and ever-increasing volume of communications of all kinds has overwhelmed agencies: even running to stand still has taxed their powers. The NSA has attempted at least to keep up with net traffic by building huge online storage systems to hold and sift e-mail. The current system, designed in 1996 and delivered in 2000, is known as Sombrero VI and holds a petabyte of information: equivalent to a million gigabytes or eight times the capacity of the Library of Congress. Its replacement will be a petaplex system with a capacity 20 times larger, designed to hold Internet records for up to 90 days.[40]

Leading the race to maintain the NSA's technological hegemony is the Agency's own in-house Supercomputer Research Center (SRC). Built in 1984 at the University of Maryland's Science and Technology Center, the SRC is actually operated by the Communications Research Division (CRD), part of the Institute for Defense Analysis. Also run by the CRD is the NSA's think tank, the Communications and Computing Center, specialising in crypto-mathematics, crypto-computing, speech research and special signals processing techniques. The NSA also operates a Laboratory for Physical Sciences containing facilities to develop miniature lasers, optical amplifiers and research exotic materials. A major focus here is on computing speed – the essential key in cryptography. Measured in operations per second, the goal has been to move from billions to more than a quadrillion – pentaflop speed. To do this, the NSA has sought ever-increasing miniaturisation. In 1994–5, a series of meetings was held with such experts as the late computer guru Seymour Cray, to explore the next generation of super-fast micro-computing. Ideas included employing processers in memory chips – these are now in series manufacture at the NSA's own plant, the Special Processing Laboratory. By 2005, the NSA aims to be working at exaflop speeds – a quintillion operations per second – and is pushing for zetaflop or even yottaflop machines, capable of a septillion (10^{24} operations per second). Already pursuing miniaturisation to the level where seventy transistors will fit on the cross-section of a human hair, the NSA is also developing a new generation of chips by bombarding light-sensitive material with ions. Built to reach exaflop speed, parts have to be shrunk to the size of atoms or even sub-atomic particles.[41]

Quantum computing, which is the emerging field, involves harnessing individual atoms. Since 1994, the NSA has invested some $4 million per year on quantum systems. The prospect here is one of uncovering pairs of very large prime numbers which are the passwords for many encryption systems. Instead of trying sequences of combinations, the great advantage is one of being able to try all possible options simultaneously. According to Bell Laboratories scientist Lov K. Grover,

> On paper, at least … a search engine could examine every nook and cranny of the internet in half an hour, a brute force decoder that could unscramble a data encryption standard – the 'DES' commonly used by banks and confidential commercial transactions – transmission in five minutes.[42]

A quantum computer could also scan a massive body of intercepts.

A breakthrough came in 1999 when researchers at Massachusetts Institute of Technology, IBM, the University of California (Berkeley) and Oxford University announced the world's first quantum computer. Four months later, scientists at Hewlett Packard had created rows of conductive wires less than a dozen atoms in diameter. The Pentagon's Defense Advanced Research Projects Agency (DARPA), long the NSA's principal partner in classified research, has speculated that it may soon be possible to fashion tiny switches or transistors from clusters of molecules only a layer deep – the result would be 100 billion times faster than today's fastest personal computer (PC). And in prospect there is the possibility of making nano-machines out of biological entities by mapping circuitry onto biological material – making processers self-reproducing.[43]

Encryption and 'backdoors'

Under 'Moore's Law' the computing power of the average desk-top PC approximately doubles every eighteen months. With the availability of commercial or freeware encryption – such as Pretty Good Privacy (PGP) – able to take advantage of such ever-increasing capability in home/office computers, intelligence agencies fear that this will more and more limit Sigint to 'traffic analysis', keeping track of simply where and when messages are sent. Moreover, sheer volume and techniques such as the rapid alternation of data across wavelengths – known as 'packet switching' – also make traffic analysis itself much harder.[44]

At the present time, the use of powerful encryption algorithms has presented great difficulties for code breakers, since decryption has entailed trying all possible keys in a 'brute force' attack. In general, the longer the key, the more likely it is that this attempt will be thwarted, even using very powerful computers, by the time it would take.

By the same token, however, the availability of strong encryption is viewed as essential for e-commerce transactions and throughout the financial sector. In response, in the US the NSA urged that firms should be offered a sufficiently secure encryption standard, but one which the NSA itself could decrypt. This was officially adopted in 1976 as *the* Data Encryption Standard (DES, mentioned above) and for the next 25 years became the official benchmark throughout America, Europe and Japan. Whilst it remains contested whether the DES algorithm has actually been broken, hardware now exists which is powerful enough to try all possible keys. In contrast, Triple DES, which has a 112-bit key, is still regarded as secure. The successor to DES, the Advanced Encryption Standard (AES), is a European process and is regarded as secure, since it incorporates no restriction on key length.[45] Concerns similar to the NSA's led France to impose a general ban on the use of cryptography until recently, granting authorisations only in individual cases. A few years ago in Germany a debate arose concerning restrictions on encryption and the compulsory submission of a key to the authorities.

During the Clinton administration, US law enforcement and intelligence agencies mounted a forceful campaign to restrict the availability of public encryption systems – particularly, the freeware PGP. Certain systems were classified as strategic and subject to export ban, and attempts were made to compel computer manufacturers to install a so-called 'clipper chip' which would expose encrypted messages to government surveillance. A further measure proposed was 'key escrow' – the holding of encryption keys in a secure storage which could be accessed by court order. Both of these measures were strongly resisted by the US business community, which pointed out the manifest commercial disadvantages of being unable to compel worldwide adherence to the scheme.

Almost from the outset of the publicly accessible Internet, it has been widely alleged that US software contains 'backdoors' permitting the covert viewing of Net traffic and the contents of hard disks. Acknowledged versions of this technology can be found in the emplacement of resident 'cookies' included in Net downloads and commercial anti-piracy software. And visitors to the CIA's official website were perhaps not surprised to learn that they were playing inadvertent host to both permanent and 'session' cookies, although the agency put this down to 'contractor error' and now claims to have discontinued the practice.[46]

The Excel company made headlines when it was suggested that half the key is revealed in the file header of the European version of its encryption programme. Microsoft also gained media attention when a hacker claimed to have discovered a hidden 'NSA key' in its Windows suite of programmes, a claim which was of course strongly denied by Microsoft.[47] Nonetheless, German government concern led to a blanket ban on the use of Windows on 'sensitive' defence and intelligence systems in March 2001.[48] The seeming tardiness of US anti-trust litigation against the company has also fuelled speculation. Since

Microsoft has not revealed its source code, the matter remains unresolved. At any event, the earlier versions of PGP and GnuPG can be said with a great degree of certainty not to contain such a backdoor, since their source text has been disclosed.

One argument repeatedly put in the 1990s encryption debate – and reappearing after 9/11 – concerns the use of encryption by terrorists. In later-declassified Senate hearings of March 2000, CIA Director George Tenet stated that, 'To a greater and greater degree, terrorist groups including Hizbollah, Hamas and bin Laden's Al-Qaida group are using computerised files, e-mail and encryption to support their operations.'[49] Computers seized from the Manila apartment of convicted 1993 World Trade Center bomber Ramzi Yousef contained encrypted details of a plot to destroy 11 US airliners on the eve of the millennium – one file took the NSA nearly a year to decode. The use of even more exotic techniques such as Steganography – the encryption of a file within a microdot or graphic image – were also said to be in use during the Al-Qaida US embassy bombings of 1998.[50] However, post-9/11 FBI briefings on 18 September 2001 revealed that, after locating hundreds of identified Al-Qaida e-mails sent 30–45 days before the attack, the Bureau had found none of them concealed or encrypted. A former NATO official was quoted as saying this was because encryption 'would have stood out like a sore thumb' to the NSA. The evidence so far is that the terrorists used a simple open code to coordinate their actions.[51]

Civil liberties groups argue that restrictions on encryption will largely target legitimate business and political dissent and be used to clamp down on human rights activities. The same can be said for inbuilt surveillance technology and software. As Jerry Berman of the US-based Center for Democracy and Technology observes, 'Terrorists are not going to buy computers with backdoors.'[52]

The economic backdoor – state surveillance and the private sector

In a major report published in June 2001, the Echelon committee of the European Parliament found that the conduct of electronic surveillance activities by US intelligence breaches the European Convention on Human Rights even when pursued, allegedly, for law enforcement purposes. It concluded that if the British and German governments fail to prevent the improper use of surveillance stations sited on their territory to intercept private and commercial communications, they may be in breach of both European law and human rights treaties. Four new studies on 'Interception Capabilities – Impact and Exploitation' were commissioned by the Temporary Committee on the Echelon Interception System of the European Parliament (EP) in December 2000. The new studies update and extend the previous EP report, *Interception Capabilities 2000*, which was prepared in 1999. They cover the use of communications intelligence for economic purposes, legal and human rights issues, and recent political and technological developments.

Long a major source of tension between the US and EU, the issue of state-sponsored commercial espionage is further complicated by intra- and intergovernmental rivalries as well as those between individual firms and multinational subsidiaries – particularly in the EU itself. Whilst divided British loyalties provide an obvious focus for MEP discontent, it has been widely accepted that others, notably France, have pursued international economic surveillance in aggressive support of domestic profit making.[53]

The declared policy of the US government, as explained by former CIA director James Woolsey, is to use the US intelligence system to spy on European companies in order to gather evidence of bribery and unfair trade practices. 'Yes, my continental European friends,' Woolsey wrote in the *Wall Street Journal*,

> we have spied on you. And it's true that we use computers to sort through data by using keywords.... We have spied on you because you bribe.[54]

The EU report traces in detail how US intelligence-gathering priorities shifted dramatically after the end of the Cold War, with the result that 'about 40 per cent of the requirements' of US intelligence collection became 'economic, either in part or in whole'. The new priorities for economic intelligence were approved by the first Bush administration in National Security Directive 67, issued on 20 March 1992. In using the CIA and NSA to spy on foreign rivals of American companies, the stated US objective was to 'level the playing field' in foreign trade.

After the new policies came into force, the Clinton administration set up a new Trade Promotion Coordinating Committee, with direct intelligence inputs from the CIA and direct links to business through a new Advocacy Center. Its declared mission was to 'aggressively support US bidders in global competitions where advocacy is in the national interest'. Intelligence from the NSA and CIA was supplied to the US government Department of Commerce through an Office of Intelligence Liaison, which was equipped to handle intercepted communications such as those supplied by the Echelon network.

How the intelligence liaison functioned in practice is illustrated in one documented instance wherein the CIA team in the Commerce Department proposed gathering information on 'primary competitors' with American business in a major Asian market. Of 16 US government officials attending a meeting on winning contracts in Indonesia, five were from the CIA.[55] Thus, the US Congress was told, as a result of 'levelling' the said playing field, American companies gained $145 billion worth of business during the 1990s, after intelligence agencies claimed to have detected and defeated bribery or unfair conduct by foreign competitors. According to reports published by the Advocacy Center, European countries have lost out massively. France lost nearly $17 billion worth of trade, and Germany $4 billion out of a total of about $40 billion. Sweden was $386 million down and the Netherlands was short by $184 million.

Despite the huge number of cases in which it claims to have detected bribery, the US government has never published any evidence to substantiate its claims. Nor has it instigated any prosecutions. Equally hard to substantiate has been evidence in specific cases where secret interception activities are alleged to have affected a major contract. All of the specific accounts of European business losses, such as the loss of an $8 billion Airbus contract in 1994, were published by the American press at a time when the Clinton administration wanted to publicise that it was doing its best for business. But when Europe became concerned about the Echelon system, such stories stopped appearing in the US media and information dried up.

Although failing to find new reports of European business losses beyond those appearing in the American media in 1994–6, the Echelon committee has found that even if it were proved that bribery was involved, this does not make NSA activities of this kind legal in Europe. The draft report points out that:

> The American authorities have repeatedly tried to justify the interception of telecommunications by accusing the European authorities of corruption and taking bribes. It should be pointed out to the Americans that all EU Member States have properly functioning criminal justice systems. If there is evidence that crimes have been committed, the USA must leave the task of law enforcement to the host countries. If there is no such evidence, surveillance must be regarded as unproportional, a violation of human rights and thus inadmissible.

Echelon committee vice-chairman Neil MacCormick (Scotland) wants to see legal changes to protect private communications; meanwhile, 'people should treat their e-mails like seaside postcards' that anyone else can read. According to the draft report,

> under the terms of the ECHR, interference in the exercise of the right to privacy must be proportional and, in addition, the least invasive methods must be chosen. As far as European citizens are concerned, an operation constituting interference carried out by a European intelligence service must be regarded as less serious than one conducted by an American intelligence service.

The report reveals that Britain undertakes to protect the rights of Americans, Canadians and Australians against interception that would not comply with their own domestic law, while offering no protection of any kind to other Europeans. This and other background papers provided to the Echelon committee have prompted it to observe that 'possible threats to privacy and to businesses posed by a system of the Echelon type arise not only from the fact that is a particularly powerful monitoring system, but also that it operates in a largely legislation-free area'.

Albeit with legislation somewhat modified after 9/11, there are still legal ambiguities surrounding the ability of the United Kingdom to spy on its citizens; likewise for the United States. Under the terms of the UK/USA agreement, Britain spies on American citizens and America spies on the British, and the two groups trade data. Technically, it may be legal, but the intent to evade the spirit of the laws protecting the citizens of those two nations is clear. Not least, this is because European citizens or companies could only get legal redress for such misconduct in national courts, not American courts. The draft committee report concludes that

> there would seem to be good reason ... to call on Germany and the United Kingdom to take their obligations under the ECHR seriously and to make the authorisation of further intelligence activities by the NSA on their territory contingent on compliance with the ECHR.[56]

Russia – 'no concept of privacy'

Whilst the US has been 'aggressively supporting' selected corporate interests and the British intelligence services, under the 1985 Interception of Communications Act, have a formal responsibility for 'safeguarding the economic wellbeing of the UK',[57] in Russia the relationship between business and intelligence activity is close to indistinguishable. With the break-up of the KGB after the failed coup of 1991, the Elint and cryptographic missions were inherited by a reconstituted Federal Security Service (Federal'naya Sluzhba Bezopasnosti, FSB) and the Federal Agency for Government Communications and Information (Federal'noye Agentsvo Paravitel'stvennykh Svyazi i Informatsii, FAPSI) – the latter being, roughly, Russia's NSA.

As the leading inheritor of the KGB mantle, with powers to conduct both intelligence and criminal investigations, the FSB is able to monitor all Internet traffic coming in and out of the Russian Federation under a regulation known as SORM (System for Ensuring Investigated Activity). This compels each Internet service provider to install a 'black box' that connects all ISP services to the local FSB through a fibre-optic cable. Although the practice is contested in the Russian business and civil liberties communities, 'there is', as one leading ISP spokesman observes, 'no concept of privacy in the Russian constitution, so strictly speaking, nothing illegal about this'.[58]

If the FSB has accumulated virtually unlimited monitoring powers, FAPSI, perhaps, has gone one better and taken over the running of communications infrastructure itself. With the demise of the old Soviet Union, FAPSI acquired the countrywide, secure communications networks of the abolished Communist Party and increasing control over the communications systems of emerging large companies and banks. These have been developed into a single Russian Business Network which claims to provide cryptologically secure business communications. Both hardware and software in this field are provided by firms staffed by former FAPSI operatives – who remain under security regulations – and all private companies specialising in IT security must obtain a FAPSI licence. 'In the increasingly privatised world of secure electronic communication in Russia,' one recent study concludes, 'FAPSI remains the undisputed ruler.'[59]

The Third World, human rights and the Internet

Human rights workers increasingly use the Internet to coordinate their actions against repressive governments. One increasingly important tool is encryption, as it allows activists to protect communications and stored information from government interception. Human rights activists in Guatemala, for example, credited their use of Pretty Good Privacy (PGP) with saving the lives of witnesses to military abuses.[60] Encryption is not the ultimate solution, however, as governments can outlaw its use and arrest those who do not comply. PGP was originally developed by a Colorado engineer and activist, Phil Zimmermann, who wanted to make strong encryption available to the public for privacy protection against government eavesdroppers. Although the software was export-controlled, someone (not Zimmermann) quickly posted it on a foreign Internet site where it could be downloaded by anyone, anywhere, despite export regulations. Since then, other encryption tools have been posted on Internet sites all over the world.

Perhaps the first large-scale instance of the impact of Internet access on human rights activism arose in the Balkans conflict of the late 1990s. After human rights organisations expressed concern that the Yugoslav government might be monitoring Internet activity, Anonymizer Inc., a provider of anonymous Web browsing and e-mail services, launched the Kosovo Privacy Project website. The site, which went online in April 1999, offered surfers anonymous e-mail and instant, anonymous access to Voice of America, Radio Free Europe, and about 20 other websites. World software giant Microsoft began a section called 'Secret Dispatches from Belgrade' in their online magazine *Slate*, where anonymous daily reports were posted of both alleged Serb atrocities and civilian suffering inflicted by NATO bombing.[61]

According to *Federal Computer Week*, Anonymizer planned to add NATO and other Western government information sites to the Kosovo list, and to launch similar projects in other parts of the world where human rights were at issue – China, for example.[62] However, the effectiveness of the Kosovo project was never established. In August, *USA Today* reported that activists said the project was little noticed inside Kosovo, where traditional media seemed unaware, while the fighting knocked out Internet trunk line connections in short order.[63]

In the late 1990s, both national and international advocacy groups specifically devoted to Internet issues sprang up. They all operate websites, where they publish policy papers and information about issues, events and membership. Many also send out e-mail newsletters and alerts. In the area of encryption policy, for example, the major players include Americans for Computer Privacy (ACP), the Center for Democracy and Technology, Cyber-Rights & Cyber Liberties, the Electronic Frontier Foundation, the Electronic Privacy Information Center, the Global Internet Liberty Campaign (GILC), and the Internet Privacy Coalition. The ACP has perhaps the largest group of constituents, being composed of 40 trade associations, over 100 companies, and more than 3,000 individual members. GILC is one of the most global, with member organisations from Europe, North America, Australia and Asia.[64]

Civil liberties and the Net – the dilemmas of 'emerging markets'
For many authoritarian regimes in the Third World, particularly those considering themselves as 'emerging markets', the spread of the Net presents a particularly acute dilemma. As the collapse of the Soviet Union demonstrated, a successful economy demands a free flow of

information, but ensuring a separation of dissident political views and information from that which is purely commercial has presented a challenge. There have been a variety of responses, from regimes where the Net is seen as an indispensable business tool – the People's Republic of China (PRC), the Gulf – and those placing a greater priority on information/social control – Cuba, Vietnam. By far the greatest emerging market is the PRC. Here, access to the Internet has grown exponentially since the first connection was established in 1993. Official PRC figures have claimed that 22.5 million people had Net access by the end of the year 2000, rising to 30 million in some estimates at the end of 2000.[65] Marketing analysts predict that China will overtake Japan as the Asian country with most Internet users by 2004. China has also witnessed a rapid growth in domains and websites – roughly 20 per cent per quarter in some estimates – and users are increasingly accessing the Net from home and office PCs as well as schools and Internet cafés. Although this has led many observers to suggest that the Net poses an insurmountable threat to authoritarian rule, the government has responded with a number of measures designed to counter potential challenges, as well as proactively to reap the technology's benefits.

Indeed, the spread of the Net in China has been largely a product of state initiative. From the outset, the Beijing authorities began a process of 'informatisation', using IT to modernise the economy and decentralise decision making, yet also making the administrative process more transparent and open to central control. In 1993, the government began its 'Golden Projects', which provided Internet Protocol (IP) connections between ministries and state-owned enterprises. In tandem, China's academic community established the first computer network in China and a direct link to Stanford University that gave it access to the World Wide Web. Whilst long the subject of turf battles between the Ministry of Posts and that of Electronic Industries – which were merged in 1998 to form a new Ministry of Information Industry – the Net has also become a means for the state itself to assert control over the bureaucracy.

After close study of other Asian approaches to the Internet – notably, that of Singapore,[66] the Chinese government has adopted two main strategies: filtering material and self-censorship. Websites deemed politically sensitive – including those of foreign news media and human rights organisations – are routinely blocked. A slew of regulations make it clear that any 'subversive' discourse, particularly dealing with such topics as Taiwanese independence and the mystical Falun Gong sect – will invite a repressive response. Recent crackdowns on Internet cafés have encouraged managements to monitor Web surfers closely and chatroom administrators hire censors – known as 'big mamas' – to screen the contents of bulletin boards. Dissidents such as Lin Hai and Huang Qi have been arrested and tried for Internet activities and their fates have been well publicised in the state media. The state has also cracked down on the fledgling China Democracy Party, formed in 1998 with the Net as a critical element in its strategy.[67]

Whether China's combination of filtering, censorship and surveillance will prevent the sort of Net-based activism credited with aiding the overthrow of Suharto in Indonesia remains to be seen. Indeed, one recent report suggests that 'political change is a determinant of Internet diffusion' rather than the other way around.[68] Elsewhere, regimes such as Cuba have tackled the issue by physically restricting access to the Net – there is one Internet café, in the Captitolio building, on the whole island – and by constructing a nationwide Intranet – Cubaweb – to facilitate acceptable commercial activity and propaganda. A combination of these approaches has also taken place in the Middle East where, typically, access relies on a single service provider, such as Bahrain's Batelco, under intense state scrutiny if not formal control.[69]

Reported efforts by the CIA to promote Internet privacy tools such as Safeweb – produced by its own proprietary company, INQTEL – in China[70] present an interesting contrast to the efforts of other US software manufacturers to market blocking, surveillance and anti-hacking products. These have been actively sought by the Beijing government at such events as the Security 2000 products fair (November 2000), sponsored by the Ministry of Public Security.[71] The CIA effort has apparently undergone something of a rethink post 9/11. INQTEL's flagship product – previously downloaded free from the Net – has not been available since November 2001.

Intelligence and law enforcement –
breaking down the firewall

With the ending of the Cold War, intelligence agencies – particularly
in the West – were faced with the prospect of radical downsizing. The
CIA, for example, did indeed suffer overall cuts of some 30 per cent in
its overall budget in the period 1990–6. The advent of the new world
order, however, also presented its own opportunities. In place of the
Warsaw Pact and order-of-battle intelligence, agencies perceived fresh
fields of endeavour. Initiatives in transnational crime fighting, terrorism and the war on drugs were eagerly grasped. Whilst the expansion
of IT in the early 1990s seemed to offer limitless scope for intelligence
in technical means of collection, a parallel but less visible change was
taking place in intelligence doctrine. The new world, it was decided,
required a change from reactive law enforcement to proactive intelligence intervention.

In the US, the debate led to a number of inter-agency and Congressional initiatives. Acts of 1984 and 1986 provided a legal framework
for extraterritorial judicial actions on behalf of the US,[72] culminating
in the Anti-terrorism and Effective Death Penalty Act of 1996.[73] We
have seen how in the European Union pressures for ever-greater
integration have resulted in an increasingly EU-wide legislative framework revolving around Europol and the Schengen Agreement for
cross-border judicial activities. This mirrors initiatives in individual
states, such as Britain's Criminal Justice Act of 1988 which brings
categories of crime within the purview of national justice whether or
not committed within the UK itself.[74]

For US policy makers – reflecting perhaps a culture more steeped
in legal mores – the debate has been especially acute. As three
knowledgeable observers have written:

> The Law Enforcement/national security divide is especially significant,
> carved deeply into the topography of American government. The national
> security paradigm fosters active, aggressive intelligence gathering. It
> anticipates the threat before it arises and plans preventive actions against
> suspected targets. In contrast, the law enforcement paradigm fosters
> reactions to information provided voluntarily, uses ex-post-facto arrests

and trials governed by rules of evidence, and protects the rights of citizens.[75]

Throughout Western countries, and indeed worldwide, a combination of tradition and bureaucratic rivalry has sharpened a clear distinction between domestic and foreign intelligence agencies. In the US, this was asserted even more firmly after the 1970s revelations of CIA domestic surveillance. In the EU, and the UK in particular, the domestic/foreign firewall and restrictions on domestic surveillance in general were a lot more fluid, maintained as much by bureaucratic 'turf' considerations as by legal safeguard. However, on 13 September 2001, the UK government asked all communications service providers to retain the following information:

- logs of all e-mails sent and received (not the content);

- logs showing the allocation of dynamic IP addresses (Internet usage);

- logs identifying the source, destination and times of all calls made or routed through their telephone networks.

Whilst cloaked in the catch-all 9/11 garb, the measures, like much else in the expanded domestic surveillance armoury, have been in preparation for some time. In April 2001 MI 5 announced the building of a new £25 million e-mail surveillance system that would have the power to monitor all e-mails and Internet messages sent and received in Britain. The government is requiring ISPs such as Freeserve and AOL to have 'hardwire' links to the new centre – codenamed GTAC (Government Technical Assistance Centre) – inside Thames House, the MI 5's London headquarters. Under powers granted in the Terrorism Act (2001), but long sought, the new centre will also handle encryption by requiring any specified individuals and companies to hand over secure 'keys'. As Caspar Bowden, Director of the Council for Information Policy Research (a civil liberties lobby), points out, with these capabilities 'the government can track every website that a person visits, without a warrant, giving rise to a culture of suspicion by association'.[76]

Indeed, the dangers have also been pointed out in the report of the government's own Intelligence Ombudsman, Sir Swinton Thomas. As official figures show that wiretapping has been increased by 20 per cent in the course of a year, errors include the wrongful tapping of the phone of a suspected kidnap victim's family, the recording of 66 calls made by a man who 'inherited' a target's phone number, and 26 wrongful taps due to operator error. One wholly innocent victim was bugged three times by the security service. 'I am concerned about the number of errors reported during the year,' Thomas observes. Under the tenure of Labour's Jack Straw as Home Secretary, 2,080 warrants were issued in 2000, an increase of 346 on 1999. Straw was signing an average of six warrants per day toward the end of his period, almost double the score of his Tory predecessor, Michael Howard.[77]

The US – 'a new way of thinking'

In the US, there has long been no restriction on claimed intercepts by the Echelon system except to exclude 'US persons' as more fully described by an NSA directive, USSID 18. Before the enactment of USA-Patriot, intercepted data could not be shared with US law enforcement agencies; now it can. Similarly, domestic agencies can now pool data with foreign intelligence agencies. Critics have drawn a close parallel between the worldwide scope of Echelon and the domestic scope of progammes such as Carnivore.

The USA-Patriot Act eased restrictions on law enforcement agencies established in the Foreign Intelligence Surveillance Act (FISA) of 1978. FISA was modified to permit exploitation of changing information technologies such as roving surveillance, pen registers and trap-and-trace authorities. It now permits the transfer of foreign intelligence information obtained from law enforcement sources to intelligence agencies in accordance with regulations established by the Attorney General in consultation with the Director of Central Intelligence – with the allowance of exceptions if/when the Attorney General determines that disclosure would jeopardise ongoing law enforcement investigations or impair law enforcement interests. Although the potential for abuse has been widely recognised, the premise is that information about foreign terrorists gathered by law enforcement agencies, including grand jury information, should be available to intelligence agencies.

Passed in great haste, and with muted opposition, the new anti-terrorism Act lays the foundation for a domestic intelligence-gathering system of unprecedented scope. By treating all available data holistically, the legislation permits genuine cross-database searching offered by technology such as Carnivore and empowers the government to shift the primary mission of the FBI from solving crimes to gathering domestic intelligence. In addition, the Treasury Department has been charged with building a financial intelligence-gathering system yielding data that can be accessed by the CIA.

Most significantly, for the first time the CIA will have the authority to influence FBI surveillance operations inside the United States and to obtain evidence gathered by federal grand juries and criminal wiretaps. Whilst the foundations for such data pooling were already in place, a 13 November 2001 directive from US Attorney General John Ashcroft established a National Law Enforcement Coordinating Committee on Counter Terrorism and ordered more comprehensive use of the existing Regional Information Sharing System (RISS). Comprising a nationwide network of six regional intelligence centres, the RISS system has created riss.net, 'the only secure, Internet-based national network for the sharing of criminal intelligence amongst federal, state and local law enforcement agencies'.[78] Ashcroft's 'sweeping reorganisation of the Department of Justice' reflects how profoundly the attacks changed the nation's thinking about the balance between domestic security and civil liberties. The Act effectively tears down legal firewalls erected 25 years ago after disclosures about presidential abuses of domestic intelligence-gathering against political activists. 'We are going to have to get used to a new way of thinking,' Assistant Attorney General Michael Chertoff, who is overseeing the investigation of the 9/11 attacks, said in an interview. 'What we are going to have is a Federal Bureau of Investigation that combines intelligence with effective law enforcement.' The new law 'should be a big step forward in changing the culture'.

In the new Act, Congress authorised a secure, nationwide communications system for the sharing of terrorism-related information with local police. 'Terrorists are a hybrid between domestic criminals and international agents,' Utah Senator Orrin Hatch, a strong proponent of the Bill, said in floor debate on 11 October. 'We must lower the barriers that discourage our law enforcement and intelligence agencies from working together to stop these terrorists. These hybrid criminals call for new hybrid tools.'[79]

A sense of how these 'hybrid tools' measures will operate in practice is provided by recent moves by the FBI. In a project called Cyber Knight, developed by the Bureau's electronic tools laboratory, a programme known as Magic Lantern would allow the secret installation of eavesdropping software over the Internet that records every keystroke on an individual computer. The software is somewhat similar to so-called Trojan software already used illegally by some hackers and corporate spies. The FBI envisages one day using Magic Lantern to record the secret unlocking key a person might use to scramble messages or computer files with encryption software.

Magic Lantern would largely resolve an important problem with the FBI's existing monitoring technology, the Key Logger System, which has required physical access into a target's home or business with a so-called sneak-and-peek warrant to attach the device to a computer. Magic Lantern could be installed over the Internet by tricking a person into double-clicking an e-mail attachment or by exploiting some of the same weaknesses in popular commercial software that allow hackers to break into computers. 'If they are using this kind of program, it would be a highly effective way to bypass any encryption problems,' said James E. Gordon, who heads the information technology division of the famous detective firm Pinkerton Consulting and Investigations: 'once they have the keys to the kingdom, they have complete access to anything that individual is doing'.[80]

The dark glass – into the future

Over the longer term, the continuing relevance, if not existence, of both imagery and signals intelligence will come into question. Within a decade, sophisticated imagery technology will come on the open market. Targets will know what they look like from the sky and take counter-measures, as India apparently did to conceal preparations for the 1998 nuclear tests. Commercial firms offer images of ever-increasing quality. One measure is resolution – how small something can be without loss of identity. In a one-metre resolution (the watershed image), a parked car would be clearly identifiable, but not its make. People can be discerned but not personally identified.

Sigint faces sharper challenges – from digitising, packet switching, fibre optics and encryption. Digitising makes it possible to send huge amounts of information over a single channel and thus vastly compounds the challenge of sorting out particulars. Packet switching means that the routing of a message may be changed in the middle of a communication and that the address of a message can be sent in a different packet to the message itself. With the improvement in cable transmission made possible by fibre optics, many fewer messages are sent into the open air, where satellites or ground stations can intercept them. If Sigint is to remain useful, it will have to get close to the communication channels it seeks to intercept.

The end of the Cold War was rightly greeted across the globe as a time of release from the threat of nuclear annihilation. But, just as in the nuclear arms race, there is a foreboding that, for intelligence agencies as for societies in general, technology is running ahead of, and indeed driving, human actions. The irony is that – as professional terrorists, criminals and drugs cartels become more adept at avoiding surveillance – the technology is increasingly targeted at civil liberties groups and legitimate protest, not to mention commercial and political targets, whose aims are those of civil society itself.

However, the human and fallible element is unavoidable. Over the last two decades, analyst James Bamford has probably done more than most to raise the veil on these matters. He observes that

> information … can be held eternally. As permanent as India ink, the mark can remain with the person forever. He will never know why he was placed on the customs blacklist, who put him there, why he lost a contract – or worse.[81]

Notes

1 See Gregory F. Treverton, *Reshaping Intelligence for the Age of Information*, Cambridge, Mass: RAND, 2001, Chapter 1.

2 See European Parliament, *Report on the Role of the European Union in Combating Terrorism* (A5-0273/20012: July 2001), p. 5/18.

3 For probably the best current overview of the NSA, see James Bamford, *Body of Secrets: How America's NSA and Britain's GCHQ Eavesdrop upon the World*, London: Century, 2001.

4 *Ibid.*, p. 475.

5 There was apparently some dispute about this in Moscow; see 'Russia Denies Closure of Sigint Center in Cuba', rferl.org/Yahoo, 22 August 2001.

6 See Vincent Jauvert, 'Espionage – How France Listens to the Whole World', *Nouvel Observateur*, 5 April 2001.

7 See Duncan Campbell, *Interception Capabilities 2000*, European Parliament, Scientific Technical Assessments Office Report (hereafter STOA Rep.), pp. 19–20.

8 *Ibid.*, pp. 16–23.

9 *Ibid.*

10 See *State Surveillance in the Internet*, bernal.co.uk/capitulo3.htm (hereafter State/Surv/net), p. 21.

11 *Ibid.*, p. 6.

12 See Bamford, *Body of Secrets*, p. 466.

13 STOA Rep., pp. 17–18.

14 See Bamford, *Body of Secrets*, p. 393.

15 STOA Rep., p. 18.

16 See Mark Urban, *UK Eyes Alpha*, London: Faber, 1996, pp. 258, 90.

17 See Desmond Ball and Jeffrey Richelson, *The Ties That Bind: Intelligence Cooperation between the UK/USA Countries*, London: Allen and Unwin, 1985, pp. 137–8.

18 STOA Rep., p. 22.

19 *Ibid.*, p. 23.

20 http://www.jya.com/crypto.htm

21 STOA Rep., p. 23.

22 *Ibid.*

23 See Bamford, *Body of Secrets*, pp. 460–3.

24 See State/Surv/net, pp. 2–3.

25 Bamford, *Body of Secrets*, p. 421.

26 Niall McCay, 'Eavesdropping on Europe', *Wired*, 30 September 1998.

27 The full series of reports are: Vol. 1, *Presentation of the Four Studies/Analysis: Data Protection and Human Rights in the European Union and the Role of the European Parliament*; Vol. 2, *Interception Capabilities 2000*; Vol. 3, *Encryption and Cryptosystems in Electronic Surveillance*; Vol. 4, *The Legality of the Interception of Electronic Communications*; Vol. 5, *The Perception of Economic Risks Arising from the Potential Vulnerability of Electronic Commercial Media*.

28 Steve Wright, 'An Appraisal for Technologies of Political Control', European Parliament Directorate General for Research (Dir. B), STOA Programme, Luxembourg, 1998.

29 *Guardian*, 15 June 2001; *Ekstra Bladet* (Denmark), 18 September 1999.

30 See Nick Hager, *Secret Power: New Zealand's Role in the International Spy Network*, Nelson, New Zealand: Craig Potton, 1996.

31 Bamford, *Body of Secrets*, p. 411.

32 See State/Surv/net, p. 4.

33 Bamford, *Body of Secrets*, p. 409.

34 This is the US intelligence community's own internal TV service; see Bamford, *Body of Secrets*, pp. 606–7.

35 See Suelette Dreyfus, 'Spies in the Forests', *Independent*, 22 November 1999.

36 Ted Brindis, 'Anti-terror Tolls Include High-tech', Associated Press, 28 October 2001.

37 See STOA Rep., p. 30.

38 See *Jane's Intelligence Digest*, 13 January 2002; for related matter, see also Colin Campbell, 'Intelligent Computer Reads Many Typefaces', *New York Times*, 19 August 1984; NSA technology factsheet, 'Information Sorting and Retrieval by Language and Topic', 1999; Berger-Liaw Neural Network, University of Southern California press release No. 0999025, 30 September 1999.

39 See State/Surv/net, p. 8. The patent was filed on 15 April 1997.

40 See Duncan Campbell, 'How the Plotters Slipped the US Net', *Guardian*, 27 September 2001.

41 See Bamford, *Body of Secrets*, pp. 604–11.

42 See 'Quantum Computing', *The Sciences*, July/August 1999.

43 John Markoff, 'Tiniest Circuits Hold Prospect of Explosive Computer Speeds', *New York Times*, 16 July 1999.

44 Seymour Hersh, 'The Intelligence Gap: How the Digital Age Left Our Spies Out in the Cold,' *New Yorker*, 6 December 1999.

45 See European Parliament, Temporary Committee on the Echelon Interception System, *Working Document*, 4 May 2001, p. 108.

46 See Brian McWilliams, 'CIA Web Site Cans Cookies after Report', Newsbytes.com, 19 March 2002.

47 See European Parliament, *Working Document*, p. 107.

48 Duncan Campbell, 'When Spies Fall Out', *Guardian*, 3 July 2001.

49 *USA Today*, 5 February 2001.

50 Ziff Davis, 'How the NSA Is Monitoring You – and Why It's Wasting Its Time', *Smart Business*, June 2001.

51 Duncan Campbell, 'How the Plotters'.

52 *Internetweek*, 2 July 2001.

53 Vincent Jauvert, 'Espionage'.

54 *Wall Street Journal*, 17 March 2000.

55 STOA Rep., Annexe 2–3.

56 See Duncan Campbell, 'Germany, UK Breaching Human Rights with NSA Spy Link-up', *Guardian*, 27 May 2001, citing the draft committee report.

57 See State/Surv/net, p. 11.

58 State/Surv/net, p. 13.

59 See Gordon Bennett, 'The Federal Agency of Government Communications and Information', paper for Conflict Studies Research Centre, RMA, Sandhurst (C105-GB), p. 17.

60 Alan Boyle, 'Acrypto Can Save Lives', @ZDNET/26/01/99.

61 Rick Montgomery, 'It's Time to Join the Cyber War', *Daily Telegraph* (Australia), 19 April 1999.

62 See *Federal Computer Week*, 19 April 1999.

63 See *USA Today*, 25 August 1999.

64 For an overview see Dorothy E. Denning, 'Activism, Hacktivism and Cyber-terrorism: the Internet as a Tool for Influencing Foreign Policy', paper for The Terrorism Research Institute, Georgetown University/Nautilus Institute, 1996–9.

65 See *Guardian*, 1 September 2001. See also Shanthi Kalathil and Taylor C. Boas, 'The Internet and State Control in Authoritarian Regimes: China, Cuba, and the Counter Revolution', Carnegie Global Policy Program, Working Paper No. 21, July 2001, p. 4.

66 Kalathil and Boas, 'The Internet', p. 6.

67 *Ibid.*, p. 9.

68 *Ibid.*, p. 2.

69 *Jane's Intelligence Review*, January 1998.

70 *Guardian*, 1 September 2001.

71 Kalathil and Boas, 'The Internet', p. 9.

72 Richard Best for Congressional Research Service, *Intelligence and Law Enforcement: Countering Transnational Threats to the US*, RL30252: 16 January 2001, p. 6.

73 *Ibid.*, p. 7.

74 *Ibid.*, p. 6.

75 *Ibid.*, p. 8.

76 *Sunday Times*, 30 April 2000.

77 *Sunday Telegraph*, 2 December 2001.

78 See Declan Mucullagh, 'USA Patriot Opens CIA, NSA, Intelligence Databases to Police', politechbot.com, p. 4.

79 See Jim McGee, *Washington Post*, 4 November 2001.

80 See Ted Brindis, 'FBI Develops Eavesdropping Tools', Associated Press, 22 November 2001.

81 Bamford, *Body of Secrets*, p. 427.

CHAPTER 3

US INTELLIGENCE

Back to the Future?

'Frankly, we weren't particularly concerned at what post-Soviet Afghanistan was going to look like.'

– Robert Gates, former CIA Director, 1995

Amidst much congratulatory drum beating, the sudden death of the Cold War was bound to raise mixed emotions within the US intelligence community. For one thing, it was largely unanticipated. Director of Central Intelligence (DCI) William Webster and his boss, former DCI George Bush, had been consistently sceptical about the increasingly desperate efforts at Soviet reformation. For some months into 1989 – the first year of the Bush administration – the consensus view was, in the words of future CIA chief Robert Gates, that Mikhail Gorbachev aimed to 'restore the Soviet Union to good health politically and economically and thereby allow it to retain its place as a superpower'.[1] The underlying assumption of an enduring, perhaps more dangerous, superpower adversary was strongly contested in the CIA's Bureau of Soviet Analysis (SOVAN). That the Bureau's views were consistently marginalised even after the dramatic fall of the Berlin Wall in 1989 was to have unpredictable consequences for US policy, particularly in regions of the Third World where the 'hot' component of the Cold War continued much as before.

By 1992, however, the shape of the new world order was universally acknowledged by the hardest sceptics in the CIA's headquarters at Langley, Virginia. For the wider US government view, the

Intelligence Reorganization Act of 1992 attempted to address the new realities. 'While the US must prepare to meet different challenges,' the Act noted, '...its attention is no longer focused upon a single predominant threat to its interests. At the same time, faced with huge budget deficits, funding for intelligence activities is certain to decrease significantly during the next decade.' With the US deficit blooming out of control, cuts were certainly on the agenda. Former DCI William Colby observed that 'the end of the Cold War had brought the chance for large cuts in the CIA, especially in its budget'.[2] In 1994, details of the overall intelligence budget were inadvertently released in proceedings from a Congressional committee. According to press reports, the CIA had requested $3.1 billion and the Pentagon agencies (NRO, NSA, CIO, DIA – see below) some $13.2 billion, while the various joint contingency efforts grouped under the acronym TIARA (Tactical Intelligence and Related Activities), sought $10.4 billion.[3]

However, if the overall intelligence budget figure of $27.7 billion was indeed down some 25 per cent from peak 1988–9 levels,[4] new missions were quickly being found for old systems. The end of the Cold War coincided with the advent of the information and microchip revolution that, in large part, had been the Soviet empire's nemesis. The vast array of satellite and global eavesdropping technology would find new applications and fresh targets amongst erstwhile allies and not only within the shrinking band of 'rogue states' in open opposition to US power.

The Gulf War and after: grasping the 'unipolar moment'

Yet the events that were to set the mould for future US intelligence priorities were not so much those trailing the dramatic collapse of the 'evil empire' as those heralding the seemingly unqualified triumph of US forces in the Gulf War against Saddam Hussein. The victory in the Gulf provided vivid confirmation of the role of intelligence in combat situations. The NSA's geosynchronous satellites, stationed at a constant 24,000 miles above the earth, had been retargeted to search out Iraqi missile launches to an accuracy of 120 seconds. The US Airforce's Talon Lance system relayed satellite information to aircraft cockpits within ten minutes.[5] Advances in digitisation technology meant that battlefield assessment pictures could be delivered swiftly to the front line. Here, amidst much talk of the 'unipolar moment' for US power, the Pentagon began a wide-ranging 'bottom up' strategic review. The findings, released in September 1993, aimed to reconfigure US forces toward 'full spectrum dominance' on any conceivable future battlefield. Clearly, the maintenance of military hegemony was nothing new for US policy. What was new was the demotion of the Pentagon's major contingency – war against an approximately equal contender represented, for all its failings, by the Soviet Union. In its place was an evolving strategy to maintain the ability to fight two major theatre wars (Iraq and North Korea, for example) simultaneously. The outcome for US intelligence, though, was decidedly mixed in terms of its overall ability to offer a broad analysis as opposed to a narrowly focused range of strategic indicators.

Throughout the Reagan and Bush administrations, the long-running Washington Beltway (inner-ring) battle between the DCI and the Pentagon for the future of intelligence gathering had reached something of a stand-off. If the Soviet demise led to a massive redundancy in the traditional Langley focus on Russian missile forces and order of battle on the central front, the Gulf War had pushed the Agency's Support for Military Operations (SMO) mission well to the fore. This, however, had become an increasingly technical exercise, focusing on real-time combat intelligence of the sort that had indeed been crucial in the desert front line and was the speciality of the now-ascendant NSA. The longstanding turf feud with the Pentagon agencies was partially resolved by DCI Gates in 1992, when he removed the order-of-battle analysis to the NSA and created a new Central Imagery Office (CIO) which became fully constituted as the National Imagery and Mapping Agency (NIMA) in 1996.

Changing priorities – PDD-35 and the eclipse of Humint

The establishment of NIMA – combining the Defense Department's Mapping Agency, the CIA's National Photographic Interpretation Center and various other technical functions with the analysis department of the CIO – marked a major withdrawal of the CIA from the ability to commission its own technical analysis and the primacy of SMO as the chief intelligence mission. If some in the Agency were to echo the worries of Senate Intelligence Vice-Chair John Kerry that the merger would be 'a big mistake' if military was to totally eclipse political and diplomatic coverage,[6] new roles would soon appear. The Clinton administration was to formalise the changing order of priorities in a classified Presidential Decision Directive (PDD) 35 of 10 March 1995. Introduced in the wake of damaging revelations of a long-term Russian mole in CIA Counter-Intelligence, Aldrich Ames, PDD-35 defines intelligence requirements from tier zero to tier four. Tier zero is strategic warning and crisis management, whilst tier four covers countries that are of virtually no interest to the United States.

The highest priority was assigned to intelligence support for military operations – SMO. The second priority was providing political, economic and military intelligence on 'countries hostile to the United States' – a category, as we shall see, capable of broad interpretation. The third priority was assigned to 'protecting American citizens from new transnational threats' such as drug trafficking, terrorism, organised crime and weapons of mass destruction.

The new guidelines, following the recommendations of the House Permanent Select Committee (January 1996), the Aspin/Brown Commission (March 1996) and the bi-partisan Twentieth Century Fund (June 1996), were to reflect the enhanced role of intelligence, and the CIA in particular, in supporting US business worldwide. The ethos 'shaping America's priorities in the new world we live in' was also reflected in a wholesale adaptation of business school management methodology in the CIA itself. In keeping with the requirements of 'customer support', the Agency's new Human Resources Oversight Council was to emphasise the meeting of targets for intelligence 'product' set in a regular Performance Appraisal Report (PAR). Chief amongst these were the Daily Economic Intelligence Bulletin, introduced in 1993 to 'support senior economic policy makers' and the Economic Executives' Intelligence Brief, produced five days a week as the economic equivalent of the established President's Daily Brief – the regular morning intelligence digest delivered to the White House. Despite the acknowledgement of the need to address 'low probability, high impact dangers and objectives', the emphasis on 'switching the analytic focus from a judgement of *whether* a certain development is likely to *how* it could come about',[7] as internal guidelines for the Directorate of Intelligence would have it, rested on a set of somewhat sanguine assumptions about 'the very hopeful nature of the post-Cold War era',[8] which were to be soon found wanting.

An official budgetary figure for US intelligence was published for the first time in 1997. At $26.6 billion, the total closely approximated the figure which emerged in 1994.[9] In some estimates, the mid-1990s budget stood at $6.2 billion for the National Reconnaissance Office (NRO), which launches and operates satellites, $3.7 billion for the NSA, with a staff of 38,000, $3.1 billion for the 17,000-strong CIA and $2 billion for the Joint Military Intelligence Program (JMIP), which combines the Defense Intelligence Agency (DIA) and the service organisations, with some 19,000 employees. The budget for the inter-agency TIARA takes up a further $12 billion.[10]

PDD-35 marked the eclipse of traditional Humint collection by the intelligence agencies. The Presidential Directive specifically identified targets that the US intelligence community would not collect against, which in the early 1990s included Afghanistan.[11] The Ames affair, in which the former joint CIA/FBI counter-intelligence head had, over a ten-year period, betrayed virtually all the Agency's double agents in the European theatre, had led to a massive mole hunt led by a serving FBI officer, Ed Curran. With more than 300 operatives under suspicion, it was viewed by insiders as a virtual death knell for the Directorate of Operations, with institutional pride only partially satisfied by the arrest, on 20 February 2001, of a further Russian mole, Robert Hansen, who had occupied a similarly senior counter-intelligence position in the FBI itself.[12]

'Redefining national security' – Clinton and the rise of economic intelligence

Whilst the full impact of what former DCI Stansfield Turner was to term 'redefining national security'[13] towards economic issues would not come about until the Clinton administration, much groundwork was laid in the last year of Bush senior. The Intelligence Reorganization Act of 1992 envisaged wide-ranging structural changes. Although some of these, including the appointment of a new Director of National Intelligence – superseding the DCI – were defeated, many other developments showed the shape of things to come. Reflecting the focus on SMO under a resurgent Pentagon, the Act provided for a new National Imagery Agency, finally established as NIMA in 1996 to oversee the equivalent of Imagery Intelligence – Imint -- for the NSA, with Fort Meade itself receiving significantly greater funding under the Department of Defense. A more radical point of departure, however, was the stress on economic intelligence. The CIA's GNP estimates had long provided a detailed breakdown of the former Soviet economy, in the form of an annual report. In the growing Langley consensus, this expertise should now be redirected to more general economic intelligence gathering, which the Bush administration duly set out to identify in National Security Review (NSR) 29 – formalised as National Security Directive (NSD) 67 on 20 March 1992.

Thus, during April 1992 testimony to Congress, incoming DCI Robert Gates observed that 'policy makers identified new requirements … the intelligence community has a wider range of customers than ever, with interests that extend beyond traditional … security concerns', and, in particular, that, 'financial and trade issues and technological developments that could adversely affect the United States were considered of major importance'.[14]

If the Bush administration had signalled its intent to employ the intelligence apparatus for 'levelling the playing field' of international trade, the full realisation would be accomplished under the Clinton presidency of 1993. Heirs to the neoliberal tradition in US politics, the new regime had strong links, both ideological and personal, with the Trilateral doctrine of Jimmy Carter. Here, pan-Western corporate solidarity was seen as the bedrock of world politics, with international relations viewed as virtually a branch of international business. Accordingly, one of Clinton's first moves was to set up a National Economic Council as a counterpoint to the National Security Council

(NSC). In a related move, a new Trade Promotion Coordinating Committee was established, with direct intelligence input from the CIA and direct links to US business through an Advocacy Center at the Department of Commerce. According to Carter's former DCI, Stansfield Turner, 'The pre-eminent threat to US national Security now lies in the economic sphere.'[15] Turner himself had pioneered this approach by establishing a secret Office of Intelligence Liaison in May 1977 to distribute commercially sensitive data from CIA and NSA sources to the Department of Commerce.[16] Renamed the Office of Executive Support in 1993, it was to assume a more public role[17] and actively promote its successes in countering 'unfair' international business practice and securing deals for US companies.

Amongst the claimed successes were the award of a $1.3 billion contract to the Raytheon Corporation for a wide-area surveillance system for the Amazon basin. The contract, originally awarded to the French consortium Thomson-CSF, was reassigned after NSA intercepts allegedly revealed evidence of bribery of Brazilian government officials.[18] Amongst many US government projects, Raytheon is responsible for maintaining the NSA's massive ground station at Sugar Grove, West Virginia. Other reported beneficiaries were the Boeing Corporation and McDonnell-Douglas, who managed to obtain the reversal of a $6 billion contract to supply the Saudi national airline by the EU's Airbus Industrie. Again, NSA intercepts of fax and phone traffic had revealed apparent evidence of bribery between the European consortium and Saudi officials.

Amidst media revelations of organised intelligence activity by competitors – France, Germany, Britain, Japan and Israel were mentioned in particular – and accusations that French intelligence was penetrating such US corporations as IBM and Texas Instruments, bugging business flights on Air France and carrying out 'ten to fifteen break-ins a day' in Paris hotels,[19] economic espionage had become the talk of Capitol Hill. Congressional concern mounted that 'Foreign intelligence agents are draining our country of its ideas like sap from a tree';[20] this was when former DCI James Woolsey justified spying on the US's 'continental European friends ... because you bribe' (see p. 54).[21] Whilst the scale of US operations is suggested by CIA claims to have uncovered 51 such cases in 1994, accounting for some $28 billion worth of contracts, the aggressive use of intelligence to further US economic interests smacked to some of a new mercantilism. Cases included 1995 trade negotiations on the import of Japanese cars, French participation in the GATT talks of 1993, and the Asia Pacific Economic Conference (APEC) of 1997. Particularly keen on the new approach was the Commerce Department of Ron Brown, which established its own 'war room' for crisis management of economic issues. 'We steal secrets for our military preparedness,' observed Stansfield Turner; 'I don't see why we shouldn't stay economically competitive.'[22]

Blowback 1: Iraq – 'enormous market potential'

If the received wisdom in the Clinton administration was, in the words of then-incoming 1993 DCI James Woolsey, that economic intelligence has indeed become 'the hottest current topic in intelligence policy',[23] there was, in the Middle East, some other clearly unfinished business for US policy. Iraq, under the strong-arm rule of Saddam Hussein, remained obstinately defiant against UN sanctions and occasional US military threats. As the new Director eased into the Washington Beltway round of press receptions and Congressional briefings, the new world order was to yield intelligence challenges a great deal less benign than European airframe constructors or the makers of Japanese luxury cars.

Whilst CIA involvement with the ruling Iraqi Ba'ath party had dated back to the late 1950s, it was during the Iran–Iraq war of 1980–8 that US intelligence agencies took on the role of virtual ally to the regime of Saddam Hussein. On 26 February 1982 the Reagan administration had removed Iraq from the State Department list of 'State Sponsors of Terrorism', ostensibly in recognition of the Saddam regime's 'improved record' in this competitive field. A further result of the 'positive trend' in Iraqi policy was the June 1982 provision of NSA satellite data on the Gulf battlefield that quite probably staved off Iraq's defeat.[24] In 1984, with the restoration of full diplomatic relations, Reagan signed a National Security Decision Directive

(NSDD) authorising 'limited intelligence sharing' with Baghdad, a programme that became the direct responsibility of then CIA Deputy Director Robert Gates.[25]

The burgeoning intelligence intimacy between Langley and Saddam would come to encompass communications intercepts, weapons data, high definition photography of Iranian targets, and near real-time troop movement data gathered from US-manned AWACS based in Saudi Arabia. A measure of the closeness was how little it was affected by the attack on the frigate USS *Stark* in May 1987 by Iraqi 'friendly fire' – an incident that recalls an earlier assault on a US Navy vessel by a Middle Eastern ally, the Israeli crippling of the USS *Liberty*, almost exactly 20 years before.

A substantive underpinning of the relationship was, of course, economic. Starting with the granting of $400 million in US Agriculture Department Commodity Credit Corporation (CCC) guarantees in 1983, the US economic engagement with Iraq would extend to some $3.4 billion in Commodity Credit outlay by 1988. Iraq was second only to Mexico as a recipient of CCC guarantees and the number one export market for US rice. Oil, too, had come to figure in the relationship, with the annual US take of 1.5 billion barrels absorbing a quarter of Iraq's total oil exports. In recognition of the 'reassurance' found in the CIA's Autumn 1989 National Intelligence Estimate (NIE)[26] and fearful of Iraq's 'enormous market potential' falling to the unscrupulous French,[27] the Bush administration signed National Security Directive 26, designed to set the course for 'normal relations between the United States and Iraq' as official US policy.

The 2 October 1989 promulgation of NSD 26 – after a pro-forma NSC meeting chaired by Robert Gates, now Deputy National Security Advisor – was to set the stage for another year of commercially driven intelligence policy. It was not that the CIA was unaware of the aggressive aims of the Iraqi Revolutionary Command Council. The collapse of the Atlanta branch of the Banko Nazionale de Lavoro (BNL) in August 1989 had revealed over $4 billion of unsecured loans to Iraq – the biggest bank fraud in US history. In the CIA's own estimates, at least $600 million had gone on weapons acquisition.[28] If the BNL had been the principal banker for Saddam's global front company network, links had also been revealed with the Chilean Cardoen arms conglomerate and the Iraqi-owned British company Matrix Churchill (see below). The voluminous international telex traffic and cash flows had been extensively monitored from the outset throughout the US intelligence community. The official US line, however, authorised by former DCI George Bush and endorsed by former Deputy DCI and NSC point man for Iraq policy, Robert Gates, was unchanging. 'The President doesn't want to single out Iraq,' the US Under Secretary of State was reported as saying after an NSC meeting on 16 April 1990. And the meeting chair, Deputy NSC Advisor Gates, was quoted as being 'leery about moving too quickly' on Saddam's worldwide weapons-buying spree and increasingly belli-cose international posture.[29]

Although accusations of 'intelligence failure' were to fly after the Iraqi blitzkrieg of 1 August 1990, the CIA could point to a growing series of reports in the 1989-90 period accurately detailing Iraq's weapons procurement programmes and a 'convincing' finding of 25 July 1990 on the Kuwait invasion plan itself by the Agency's chief national intelligence officer (CIO) for warnings.[30] Whilst the CIA resisted the Pentagon's efforts at full incorporation of the Agency's participation within the Joint Intelligence Center (JIC), its main role remained restricted to military support during the conflict, notably the tracking of Saddam's movements in his six US-made Winnebago camper vans, three of which were successfully targeted by the US Airforce. In some accounts, however, the Agency kept its hand in with a series of covert CBW (chemical and biological warfare) bombing missions on Iraqi bio-weapons facilities.[31]

The main US failure both before and after the Gulf War was one of policy, not intelligence. In its determination to complete the '100 hour war' on schedule for Bush's re-election, the administration called an arbitrary halt to hostilities on 27 February 1991. On 1 March, however, mass uprisings in the Shi'ite Southern areas of Iraq and the Kurdish North took place in response to Bush's urgings to 'put him (Saddam) aside' and 'bring Iraq back into the family of peace loving nations'. Unfortunately, the President's exhortation had been aimed at inspiring dissident Iraqi generals rather than popular insurgency. To this end, US bombing had deliberately left the most capable elements of the Iraqi army – the Republican Guard – intact in their rear-deployed positions in Northern Iraq. Central Command commander H. Norman Schwartzkopf had explicitly offered US support to his Iraqi counterparts at the Safwan ceasefire talks of 3 March. And in order to facilitate a rapid conclusion to the expected coup, the US prohibition on Iraqi air traffic had deliberately excluded the use of helicopters. In the event, the untouched Mi 24 *Hind* helicopter gunships were critical in suppressing a rebellion of genuinely broad-based opposition forces, which at one stage had seized control of 16 of Iraq's 18 provinces.

If, for many observers, US inaction was totally inexplicable, the outcome was perhaps the least worst option for the Bush White House. A 'defanged' Saddam was preferable to continuing turbulence in Iraq, which could expand the influence of Washington's true *bête noire*, Iran. Conservative US allies in the Middle East – in effect, all the states, and the Saudis in particular – were horrified at the prospect of nascent democracy offered by the umbrella Free Iraqi Council (FIC) gathering at the Hotel Bristol in West Beirut under the sponsorship of the CIA. The Agency was soon to backtrack on the FIC. And Bush's refrain had changed overnight from overthrowing the 'evil dictator' to 'bring the boys home', an order duly accomplished with great haste and much bunting.

'Regime change?' – Northern Iraq, the INC and the CIA
With the Iraqi rebellion comprehensively crushed and the FIC descending into the familiar pattern of exile parochialism, a coup from within the Iraqi military seemed again the likely option for a Baghdad 'regime change' that would be congenial to Washington. Although Bush signed a top secret intelligence 'finding' authorising the removal of Saddam on 18 August 1990, it had not been pursued with any great success. Intelligence from inside Iraq was, in the words of one former operative, 'a black hole'.[32] Accordingly, Bush notified Congress of a further finding in May 1991, with the allocation of some $15–20 million.[33] Whilst the CIA's efforts were still focused on sponsoring

action by dissident generals from what were known to be restive major Iraqi tribal groups – the al-Juber and al-Dulaim – with a serious coup attempt indeed taking place in July 1992, a second track was also emerging. A fresh coalition of opposition forces had assembled – the Iraq National Congress (INC).

The INC was formed when the two major Kurdish factions, the long-established Kurdish Democratic Party (KDP) headed by Massoud Barzani and the Patriotic Union of Kurdistan (PUK) of Jalal Talibani, decided to participate in a broad-based opposition conference in Vienna in June 1992. The Vienna gathering included over 200 delegates from 19 separate groups and spanned the spectrum of Iraq's opposition, from communists to representatives of the Tehran-based Supreme Assembly of the Islamic Revolution (SAIRI). Adopting a platform of democracy and minority rights within a federated Iraq, the INC was to follow the successful debut with the election of a full national Assembly of 234 members in October, meeting for the first time on Iraqi soil in the Kurdish safe haven of Salahuddin.

With an international profile bolstered by meetings with US Vice-President Al Gore and British Prime Minister John Major, the INC became the favoured recipient of US aid – voted by Congress at $40 million in 1993 – and also the focus of the CIA's increasingly ambitious operations. As a first step, the Agency hired Washington public relations consultants the Rendon Group to handle worldwide lobbying and propaganda. Rendon, run by a former Jimmy Carter campaign manager, had already been employed by Kuwait to rally support for the Emirate after the Iraqi invasion. While CIA-run radio stations were set up in Amman (Jordan), Cairo, Kuwait and Jeddah (Saudi Arabia), in October 1994 the Senate Intelligence Committee cleared the Agency to establish a semi-permanent ground presence in Kurdistan. Over the next two years, some 50 agents would be rotated over six-week periods in teams of four to ten, based in a fortified compound in the Salahuddin opposition enclave.

Drawing on previous Agency experience in Afghanistan, the plan drawn up by the CIA's 35-person Iraq Operations Group and its chief field officer, Robert Baer, envisaged the gradual strengthening of the Kurdish enclave and eventual reduction of Saddam to 'nothing more

US INTELLIGENCE: BACK TO THE FUTURE? 83

than the Mayor of Baghdad'.[34] Given a united opposition effort and strong US military support, the plan had, in the eyes of many observers, considerable merit. Neither of these conditions, however, were to obtain.

In late 1994, the direction of Iraqi operations was contested within the CIA by 'pressure from the top for a quick kill', which a faction within the INC – the al-Wifac or Iraq National Accord (INA), drawn from former Ba'athist military officers – were promising was just around the corner. The prospects of such a 'silver bullet coup' held undoubted attractions for the Clinton administration. US allies – particularly Turkey – were never happy with the INC's reliance on a strong, US-armed, Kurdish militia, which could easily form the backbone of an independent Kurdish state. Under the most optimistic scenario, the extension of INC territory would need large-scale US air support and, probably, special forces, confronting the White House with an unpalatable 'body bags problem' in the run-up to an election. Meanwhile the Kurds themselves, always uneasy allies, had been engaged in an increasing violent internecine struggle over territory and the lucrative smuggling traffic through Northern Kurdistan.

Events were to come to a head in March 1995. The Baer plan had called for a large-scale assault on Iraqi garrisons at Mosul and Kirkuk – the latter some way into Iraqi-controlled territory. With a target date of 4 March, the plan envisaged a coordinated attack by 20,000 Kurdish guerrillas, 1,000 INC troops and a further 1,000-strong contingent from the Iraqi Communist Party. It was to be directed by a former chief of Iraqi military intelligence, General Wafic Samarai. However, rivalry between the PUK, who had infuriated the other factions by occupying the regional capital, Irbil, the previous December, and the numerically stronger KDP had reached such a pitch that KDP leader Barzani refused to take part, leading to the cancellation of the operation. The White House too, categorically refused any sort of support, claiming to have only heard the full details of the plan from intercepts of CIA negotiations with PUK backers Iran on possible diversionary moves on the border.[35]

What military action did take place, however, was a large-scale incursion into Northern Kurdistan by Turkey. On 20 March, 35,000

Turkish troops, assisted by Barzani's KDP militia, seized a wedge of Kurdish territory in pursuit of their own insurgents, the Kurdish Workers Party (PKK). With the Baer 'liberated zone' plan clearly in ruins, attention at Langley turned again to the INA and the 'silver bullet' option. Indeed, a move in this direction had been proceeding concurrently with the Baer plan. In January 1995 a secret meeting was held at London's Heathrow Hilton between three Iraqi officers and intelligence staff from the US, Britain and Jordan. Whilst the organisers had successfully managed the journey, with the Iraqis returning home via Jordan with unmarked passports within 24 hours, Mukhabarat penetration of the conspirators led to mass arrests of some 122 officers and the execution, in March, of the coup leader, Air Force General Mazloum al-Dulaimi.[36]

Hostile penetration of the Iraqi opposition groups is perhaps unsurprising, considering pervasive Iraqi clan and tribal rivalries, the usual febrile atmosphere of exile politics, and interest from the intelligence services of Iran, Turkey, Saudi Arabia, France, Britain, Jordan and a host of freelance operators. On the US side, however, a clear set of goals for Iraq was clearly lacking. Aside from intermittently desperate essays in crisis management, policy was driven throughout the Clinton administration, as in the closing years of Bush, by the requirements of 'dual containment' of Iraq and Iran, with priority inevitably falling on the latter. If the Bush presidency could not escape the humiliations of Iran/Contra, the Clinton administration, under the State Department of Warren Christopher, was still haunted by the 1979 hostage crisis which had destroyed the last Democratic presidency of Jimmy Carter. An example of the prevailing Washington view can be found in a classified report of the 1992 Republican Task Force against Terrorism. Based on selective intelligence leaks and much speculation, this posited a 'New Axis Pact' between Baghdad, Tehran and the Syrian regime of Hafiz al-Assad which aimed to create a 'Tehran-controlled strategic axis stretching from the Mediterranean to Iran'.[37]

Regime change in the Beltway – the Iraq Liberation Act

With the replacement of James Woolsey by John Deutch as DCI in May 1995 the INA were again centre-stage in US planning. Deutch, transferred from the Defense Department, pressured the Agency to set up 'milestones' for another attempted coup, timed to take place before the November 1996 US elections. Whilst the CIA was to retain its presence in Salahuddin and Zackho on the Turkish border, the INA operation was to remain compartmentalised in a 'special channel'. If CIA caution in this respect was perhaps understandable, the Agency's multiple operations were beginning to resemble the tangled web of Middle East politics itself.

In June 1996 Saddam rolled up the plot by arresting 100 of the INA's military contacts and executing 30 officers. Saddam was to follow this US setback by striking at the INC. In August 1996, renewed fighting between KDP and PUK forces led to Barzani inviting in the Iraqi leader. Seizing the chance, some 40,000 Iraqi troops accompanied KDP fighters in the capture of Irbil on 31 August. By 9 September they had taken the last PUK stronghold, Sulaymaniyah. With detailed maps and lists, the black-windowed Range Rovers of the Iraqi Mukhabarat toured the streets of Irbil, headquarters of the INA, and the INC facilities at Salahuddin. Some 200 activists were executed and 2,000 transferred to Saddam's notorious interrogation centres. In scenes reminiscent of Vietnam, CIA field operatives and 650 local employees underwent a rushed evacuation to Turkey.[38] Whilst Iraq then withdrew its forces, and the US vented its frustration with a launch of 44 cruise missiles on Southern Iraq on 4 September, Washington's policy was in clear disarray.

If its position in Kurdistan remained uncertain, the INC and its leader, former banker and Chicago University mathematician Ahmed Chalabi, were to have continued success on Capitol Hill. The INC put its Rendon experience to good use in lobbying Congress for a further $58 million in direct aid and secured the passage of the Iraq Liberation Act, signed into law on 31 October 1998. In it, the administration was authorised (but not required) to provide training and up to $97 million in military supplies to likely-looking opposition groups.[39]

Overall, the administration could at least claim to have avoided total disaster in its Iraq policy, albeit more by default than intention. The Kurdish 'safe haven' remained essentially intact after Saddam's incursion. A steady stream of high-profile defectors, including, in

August 1995, Kamal al-Majid, Saddam's own son-in-law, provided fresh intelligence on Iraq and indications that there was indeed continuing unrest in the Iraq armed forces. Further intelligence was provided, more controversially, by CIA personnel among the 104 UN weapons inspectors, mandated to ensure the dismantling of Iraq's weapons of mass destruction (WMD). And in October 1998 the State Department achieved a partial reconciliation of opposition forces at a Washington meeting between the Kurdish leaders, Barzani and Talibani. For the CIA, though, despite an additional $1.8 billion supplemental voted by Congress at the time of the Iraq Liberation Act, priorities were still set by the four tiers of NDD 35, with Iraq's liberation a low third on the scale of 'national security'.

Indeed, notwithstanding the efforts in Kurdistan, many Arab observers believed that US policy actually aimed to *preserve* the Iraqi dictator. Following the 1996 debacle, commentary in the respected London-based Arab daily *al-Hayat* discerned 'the practical application of what was hitherto considered merely a theory – namely, that the United States has an interest in Saddam Hussein and his regime surviving, because it looks to him to confront Iran'.[40] More concrete proof yet for Middle East conspiracy theorists could be found in the fate of former CIA Chief of Station in Kurdistan, Robert Baer. In March 1995 he was recalled to Washington and charged by the FBI with violating Executive Order 12333, the 1983 Reagan injunction on assassinations. The indictment was for the attempted murder of Saddam Hussein.[41]

Blowback 2 – Afghanistan, Pakistan and the legacy of William Casey

For years afterwards, the CIA's $6 billion covert operation in Afghanistan was viewed as being instrumental in 'winning' the Cold War and as one of the Agency's greatest successes. Even after the Soviet withdrawal in 1989, massive US aid continued flowing to Islamist insurgent forces fighting the Moscow-backed regime of former communist President Najibullah. With the latter's final fall in 1992, little thought was given in Langley to the possible after-effects of 'positive symmetry' in arms deliveries supposedly to counter Russian support for their Afghan protégé. 'Frankly, we weren't particularly concerned at what post-Soviet Afghanistan was going to look like,' former DCI Robert Gates later observed, 'the truth of the matter was that we expected it to look like pre-Soviet Afghanistan.'[42]

The Agency's insouciance over its flooding of arms to the Afghan war zone was fuelling a convoluted regional power struggle, whose scope was ill-understood in Washington. Here, feuding amongst the concerned agencies was combined with post-Cold War feelgoodery and the customary Beltway premium on the interests of regional clients – notably Saudi Arabia. The Saudis had matched the US in arms funding for the Afghan Jihad, providing some additional $5 billion by 1992.[43]

Riyadh, however, like its close allies in Islamabad, was intently pursuing its own agenda in Central Asia. And whilst the CIA and even the DEA were content to leave the shattered Afghanis to their own devices after 1992, Pakistan's powerful Inter-Services Intelligence (ISI) was massively expanding its operations. Flush with US arms and technical support, the ISI grew from some 2,000 operatives at the start of the 1980s to 20,000 at the end of the Cold War. Even after the tailing off of US funding, the organisation continued to grow, rising to an estimated 40,000 and a $1 billion annual budget by the mid-1990s.[44]

A network of ISI-run training camps in both Pakistan and Afghanistan itself had instructed over 35,000 foreign Mujahidin from throughout the Islamic world by the early 1990s, a significant proportion from Saudi Arabia.[45] They were to continue their activities, often taking would-be Jihadis directly from Pakistan's 20,000 Saudi-financed *madrassas*. In 1989 the Makhtab al-Khidmat or services centre, the Peshawar-based Saudi–ISI headquarters coordinating the Afghan Jihad, was supplanted by a more clandestine body, the military base or Al-Qaida. In some estimates, over 100,000 Islamist radicals were to emerge out of the Afghan conflict to form a loose, globally connected network.[46] The impact of the 'Arab Afghans' would soon be felt in a range of regional conflicts, spanning Algeria, Bosnia, Chechnya, Egypt, Kashmir, the Philippines and Southern Sudan. More worrying for Western intelligence agencies, cells were also being established throughout the US and the European Union.

The legacy comes home

Early indications of the Afghan legacy coming home appeared in the foiled attempt by Sheikh Omar Abdel Rahman to place bombs in the United Nations, the FBI's New York office and the Lincoln and Holland road tunnels in June 1993, and the earlier efforts of Ramzi Yousef to blow up the World Trade Center on 26 February. Yousef, arrested in April 1997 in Pakistan, had been trained in Afghanistan. Abdel Rahman, spiritual leader of Egyptian Islamic Jihad, had directed the US end of Mujahidin recruitment and fundraising from his Brooklyn headquarters in concert with the CIA, who reportedly had facilitated his US visa.[47] In the same year, Langley itself was to come under attack when another former Mujahid, Mir Aimal Kansi, opened fire on a car carrying CIA employees.[48]

Abroad, attacks on US facilities and personnel continued, with the assassination of two US diplomats in Karachi, Pakistan, in March 1995 and the bombing of a training facility in Riyadh in November. Three of the four Saudi nationals who publicly confessed were Afghan veterans.[49] The enduring US military presence in Saudi Arabia was a particular source of conflict. On 25 June 1996 the Khobar Towers US military housing complex near Riyadh was destroyed by a massive truck bomb, killing 19 US personnel. Whilst suspicion fell on Saudi Shi'a radicals linked to Lebanon-based Hamas, rather than directly on Al-Qaida, it was clear that previous sectarian distinctions were breaking down in the call for global Jihad. Worryingly for the US, the Saudi authorities imposed strict limits on cooperation and questioning of suspects by FBI and CIA investigators, and refused point blank to consider extradition.[50]

Despite US protests at being 'repeatedly stiffed' by Riyadh over the Khobar Towers bombing,[51] Washington was still closely supportive of Saudi designs in Central Asia. A new Islamist movement – the Taliban – was seizing power in Afghanistan, with strong support from the Saudi Istakhbarat and Pakistan's ISI. The Saudi intelligence chief, Prince Turki al-Faisal, had visited Kandahar and Islamabad in July

1996 to coordinate funding, supplies and the delivery of the Taliban's favoured Japanese pick-up trucks, which would help secure the capture of Kabul that September. Whilst the Saudi and Pakistan interest in the Taliban was ideological, more material factors were drawing Washington back to the North West Frontier. Saudi-owned Delta Oil and its partner US giant Unocal were pressing to construct a major gas pipeline from Turkmenistan to Pakistan and the Gulf. The transit via Afghanistan would require a stable government which, the US was assured, would be provided by a Taliban victory.

As ever in the Clinton administration, intelligence assessments were coloured by the top tiers of NDD 35. The Foreign Oil Companies Group, set up to lobby in Washington in early 1995, had hired as consultants a range of former Bush- and Carter-era officials. The latter, including Carter's National Security Advisor Zbigniew Brezinski, former Assistant Defense Secretary Richard Armitage, and former Secretaries of State Lawrence Eagleberger and Henry Kissinger, retained their high security clearances and were thus admitted for top-level briefings by the Advocacy Center. Clinton's Deputy National Security Advisor, Sandy Berger, had also established a special working group, including the CIA, to provide such briefing and coordinate policy for the Caspian area.

During official visits to the region in April and August 1996, Assistant Secretary of State Robin Raphel voiced open US support for the Unocal project, and State Department announcements at the time of the Taliban victory – later retracted – seemed to imply diplomatic recognition.[52] Yet if the impression in Tehran, Moscow and New Delhi, who strongly opposed the Taliban, was that the old Saudi/CIA/ISI alliance was again up and running in Afghanistan, the reality was more complex, if scarcely less reprehensible. Deputy National Security Advisor Sandy Berger, head of the inter-agency group on Caspian oil policy, had tasked Sheila Heslin, Deputy for Intelligence Programs at the NSC, to focus the CIA's intelligence gathering on 'derogatory' information on corporate rivals to the Foreign Oil Companies Group, rather than on the escalating political turmoil in the region.[53]

Whilst Unocal and their high-profile Beltway alumni were indeed hiring 'every available member of the inner circle of those Americans involved in Afghan operations during the Jihad years',[54] other sections of the US intelligence community were watching the emergence of a new Islamist alliance, in which Saudi funding matched strident anti-Americanism, with mounting alarm. The focus of the emergent group was a former US Afghan war protégé, Saudi construction millionaire Osama bin Laden.

Enter bin Laden

First introduced to the Afghan conflict in 1980 by Prince Turki, at the instigation of senior ISI Chief Hamid Gul, bin Laden had become progressively estranged from the pro-US policies of the Saudi regime after his return to the kingdom in 1990. After living in the Sudan from 1992 under the protection of National Islamic Front strongman Hassan al-Turabi, bin Laden returned to Afghanistan in May 1996, again under the wing of the ISI, who were anxious to retain the use of the cross-border training camps at Khost – built in 1986 by bin Laden with Saudi and CIA funding – for militants fighting India's forces in Kashmir.

In August 1996 bin Laden issued his first public declaration of Jihad against the United States and vowed the 'humiliation' of US bases in Saudi Arabia; he now featured as 'one of the most significant financial sponsors of Islamic extremist activities in the world' in the State Department's annual *Patterns of Global Terrorism*. The administration also attempted unsuccessfully to use the new Anti-Terrorism and Effective Death Penalty Act to seize control of the estimated $300 million assets of the Saudi renegade.[55] Shortly afterwards, the CIA attempted to use the Act's provisions for 'rendering' terrorist suspects to launch a snatch squad from Peshawar, which foundered on the ambivalence of their hosts in the ISI.

On 23 February 1998, bin Laden convened a large gathering of Islamists at the Khost training camp under the banner of the 'International Islamic Front for Jihad against Jews and Crusaders' and issued his most forthright declaration to date. It was, the *fatwa* stated, 'the individual duty of every Muslim' to 'kill the Americans and their allies ... in any country in which it is possible'.[56] With US business enthusiasm for the Unocal deal waning – partially due to the collapse in world gas prices at this time – and a more proactive Secretary of State, Madeleine Albright, replacing the lacklustre Warren Christopher, Washington was beginning to change its view of the Taliban. The Kabul regime's evident closeness with bin Laden and the Arab Afghans and the increasing radicalisation of Pakistan were beginning to creep up the agenda at the NSC. The coordinated bombing of US embassies in Kenya and Tanzania on 7 August 1998 was to bring Islamist terrorism and bin Laden in particular to the forefront of policy. The US launched 70 cruise missiles on Al-Qaida bases in Afghanistan in retaliation, and arrested over 80 militants worldwide. Bin Laden, the subject of a $5 million reward, was indicted in a New York court for the embassy bombings and on a range of other charges, including the Riyadh and Dhahran bombings in Saudi Arabia. The administration gave an additional $6.7 billion in anti-terrorism funding, while the FBI's counter-terrorism budget grew from $118 to $286 million, and the Bureau doubled its counter-terrorist staff to 2,650. Overall, the US has spent some $50 billion in anti-terrorism funding since 1996, with the FBI's dedicated budget rising nearly six-fold to $609 million by the year 2000.[57]

In the view of many in the intelligence community, however, the influx of funding – overwhelmingly committed to increasing technical capabilities – merely served to compound existing structural failings rather than address the 'cinder-block, mud-brick side of the Muslim world',[58] as one agent put it, the success of a few high-profile operations like the 1997 Ramzi Yousef 'snatch' notwithstanding.[59] By 1996 the CIA had reduced the clandestine Directorate of Operations by 25 per cent, with cuts falling disproportionately on overseas postings. In an arrangement known as 'homebasing', most of the counter-terrorism case officers were based at Langley, with a restricted brief for visits to the field. The Agency had a station chief and a small number of case officers in Islamabad, treading the diplomatic/business circuit, whilst the CIA's station officer in Karachi, the largest city in Pakistan and a world centre of espionage and arms and drugs dealing, was reportedly a contract employee whose term included regular six-month spells back in Virginia.[60] More field operators were pulled out of Europe after the public clashes with French and German intelligence over the

Airbus and IBM affairs, hampering efforts to monitor the growing
Islamist network in the EU. Back at Langley, the Bin Laden Operational Unit, set up to track bin Laden's increasingly public activities,
was relying in the main on allied services for its intelligence. The one
genuine coup – the ability to tap real-time communications on bin
Laden's US-made satellite phone – was compromised after media
revelations of its role in the cruise missile attacks.

The obvious source of Humint in Afghanistan, the still-resisting
opposition forces of Tajik leader Ahmed Shah Massoud, were not
contacted directly by the CIA until October 1999. An annual $50,000
subsidy, earlier authorised from CIA funding, was delivered to
Massoud by British agents to ensure US 'deniability'.[61] After Russian
forces, furious at open Taliban support for the insurgency in Chechnya,
threatened military action against the Taliban in May 2000, tentative
plans were laid for a joint US/FSB special forces strike against Al-
Qaida bases from Uzbekistan. The putative Operation Gateway was
to remain at the planning stage, however, sidelined by the Clinton
administration's perennial fear of body bags and the US military's
preference for 'TLAM [cruise missile] therapy'.

Latin America – business as usual?

During the 1990s, US policy in the Western Hemisphere was lauded
as a success. One by one, the generals and *caudillos* had departed the
scene, replaced by lip service (at least) to democracy and the rule of
law and a more concrete commitment to the rule of market economics.
The entry of Mexico into the North American Free Trade Association
(NAFTA) in January 1994 seemingly had set the seal on the continent's emergence from the era of coups, death squads and covert
operations.

The arrest and trial of former Peruvian intelligence chief Vladimiro
Montesinos in June 2001, however, was to reveal that, for the old
alliance of US intelligence agencies and local strongmen involved in
kidnappings and disappearances, it was very much business as usual.
Montesinos, a former army officer and well-connected Lima lawyer,
was appointed head of Peru's Servicio de Inteligencia Nacional (SIN)

in 1989 after helping secure the election of President Alberto Fujimori. As Fujimori's rule became increasingly autocratic after the suspension of the constitution in 1992, so the power grew of Montesinos's intelligence empire, which included the direction of anti-drugs operations in close collaboration with the US Drug Enforcement Administration.

Whilst Fujimori, until his flight to Japan in November 1999, was to remain a World Bank and IMF favourite for his privatisation policies, documents revealed at the trial show that Montesinos had been of growing concern to his US handlers from the outset. A declassified US Army Intelligence report of July 1991 warns that – despite some success in routing the Maoist Sendero Luminoso (Shining Path) guerrilla movement, who were also rivals in the drugs trade – Montesinos was 'playing both sides', and trying to 'frustrate joint US–Peruvian counter drug efforts'.[62] It was also to emerge that Montesinos had first approached US intelligence in the 1970s, leading to his dismissal at that time from the Peruvian army. Once in power as intelligence chief, he received an annual $1 million payment from the CIA and was regarded as 'the go-to guy, short of the President himself, on any key issue'.[63]

Of the 57 cases and 168 criminal investigations levelled against the former spymaster, the most serious included the organisation of death squads, massacres of suspected Maoist sympathisers in 1991 and 1993, and personally ordering the killing of 14 surrendering Tupac Amaru fighters, who had occupied the Japanese ambassador's Lima residence in 1997. Evidence of a suspected $800 million personal fortune provides some indication of the breadth of Montesinos's involvement in illegal drugs and arms trafficking. His most ambitious scheme, aborted in August 2000, was the shipment of 50,000 AK 47s to the Revolutionary Armed Forces of Colombia (FARC) insurgents. The weapons were to be transferred from Jordan under phoney Peru end-user documentation. Unfazed by the courtroom revelations, and indeed by his own department's acknowledgement of the 'significant amount of negative baggage' attending Montesinos, US ambassador John Hamilton stated: 'He [Montesinos] was a reality. I think we dealt with him in a way consistent with our commitment to democracy and human rights throughout the ten years.'[64]

Elsewhere in the hemisphere, too, much negative baggage has been accumulated. Guatemala, a focus of US attention since the original 'banana republic' coup of 1954, became a public embarrassment to the Clinton administration when it emerged that an American nun, abducted by Guatemalan forces in 1989, had been tortured in the presence of an alleged US adviser.[65] G2, the army unit running counter-subversion, was trained by the CIA and had many US assets on its payroll.[66] It was further revelations – of the role of CIA contract personnel in the murder of US hotel owner Michael Devine in 1990 and of URNG (Guatemalan National Revolutionary Unity) guerrilla leader Efrain Velasquez, married to US attorney Jennifer Harbury, in 1992 – that led to the proscription on CIA recruitment of 'unsavoury' local contacts set down in 1995. DCI John Deutch, however, still refused to reinstate the security clearance (and career prospects) of State Department whistle blower Richard Nuccio, who had first revealed the suspected murderer on the CIA's payroll in Guatemala.

The old-established duo of oil and old-fashioned anti-Marxism are playing their roles in the US relationship with Colombia. The State Department's foreign aid request for 2003 included $98 million to train local troops to protect the Caño Limón oil pipeline, which has been attacked regularly by rebels, especially by the left-wing National Liberation Army (ELN). The administration also wants permission from Congress to provide US arms and training in military action against the FARC insurgency. The official rationale is that the aid supports counter-terrorism, since FARC is on the US list of terrorist organisations. But if this were truly its principal concern, Washington would focus its efforts on the right-wing paramilitaries, which are closely tied to the Colombian military but are responsible for the vast majority of political assassinations in Colombia.

There have, to be sure, been some changes in Washington's relations with its hemispheric interlocutors, with the Pentagon taking an increasingly assertive role. Foreign Military Financing (FMF) grants for countries to buy US military equipment and services rose from $3.57 billion in 2001 to a requested $4.12 billion for 2003. The administration's 2002 supplemental appropriation request included another $372.5 million in counter-terrorism-related FMF for a wide range of countries including Oman, Nepal, Ethiopia and Djibouti. Funding for International Military Education and Training (IMET), one of many US foreign military training programmes, rose from $58 million in 2001 to a requested $80 million for 2003, a jump of 38 per cent.[67]

Particularly after the 1995 ban on 'unsavoury' recruitment, the Defense Department's Special Operations Command has replaced the CIA's slimmed-down Directorate of Operations as the main avenue for covert action. This has been taken on by the Joint Combined Exchange Training Program (JCET). Set up in 1991, this allows US special forces to deploy overseas on a virtually unlimited basis, as long as the avowed purpose is the training of host military personnel. As of 1998, some 110 JCET missions had been established.[68] With a focus on 'foreign internal defence' – or, as some would say, repression – JCET is being increasingly conducted by private contractors made up of ex-military personnel.[69] The advantage here lies in both deniability and the crucial factor that commercial activities are not covered by the Freedom of Information Act. That they could, conceivably, fall under the purview of an International Criminal Court perhaps helps explain the vehemence of US opposition to such a body.

Intelligence without policy or policy without intelligence?

Despite the mounting evidence of misplaced memos and virtually non-existent coordination between the several branches – CIA, Customs, FBI – charged with conducting the war on terrorism, the US intelligence community has so far been spared the sort of all-out witch-hunt that might have been predicted after the events of 9/11. Adroit footwork by DCI George Tenet and open revolt in the ranks of the FBI have kept the spotlight shifting, notably to the Oval Office itself.

With Congressional funds flowing as never before and a reported 60,000 new applicants queuing up to join the CIA, the lean days of the early 1990s are as well and truly over as the prospects for a 'new and hopeful world' foreseen by President Clinton in NDD 35. But while things look rosy for the CIA's long-neglected Directorate of Operations, truly engaging with the 'cinder-block, mud-brick side of the Muslim world', or the world outside America in general, will require more than just a crash course in demotic Arabic and primers on the more recondite strains of Islamic fundamentalism. The queue of 'unsavoury' Third World recruits waiting for the administration's four-billion-dollar arms bonanza suggests that, for all its sophistication, US intelligence is still locked into a mindset that will not be remedied by the repeal of EO 12333 and a return to the buccaneering, gloves-off, drugs-and-assassination days of William Casey.

Indeed, US actions like the flip-flop support for the 'Two-day Coup' which temporarily unseated Venezuelan President Hugo Chavez in April 2002, the similarly unsubtle pressure on Bolivian Presidential hopeful Evo Morales, and the blank cheque offered Colombian strongman Alvaro Uribe in suppressing dissent under the 'war on drugs' catch-all could easily leave the impression that Casey and Oliver North have never been away.

As evidence before the House–Senate investigating committee has shown, much of the information concerning motive, methodology and personnel for the attacks of 9/11 was present in the President's Daily Brief of 6 August 2001 – apparently under the title 'Bin Laden determined to strike at US'.[70] FBI agents had strong suspicions about the now notorious Phoenix flying school and the determination of its inmates to 'bring the fight to America'. But as the FBI takes on counter-terrorism as its top priority, with some 3,700 agents working full-time, and the CIA seeks fresh allies amongst the all-too-unsavoury post-communist regimes of Central Asia, the issue of what guides and informs intelligence policy remains unresolved. The widespread – if often self-serving – opprobrium confronting the US will not yield to homilies about American values while these are undermined by self-imposed blindspots like refusing to question the policies of Israel, or the fact that no national intelligence estimate was written about Saudi Arabia throughout the 1990s.[71] Perceiving the mud-brick world with any clarity will require an effort of engagement – and, indeed, empathy – that still has some way to go.

Notes

1 See Robert M. Gates, *In from the Shadows: the Ultimate Insider's Story of Six Presidents and How They Won the Cold War*, New York: Simon and Shuster, 1996, p. 566.

2 Walter Pincus, 'EX CIA Chief Backs Smaller Spy Agency; Gates Plan for Pentagon', *Washington Post*, 10 December 1994.

3 *New York Times*, 5 November 1994.

4 See US State Department, *Strategic Assessment 1996 – Elements of US Power*, p. 2.

5 See *Aviation Week and Space Technology*, 8 April 1991, p. 44.

6 See Walter Pincus, 'CIA, Pentagon Back NIMA Concept', *Washington Post*, 29 November 1995.

7 See CIA Directorate of Intelligence, cià. gov /cia/di/index.html, pp. 24–5, 99.

8 See White House, Press Briefing by Mike McCurry, 10 March 1995.

9 See *Washington Post*, 12 June 1994, p. A8, which listed the CIA at $3 billion, the Pentagon agencies (NRO, NSA, CIO, DIA) at $13.2 billion and TIARA at $10.4 billion.

10 See Gregory F. Treverton, *Reshaping Intelligence for the Age of Information*, Cambridge, Mass: RAND, 2001, pp. 66–7.

11 See 'America's Intelligence Services: Time for a Rethink', *The Economist*, 20 April 2002.

12 See 'The Hansen–Ames Connection Uncovered', *DEBKA-Net-Weekly*, February 2001.

13 See Stansfield Turner, 'Redefining National Security', *Foreign Policy*, August 1991.

14 See testimony before the Senate Select Intelligence Committee, *Intelligence Reorganization Legislation*, 1 April 1992.

15 Peter Schwietzer, *Friendly Spies*, New York: Atlantic Monthly Press, 1993, pp. 292, 30–1.

16 See Duncan Campbell, *Interception Capabilities 2000*, European Parliament, Scientific Technical Assessments Office Report (hereafter STOA Rep.), p. 35.

17 See Scott Shane, 'Mixing Business with Spying', *Baltimore Sun*, 1 November 1996.

18 See STOA Rep., p. 35; Amy Borus, 'The New CIA: I Spy for Business', *Business Week*, 17 September 1994, p. 23.

19 See Jay Pretzerel, 'When Friends Become Moles', *Time Magazine*, 28 May 1990.

20 Congressional Record, Senate, S8732, 24 June 1992.

21 James Woolsey, 'Why We Spy on Our Allies', *Wall Street Journal*, 17 March 2000.

22 See Amy Borus *et al.*, 'Should the CIA Start Spying for Corporate America?', *Business Week*, 14 October 1992.

23 See R. Jeffery Smith, 'Administration to Consider Giving Spy Data to Business', *Washington Post*, 3 February 1993.

24 See Howard Teicher and Gayle Radley Teicher, *Twin Pillars to Desert Storm: America's Flawed Vision in the Middle East*, New York: William Morrow, 1993, p. 207.

25 See US Senate, Select Committee on Intelligence, 'Nomination of Robert M.

Gates to be Director of Central Intelligence', *Executive Report 102-19*, 102 Congress 1st Session, 24 October 1991, pp. 179–80.

26 See R. Jeffrey Smith and John Goshco, 'Ill-Fated Iraq Policy Began Shortly after Bush Took Office', *Washington Post*, 27 June 1992.

27 See US Department of Agriculture, *Congressional Record*, p. H517, 19 February 1992.

28 See CIA, Directorate of Operations, 'Iraq–Italy Repercussions of the BNL–Atlanta Scandal', *Congressional Record*, 31 July 1992, pp. H7142–4.

29 See Robert S. Greenberger, 'How Baker Plan for Early Sanctions against Iraq Failed', *Wall Street Journal*, 1 October 1990.

30 See US Congress, Nomination of Robert M. Gates, vol. 2, p. 30; see also Ruth Sinai, 'Administration's Support for Iraq Ignored Multiple Warnings', Associated Press, 4 June 1992.

31 See David Guyatt, 'Operation Black Dog', *Lobster 35* (Summer 1998).

32 See Jeff Stein, 'Diminished Intelligence', Salon.com, 12 September 2001.

33 See Elaine Sciolino, 'Greater US Effort Backed to Oust Iraqi', *New York Times*, 2 June 1992.

34 Former CIA operative Warren Marik cited in Jim Hoagland, 'How the CIA's War on Saddam Collapsed', *Washington Post*, 26 June 1997.

35 *Ibid.*

36 See Helga Graham, 'How America Saved Saddam', *New Statesman*, 20 September 1996.

37 See 'Tehran, Baghdad and Damascus: the New Axis Act', 10 August 1992, Federation of American Scientists, fas.org/index.html.

38 See Kenneth Katzman, 'Iraq's Opposition Movements', *CRS Issue Brief*, 26 March 1998.

39 See Veronica Loeb, 'US Revives Old Dream of Saddam Overthrow', *Washington Post*, 21 October 1998.

40 See Abdel-wahab Badrakhan, *al-Hayat*, 11 September 1996; see also John Simpson, 'Are the Americans Protecting Saddam?', *Sunday Telegraph*, 15 September 1996.

41 See Robert Baer, *See No Evil*, New York: Crown, 2002, p. 217.

42 See Robert Gates interviewed by Fred Halliday, 'Conversations with Cold Warriors', BBC Radio Four, 28 April 1995.

43 See Barnett Rubin, 'Afghanistan – the Forgotten Crisis', *Refugee Survey Quarterly*, 15, 2 (UNHCR, 1996).

44 See Robert Marquand and Scott Baldauph, 'Will the Spies Who Know Tell the US?' *Christian Science Monitor*, 25 September 2001.

45 See *Los Angeles Times*, 4 August 1996.

46 See Ahmed Rashid, *Taliban*, London: Penguin, 2001, p. 130.

47 See 'Brooklyn Link in World Terror Network', *New York Times*, 22 October 1998; Mary Anne Weaver, 'Blowback', *Atlantic Monthly*, May 1996.

48 See Mary Anne Weaver, *New Yorker*, 13 November 1995, pp. 62–4.

49 See Kenneth Katzman for CRS, *Terrorism: Near Eastern Groups and State Sponsors,*

2001, RL31119: 10 September 2001, p. 10.

50 See US Congress, House, 'The FBI Investigation into the Saudi Arabia Bombing and Foreign FBI Investigations', *Hearings*, 105 Congress 1st Session, 12 February 1997.

51 See John Deutch, 'Terrorism', *Foreign Policy* (Fall 1997), pp. 16–18.

52 See Michael Dobbs, 'Kabul's Fall to Halt the Anarchy', *Washington Post*, 29 September 1996.

53 See Baer, *See No Evil*, p. 244. In some reports, leading NSC figures had substantial holdings of oil company stock.

54 See Richard Mackenzie, 'The United States and the Taliban', in William Maley (ed.), *Fundamentalism Reborn?*, London: C. Hurst, 1998.

55 See Carol Giacomo, 'US Lists Saudi Businessman as Extremist Sponsor', *Washington Post*, 14 August 1996.

56 Rashid, *Taliban*, pp. 134–5.

57 See Robert Dreyfus, 'Dim Intelligence', *American Prospect*, 12, 18 (22 October 2001).

58 See Reuel Marc Gerecht, 'The Counterterrorist Myth', *Atlantic Monthly*, July/August 2001.

59 See 'Where Does US Intelligence Go from Here?' *Jane's Intelligence Weekly*, 27 September 2001.

60 See David S. Cloud, 'For a Shrunken CIA, War in Afghanistan Was a Call to Arms', *Wall Street Journal*, 15 April 2002.

61 *Ibid.*

62 See Kevin G. Hall, 'Peru Spy Chief Drags CIA into Scandal', *Knight Ridder News Service/Philadelphia Enquirer*, 8 August 2001.

63 See 'US/Peru Spy Relations Disclosed', Associated Press/*Guardian International*, 8 January 2002 .

64 *Ibid.*

65 See *Washington Post*, 12 May 1996, p. C1.

66 See Alan Nairn, 'CIA Death Squads', *Nation*, 17 April 1995.

67 See Tamar Gabelnick, 'Security Assistance After September 11' *Federation of American Scientists Bulletin*, Volume 7, May 2002, http://www.fpif.org/form_feedback.html.

68 See Dana Priest, 'Free of Oversight, US Military Trains Foreign Troops', *Washington Post*, 13 July 1998.

69 See Ken Silverstein, 'Privatising War: How Affairs of State Are Outsourced to Corporations beyond Public Control', *Nation*, 28 July 1997.

70 See David Wastell, 'Fresh September 11 Revelations Rock Bush', *Sunday Telegraph*, 19 May 2002.

71 See Baer, *See No Evil*, p. 234.

CHAPTER 4

THE EUROPEAN UNION
New Purpose, Old Methods?

'We now have a political system at the national and EU levels which not only lacks content and accountability, but more importantly, lacks a belief in the liberal democratic culture itself.'
– Tony Bunyan, *The War on Freedom and Democracy*

Intelligence is one area in which the EU may hope to realise its drive for a Common Foreign and Security Policy (CFSP). Though enduring national rivalries remain, there are some positive signs, if only at the level of mutual empire building. The avalanche of EU-wide security measures brought in after 9/11 has given a new lifeline to agencies hitherto facing tough financial questioning – as, indeed, has the existence of a more palpable threat than football hooligans, anti-globalisation protesters and bugged corporate executives. The events of 11 September, and the realisation that the EU – and Germany in particular – had provided the rear assembly area for a decade of Islamist terrorist operations have certainly brought a new sense of common purpose to the fore. And this has helped sideline issues such as the contested nature of trans-Atlantic intelligence relations, which seemed to be about to explode into the public spotlight at the time of the European Parliament's enquiry into the Echelon global monitoring system.

In the words of one recent survey of European trends, 'We now have a political system at national and EU levels which not only lacks content and accountability, but more importantly, lacks a belief in the liberal democratic system itself.'[1] In such a climate, secrecy and misinformation thrive, and the knowledgeable flit seamlessly from covert conclave to corporate boardroom. This chapter considers how some leading EU intelligence services have adapted to new realities and questions whether in the war on terrorism – as in war in general – 'truth is the first casualty'.

The UK

During the 1990s, Britain's intelligence apparatus, the Security Service (MI 5), the Secret Intelligence Service (SIS – MI 6) and the signals intelligence arm, Government Communications Headquarters (GCHQ) all emerged blinking out of the shadows of the Cold War. The Security Services Act of 1989 established a legal identity for MI 5, ahead of a high-profile civil liberties challenge by future Labour ministers Patricia Hewitt and Harriet Harman, and pending judgements by the European Court of Human Rights. The foreign intelligence service, SIS, was first acknowledged officially in the House of Commons on 6 May 1992 and put on a statutory footing with the Intelligence Services Bill of 24 November 1993 (brought in as an Act in 1994). An oversight board – the parliamentary Intelligence Oversight Committee (ISC) – was established for the first time. Although the structure of the ISC was strongly criticised by Labour in opposition,[2] no radical adjustments were made when the party came to power. At this writing, a directly accountable House of Commons committee and a US-style Freedom of Information Act are as far away as ever. Currently, the nine members are nominated by the Prime Minister and sit *in camera*. With a small staff of three Cabinet Office officials (and one part-time investigator), the ISC is physically confined to the Cabinet Office. It has no powers to call witnesses individually and all proceedings and reports are vetted by the Prime Minister. The Act also established a framework for GCHQ, officially unacknowledged even by name until the 1970s.

Despite the nod towards oversight – and the undeniable presence conveyed by glitzy new London office buildings – Britain remains the most secretive state in the Western hemisphere. Under the UK's 'unwritten' constitution, 'rights' do not exist independently of the laws passed by governments. British courts are required to uphold the legality of Parliament's legislation, but it is Parliament itself which has the last word. This, in effect, allows the government of the day an almost unlimited discretion which, to date, no government has been willing to give up. The principle of 'ministerial responsibility' offered in place of direct oversight and freedom of information relies on the assumption that ministers give true answers to questions put by Members of Parliament (MPs). However, even leaving aside the record of ministerial 'economy with the truth', these provisions are somewhat hobbled by the longstanding convention that ministers are excused from parliamentary answers when matters of 'national security' are involved. Even this state of affairs, though, can be counted as a step forward. For most of their existence, the intelligence services have operated under the shadowy 'Crown Prerogative' which, in practice, left them as effectively 'self-tasking' entities.

The declared purpose of Britain's intelligence services was set forth in 1963 by then Master of the Rolls, Lord Denning:

> their operations are to be used for one purpose and one purpose only, the Defence of the Realm. They are not to be used to pry into any man's private conduct … or even political opinions, except in so far as they are subversive, that is, they would contemplate the overthrow of the government by unlawful means.[3]

Both before and after Denning's much-quoted dictum, however, the record on all these counts has often been found wanting. The definition of 'subversion' became particularly elastic during the Thatcher years, with lawyers, trade unionists and opponents of government policies of every stripe falling foul of MI 5's burgeoning 'F' (counter-subversion) branch. And, as numbers of disillusioned former agents were to reveal, there was a growing tendency for MI 5 operations and resources to be used for partisan rather than simply government ends.[4]

In addition to the Hewitt and Harman cases, files were also open on future Labour cabinet minister Peter Mandelson and 1997 Home Secretary – and thus, theoretically, boss of the Security Service – Jack Straw.[5] The 1989 Act does provide for an appeals tribunal, made up of senior lawyers, for people feeling 'unfairly' targeted. However, it also states that 'the complaint will only be upheld … if the targeting was based on information that MI 5 had no reason to believe was true'.[6] As the burden of proof is clearly incumbent on the complainant (who is legally denied access to any evidence), it is perhaps not surprising that of the 81 complaints lodged in the tribunal's first two years of existence, not one was upheld.[7] In a further Kafkaesque twist, the Act even enjoins MI 5 action on the basis of complaints themselves, if they come from a person or group 'regarded by the service as requiring investigation'.[8]

With the 1994 Act, MI 5 published a glossy brochure about its activities. Whilst drawing a veil over some of the more controversial episodes in its past – notably the infiltration of trade unions and the 'Wilson Plot' of the 1970s[9] – the Security Service admitted targeting 'the subversive element within' legitimate protest groups. In 1998 Home Secretary Jack Straw told the Commons that MI 5 held 440,000 files, of which some 290,000 related to individuals investigated since the service was set up in 1909. Only about 13,000 are 'Green' or active files on British citizens, largely for terrorist connections – though this figure will have grown since 11 September.[10] Although their party had been subject to many hostile actions by the security services in the past, the New Labour governments of 1997 and 2001 have showed no more inclination toward democratic accountability than their predecessors. In the wake of damaging allegations by former agents, then Home Secretary Jack Straw refused to countenance a 'public interest' addition to the 1989 Official Secrets Act, brought in by the Thatcher government to plug loopholes unforeseen in the draconian measures of 1911. 'If there were a public interest defence,' Straw was to claim, 'it would be open to any officer to decide for themselves when they thought the release of information was in the public interest.'[11] The Anti-Terrorism, Crime and Security Bill rushed through in November 2001 – a Whitehall wish-list of measures, which gave every indication of being ready prepared on departmental shelves pre-9/11 – faced opposition even from the opposition Conservative Party (see above, Chapter 1). And the Regulation of Investigatory Powers Act (RIPA) of October 2000 had the main aim of *extending* the powers of surveillance of a range of 'designated' authorities, in order to catch up with the Internet, largely by abolishing the existing, largely *pro forma* requirement for judicial sanction.

Under RIPA 2000, the oversight of the issue of a warrant for surveillance was transferred to the Office of Surveillance Commissioners – although the OSC, which has commissioners for the Intelligence Services, Surveillance, and Interception of Communications, is woefully understaffed for its task. In his annual report, the Chief Surveillance Commissioner, Sir Andrew Leggatt, observes,

> There are about 950 public authorities (including local authorities and Health Trusts) which are entitled to conduct covert surveillance under the provisions of the 2000 Act ... I clearly cannot carry out meaningful oversight of so many bodies without assistance.[12]

The proposal by Straw's successor as Home Secretary, David Blunkett, to extend these powers to a still further 1,039 'designated' authorities – excoriated across the UK press as a 'snoopers' charter' – was defeated in June 2002 when the usually quiescent Labour majority rebelled.[13]

Overall intelligence coordination – of MI 5, MI 6, GCHQ and Defence Intelligence Staff (DIS) – is undertaken by the Cabinet Office Joint Intelligence Committee (JIC). With a full-time staff of about thirty, including Foreign Office and Ministry of Defence personnel on four-year secondments, it prepares weekly intelligence evaluations – usually by topic – drawn from specifically tasked Current Intelligence Groups (CIGs). The 'Red Book' current intelligence digest, containing open-source as well as sanitised agency material, is circulated to principal ministries of state and bodies like the Bank of England.

Aside from Mrs Thatcher, ministers have rarely attended the Thursday JIC meetings. By convention, however (and this is a source of irritation in the EU), there is usually representation from the UK/USA states – Australia, Canada, New Zealand and, for the US, the CIA.[14] An innovation of the Major years was the creation of the Ministerial Committee on the Intelligence Services, with a brief to 'keep under review policy on the intelligence and security services': this, however, is focused on inter-agency matters rather than intelligence as such.

Intelligence funding – the 'greatest secret'

The most consistent oversight of the intelligence community has, however, been exercised on a somewhat *ad hoc* basis by the Treasury. The bitter backstairs struggle between successive Chancellors and intelligence chiefs is almost legendary in Whitehall. Of all the organs of government, the intelligence services were the most successful in resisting the public sector cuts of the Thatcher years. It was not until Kenneth Clarke and, latterly, Gordon Brown – both in commanding positions regarding their respective Prime Ministers – that the balance began to shift. The cost of Britain's intelligence services – the 'greatest secret' – has been officially admitted at £776 million for the financial year 1999/2000 (with a capital budget estimate of £144 million), rising to £876 million for 2001–2 and an overall bill of £1 billion.[15] Treasury reviews of 1993 began making some inroads in the secret budget – with GCHQ in particular facing rolling three-year 2–4 per cent cuts and a staff reduction from 7,000 to 6,000[16] – and in 1998 the Treasury succeeded in introducing the standard model of 'zero based budgeting'. However, as leaks from the National Audit Office make clear, overspends – from £140 to £250 million (MI 6) and £85 to £227 million (MI 5)[17] – on high-profile city offices and a range of other scandals involving IT contract overruns (not, to be sure, unknown in other government departments), make the unofficial estimate of £2.5 billion closer to the mark.[18]

Whilst it is now claimed that the many items formerly hidden in other government budgets – notably, those of the Ministry of Defence and the Foreign Office – are now all included in the 'secret vote', the proliferation of front companies and deniable contract personnel glimpsed in the 1990 'arms to Iraq' scandal makes this unlikely. Indeed, given the Blair government's mania for outsourcing and the traditional security service practice of stationing retired officers in corporate management, it is probable that the budgetary take has shifted quite significantly in this direction. This, as we see from the US, Russian and South African experiences, is part of a worldwide trend. Front companies might actually *make* money and contract personnel are, of course, subject to rigorous confidentiality clauses.[19] In the summer of 2001, reports – undoubtedly based on Treasury leaks – began to surface in the UK press of a £1.4 billion intelligence 'slush fund' which was attracting the eyes of the Treasury.[20]

It is clear that the official injunction for SIS to operate 'in the interests of the economic well-being of the United Kingdom', set forth in the 1994 Act, began to be taken very seriously in the 1990s. With its Terry Farrell-designed offices in Vauxhall Cross and newly acknowledged public profile, SIS, like its French and US counterparts, scrambled to rebrand itself as business-friendly. To be sure, a network of private consultancies – Control Risks, Sandline, the Hakluyt Foundation[21] – was already known for recruiting retired intelligence personnel. The dramatic emergence of SIS into public view demonstrated more than anything the change of priorities from Cold War to globalisation. Internally, the Service, under Director Sir Colin McColl, reorganised its six geographically based controllerates to emphasise Global Tasks – the department set up in the 1980s as a co-ordinating function for terrorism, narcotics and financial affairs. As well as the perceived shift in emphasis – away from the old Soviet Union, for example – the changes reflected the Treasury axe. In some accounts, SIS staff numbers were cut from 2,400 in 1993 to 2,150 in 1996,[22] with overseas stations reduced from 60 to 51. The new trend, heavily and somewhat hypocritically attacked in Europe – notably by France – was alleged to be the direct provision of intelligence to UK companies. This, as we have seen, was a particularly sore point on the Quai d'Orsay, given the input to British intelligence from the Echelon eavesdropping system. In one recent account, it is claimed that

> useful commercial intelligence collected and collated by MI 6 is passed on to Britain's major companies, including city banks, defence exporters such as British Aerospace, the oil companies Shell and BP and other global companies such as British Airways, code-named 'Bucks Fizz'.[23]

Many claims surround the £20 billion 'Al Yamamah' arms-for-oil deal to Saudi Arabia in the 1980s and the £1.7 billion Tornado/Hawk sale to Malaysia, linked with the £234 million Pergau dam affair.[24] In a world of multinationals, commercial spying could also bring diffi-culties – notably, between domestic and overseas parent companies – and GCHQ has denied such partisan 'tendering of its services'.[25]

MI 5, though, continued to blur the line between intelligence and commercial risk consultancy in a seminar for selected guests held in August 2001. Gathered to discuss 'Secret Work in an Open Society', 64 executives from such blue-chip outfits as Ernst and Young, Cadbury Schweppes and HSBC were treated to buffet lunch and a talk by then MI 5 Director Sir Stephen Lander.[26] Earlier that year, evidence emerged of what such secret work could involve. The *Sunday Times* reported on what appeared to be an MI 5 investigation of the Royal Society for the Protection of Birds (RSPB) on behalf of the Tesco supermarket chain. The information – apparently leaked by a disgruntled Special Branch officer – claimed that 'RSPB's "political"' campaigning was posing a threat to the "economic wellbeing" of British companies', and there was concern that the campaigns were 'aided by foreign agents'.[27]

Spin and the Supergun

In the past, however, some companies have found the aid of the intelligence services something of a mixed blessing. Due in the first place, it is true, to the enthusiasm of Her Majesty's Government for selling British weapons, infiltration of Iraq's massive arms procurement programme of the 1980s was, in some ways, a resounding intelligence success story. The sheer volume of the trade, though, as exemplified in the 'Supergun' ordered by Iraq in 1990, eventually conflicted with the needs of intelligence gathering and led to the seizure of the giant artillery piece by HM Customs – traditionally at odds with the secret services – who were out of the loop on some of the finer points of the deal. The central player in the 'Arms to Iraq' affair was British machine tool firm Matrix Churchill, bought by the Iraqi government front company TDG in 1987. On hand were informants from SIS (Managing Director Paul Henderson), MI 5 (Sales Manager Mark Gutteridge) and Special Branch (John Grecian, Managing Director of Matrix partner Ordtec).[28] Directors of other companies involved – casting firm Sheffield Forgemasters in particular – had repeatedly checked with the Department of Trade and Industry (DTI) and 'other agencies' on the legality of the deal. Nonetheless, charges were brought against the Matrix Churchill directors and numerous others in connection with breaking arms export guidelines. In November 1992, after a month of increasingly embarrassing courtroom revelation, charges were dropped. Despite their evident responsibility, the various agencies reacted in typically defensive bureaucratic fashion. Rather than acknowledgement of valuable work done at considerable personal risk, a sorry tale ensued of denial, bitter inter-agency squabbling, attempted cover-up by 'public interest immunity' certificates and the persecution of erstwhile agents in the field.

If the disclosure of the Supergun affair revealed a great deal more about 'sources and methods' than was thought desirable, Whitehall did succeed in closing ranks over perhaps even murkier aspects of the intelligence/arms trade tar-baby. Concurrently with the Customs enquiry into Matrix Churchill et al., the DTI launched a £2.5 million inquiry into arms manufacturers Astra Holdings. Originally a well-known fireworks maker in the UK, Astra had grown in the 1980s into a £350 million operation at the very heart of international weapons dealing. Selling everything from munitions to complete arms production lines, it included subsidiary BMARC, the only organisation outside government authorised to store nuclear weapons. Trouble began when Astra group chairman Gerald James began taking too close an interest in some of the recent corporate acquisitions – BMARC in particular. According to James,

> I became aware that certain plants were used to secretly store and ship goods; that monies were being secretly transferred to other operations without book records or board approval ... that our paperwork and parallel bank accounts were being used to process arms shipments from major UK defence companies ... it also became clear that ... Astra had inherited a hard core of MI 6, MI 5, DIS agents who operated behind the backs of the original directors and who treated them as 'useful idiots'.[29]

James's probing, which had first alerted Customs to the Supergun, threatened to unravel a vast covert network and led to 'harassment, burglaries ... surveillance, threats, bugging, telephone tapping, a DTI Inquiry ... and a DTI prosecution.'

Formally exonerated after a four-year hearing, James had seen his hitherto profitable company go into liquidation in 1992. In 1990, however, as the Supergun affair – precipitated by his own whistle-blowing – began to surface, James was ousted as company chairman by BMARC managing director and Midland Bank Industrial and Trade Services (MITS) consultant Stephan Kock. The evident aim was to resume (arms) business as usual. A fellow director at BMARC was future Minister for Defence Procurement and arms industry impresario Jonathan Aitken. Like the disgraced Aitken, Kock is widely reported to have intelligence connections[30] and was, in concert with MITS, chief negotiator for the £2 billion arms deal to Malaysia which led to the Pergau dam affair.[31] MITS is not the only city consultancy favoured by the intelligence agencies. NatWest Markets had on its board former JIC chair Dame Pauline Neville-Jones. Responsible for intelligence coordination on the Balkans during the Major government, Neville-Jones oversaw what veteran *Guardian* correspondent Ed Vulliamy described as 'an ill-disguised [propaganda] agenda: the Foreign Office's determination that there be no intervention against Serbia's genocidal pogrom'.[32] Vulliamy's experience of FO/MI 6 'spin' on the Balkans was not untypical. US forces in Bosnia accused British intelligence of not recording the full extent of Serb military dispositions, and MI 6-inspired smears against the Bosnian government began circulating in the UK press.[33] After leaving government, Neville-Jones, along with former Foreign Secretary Douglas Hurd, met with Serbian dictator Slobodan Milsosevic on the morning of 24 July 1997. The discreet breakfast was to celebrate the signing of a £10 million deal brokered by NatWest Markets for the privatisation of Telekom Serbia.[34]

The rash of 'Bosnia mortars its own people' allegations in circulation in the mid-1990s[34] reflected a new media activism on behalf of Vauxhall Cross. In keeping with the new public profile, Director Colin McColl established a new unit to handle media liaison. Information Operations (I/OPS), set up with a staff of twenty in 1992, was in structure and practice a similar body to the old Information Research Department (IRD), an in-house propaganda cell established during the Cold War. IRD had gained such notoriety for media manipulation that it was finally disbanded by Labour Foreign Secretary David Owen in 1977. Like the IRD of old, I/OPS specialises in planting stories in the press traducing its critics, seeing off 'turf' threats from other agencies and spinning the current Whitehall policy line. Off-the-record briefings to sympathetic journalists are a favourite route, as is the 'double sourcing' of stories planted abroad which are then picked up by the UK media. Recent examples include the supposed assassination team of Iraqi belly dancers, Iraqi anthrax in duty free perfume and, still with Iraq, 'Saddam's son made millions shipping cocaine to Britain'.[35] Whilst it is unlikely that Uday Hussein will soon be engaging learned counsel, I/OPS does sometimes come unstuck. In June 2000 Saif Gaddafi, son of the Libyan colonel, launched a libel action against the *Sunday Telegraph*. The writ stemmed from a 1995 article by that paper's chief foreign correspondent, claiming Gaddafi junior as the mastermind of 'an outrageous international conspiracy to launder Libyan currency' and import fake currency into Iran. As it emerged in court that the sole source for the story was a 'Western government security agency', lawyers for the plaintiff observed, correctly, 'that it was, in truth … a story of security service incompetence, a story of black propaganda'.[36]

Colonel Gaddafi himself has, indeed, reportedly been the recipient of more robust attention from SIS. In 1997, renegade MI 5 agent David Shayler revealed details of an alleged MI 6 plot to assassinate the Libyan leader. The plan involved covert funding to a Libyan dissident, codenamed 'Tunworth', whose contacts inside Libya would then launch a grenade attack on Gaddafi's motorcade outside the town of Sirte. In February 1996, this duly happened, but apparently the assailants struck the wrong car.[37] Despite studied government denials, the £100,000 in covert funding had ended up bankrolling a militant Islamist group – Jamma al-Islamiya al-Muqatila – drawn from 'Arab Afghans', whose aim was to force Libya toward a Taliban-style fundamentalism.

A similar assassination proposal, from the same offshoot of the Egyptian Muslim brotherhood, had been made to the CIA some years earlier. CIA field agent Robert Baer was contacted in Khartoum by Egyptian Ja'amiat in 1986, but cautioned against them, observing that, 'while Gaddafi might be as crazy as a tree full of owls, the Muslim Brothers in power in Tripoli would be a whole lot worse'.[38]

The 'King's Road Irregulars'

SIS maintains a reserve capacity for direct operations. Helicopters, a Hercules transport aeroplane and a small Special Boat Service (SBS)/ Special Air Service (SAS) detachment known as the 'increment' are permanently on call. This was beefed up under the auspices of the Operational Support Directorate after the 1994 reorganisation and has recently been augmented further with operations in Iraq and Afghanistan.[39] The main avenue for unconventional warfare, though, is through ostensibly private sector organisations. While these companies trade on their intelligence connections, a line of deniability is always maintained. An inadvertent exposure of the corporate/covert nexus was given by the activities of the UK-based 'security consultancy' Sandline International in recent conflicts in Papua New Guinea and Sierra Leone. Established by former intelligence and special forces personnel, Bahamas-registered Sandline shared offices in London's King's Road with 18 other companies involved in mining, minerals, construction, air transport and related activities. Also located at 535 King's Road was a South African firm well known on the 'circuit', Executive Outcomes. Whilst linked in multifarious business arrangements and overlapping personnel, Sandline has always strenuously denied formal connection with its King's Road cohorts, especially Executive Outcomes.

In January 1997 Sandline was hired by Prime Minister Julius Chan of Papua New Guinea at the behest of Rio Tinto Zinc. The £36 million contract was to regain control over RTZ's vast nickel mine on the island of Bougainville, where a rebel movement had taken over the island in protest at RTZ's and the government's reneging on royalties and compensation payments. However, popular anger over the Sandline deal led, in March, to the Chan government being replaced after an abortive coup. The new government of Bill Skate cancelled the deal and arrested leading Sandline operatives. It later emerged that they had enjoyed Sigint support from both New Zealand's Government Communications Security Bureau (GCSB) from its NSA-linked Waihopai facility and the Australian Defence Signals Directorate (DSD) operating from Cape York, Northern Queensland.[40] Both facilities are integral to the UK/USA Echelon network.

The cross-over of transnational mineral corporations, global Sigint and the 'King's Road Irregulars'[41] crops up again in Sierra Leone, again leaving many questions unanswered. Executive Outcomes had been contracted by the Freetown military government to take back lucrative diamond concessions in Kono, near the Guinean border (see also below). These efforts were close to success by spring of 1996, when further military coups plunged the country back into anarchy. A new President, Ahmed Tegan Kabbah, was elected in May 1996 during a civilian interregnum lasting a few months, before being exiled by a new junta under warlord Johnny Koromah. As this left the country divided up between rival factions and outside interests – notably Nigeria and Liberia – and the diamonds again unavailable, Executive Outcomes and their backers looked to regain control. However, with Pretoria becoming increasingly uneasy at the company's high public profile, the contract was passed to Sandline International. Despite sharing telephone lines and the same King's Road offices, Sandline was always quick at denial, backed by legal threats, of any corporate relations with Executive Outcomes. It is clear, though, as presiding Australian Justice Warwick John Andrew observed in hearings on the Bougainville affair, that 'the information provided by Sandline Holdings that they are entirely separate from Executive Outcomes cannot be correct, but the exact nature of their relationship seems clouded behind a web of interlocking companies whose ownership is difficult to trace'.[42]

By July 1997, with a Labour government newly elected in London, moves were in train to restore the Kabbah government back to power in Sierra Leone. With Sandline in pole position, British High Commissioner Peter Penfold oversaw an intelligence gathering mission in Freetown[43] and Kabbah's government was officially endorsed, by Prime Minister Tony Blair, at the October Commonwealth Leaders' conference in Edinburgh. The key to Sandline's planning was the shipment of 30 tonnes of weapons, bought from Bulgaria, to Kabbah's loyalist forces. This was, however, in contravention of a blanket UN arms embargo. The arms were publicly seized by Nigerian troops of the ECOMOG West African peacekeeping mission, who themselves reinstalled the Kabbah regime – a move widely unpopular in Sierra

Leone and which led to more years of anarchy. Sandline became subject to a Customs investigation and official parliamentary inquiry, amidst heated denials of any knowledge of its activities by Foreign Secretary Robin Cook.[44] Both Customs – burned before by the Supergun affair – and the Commons Foreign Affairs Select committee failed to establish a cast-iron chain of command between the government and Sandline. Requests to interview MI 6 Director David Spedding *in camera* were denied[45] on the grounds that 'the Intelligence and Security Committee (ISC) ... was the appropriate committee to examine the work of MI 6'.[46] Under the terms of the 1994 Intelligence Services Act, the ISC has neither powers to call for 'papers and persons', nor the staff to evaluate them. The accompanying judicial inquiry, by the long-serving Sir Thomas Legg,[47] managed to compile 160 pages with only one mention of MI 6.

Like the Supergun affair, the Sandline inquiry afforded a brief glimpse of the tangled world of intelligence, multinationals and covert arms dealing. And once again official deniability was the name of the game. 'There is a curious convention in Whitehall,' former MI 6 Deputy George (G. K.) Young once observed. 'You can inform the Prime Minister without telling him.'[48] Like the embattled Robin Cook, Tony Blair managed to escape censure and, indeed, regained some good name for the UK by using regular British troops, rather than mercenaries, to restore (yet again) Ahmed Tegan Kabbah and an approximation of the rule of law to Freetown in May 2000.[49] However, with British forces overstretched and signs of fresh government enthusiasm for a 'constructive' role for the military private sector, it is likely that Sandline or their successors will be back in business before long.[50]

Taking on the terrorists

The early 1990s saw a wholesale reorganisation of the intelligence services, instigated by outgoing SIS Chief Sir Colin McColl and incoming MI 5 new broom Stella Rimington. Moves included joint sections between the old rivals to cover nuclear proliferation, Russia and the Middle East. In defining further common ground, terrorism, drugs and organised crime were identified as growth areas. For MI 5, counter-espionage, protective security and the old cash-cow of the Thatcher years, counter-subversion (K, C and F branches) were amalgamated into a new D branch. Rimington's old department, G branch, which had hitherto dealt with terrorism, was given a new overseas role against the IRA, while a new directorate – T branch – was formed in 1992 with the aim of coordinating anti-terrorist strategy across the UK. The birth of T branch had provoked fierce resistance from the Army, the Royal Ulster Constabulary (RUC) and the Metropolitan Police Special Branch, originally formed specifically to tackle Irish Republican terrorism some 100 years before. MI 5 was to claim success for its efforts, with a string of IRA operatives arrested between 1992 and the December 1993 signing of the Anglo-Irish Downing Street Declaration.[51] Police and other interested agencies put it down to resources, and here there was no doubt of the success story. Alone amongst the agencies, MI 5 saw expansion during 1992–4 (from 1,900 to some 2,300 personnel), with counter-terrorism taking up three-quarters of its capability.[52]

The inter-agency feuding had inadvertently lifted the veil on some highly secretive operations of the past. In early 2000, *Sunday Times* journalist Liam Clarke wrote a series drawn from some inside sources – apparently in the RUC – on the activities of the shadowy Forces Research Unit (FRU) run by Army Intelligence in Northern Ireland[53] and became subject to legal threats and a court injunction. The FRU was alleged to have been 'running' Loyalist paramilitaries in the 1980s by providing targeting information on prominent Republicans and IRA activists. An internal police inquiry – one of three conducted by Metropolitan Police Commissioner Sir John Stephens – had its offices mysteriously gutted by fire in 1992.[54] In March/April 1998, however, influential BBC journalist John Ware produced several high-profile pieces on the FRU and 'the Army's role in the dirty war', said to be based on 'secret files', which covered much of the same territory.[55] The official ambivalence about the Northern Ireland intelligence war remains. Fifteen former Army agents who had infiltrated the IRA have launched a civil action against the Ministry of Defence, alleging they have been simply abandoned to their fate after years of extreme danger serving under cover.[56]

Global Tasks and anti-globalisation

With the IRA ceasefire holding after 1994, the focus of threat began shifting to drugs, organised crime and money laundering. Along with their US cousins, GCHQ and MI6 Global Tasks were firmly established in this territory and the police National Criminal Intelligence Service (NCIS) was set up for precisely this purpose in April 1992. Police in the UK, moreover, were actively expanding their international links through Interpol and the emergent EEC police intelligence body, Europol. The Chief Constables, however, lacked MI 5's Whitehall imprimatur. With the support of headline-hungry Deputy Prime Minister Michael Heseltine, John Major was to announce MI 5's 'unique' contribution to this expanding field to the 1995 Tory Conference.

As we have seen, the rise of anti-globalisation protests – dramatically brought out in the confrontations at Seattle and Genoa – mobilised a concerted response from EU police and intelligence services. Closer to home, MI 5 was expanding its coverage of Green groups, roads protesters and animal rights activists.[57] 'Subversion', it seems, was making a comeback, and if the bombings and intimidatory tactics of the Animal Rights Militia were clearly a legitimate target for law enforcement, the involvement of largely unaccountable intelligence services is less clear-cut. A recent example of possible line crossing, which raised protests in the UK parliament, concerns a German freelance hired by the UK-based Hakluyt Foundation to spy on environmentalist groups on behalf of major oil companies.[58]

The agent, one Manfred Schlickenreider, had been on the fringes of European protest movements for the past 20 years, posing as a radical film maker. He was also on monthly retainer from the Bundesnachrichtendienst (BND), whose generosity had gained him a Munich duplex and BMW sports car. Shlickenreider, codenamed 'Camus', was subcontracted on behalf of Shell and BP to gather intelligence on forthcoming protests by Greenpeace against oil drilling in the North Atlantic. Over a three-year period (1996–9), Greenpeace admitted losing ground to the oil companies, particularly in terms of the latter's prior knowledge of Greenpeace's moves to protect its assets from legal sequestration. Camus had also sought information from

Anita Roddick's Body Shop chain on their campaign against oil company exploitation in Nigerian Ogoniland. Although espionage is becoming commonplace in corporate practice, what concerned then Liberal Democrat Home Affairs spokesman Norman Baker was 'the fact that this organisation [Hakluyt] is staffed by people with close ties to MI 6 suggests it was semi-official'.[59]

Set up in 1995 with Sir David Spedding's semi-official blessing, Hakluyt is indeed top-heavy with Vauxhall Cross alumni, as, indeed, is the oil industry. Managing director and founder Christopher James was head of MI 6 corporate liaison. Camus himself was recruited by a Hakluyt director who was a former MI 6 head of station in Germany, whilst John Gerson, BP's director of government and public affairs, was once seen as a leading candidate to succeed Spedding as head of MI 6. Hakluyt was co-sponsored by Sir Peter Cazelet, then BP deputy chairman, with Sir Peter Holmes, former chairman of Shell, as head of the foundation.[60]

Aside from representing an attractive retirement package for former agents, however, the close relationship between MI 6 and big business must raise questions of primary purpose. The focus on corporate issues which so adulterated the US experience prior to 9/11 has similarly undermined SIS's function as an *intelligence* service. Throughout the foreign service in general, the overwhelming emphasis in the 1990s was on aiding British business. This was coupled with the introduction of commercial targets and management methodology internally, which coloured priorities to the detriment of spies and diplomats alike. The current recruitment drive 'on the back streets of Bradford' suggests some belated recognition of this, but as the US cousins discovered, the price still to be paid is a steep one.

GCHQ – 'enjoying the best of both worlds'?

Like its US counterpart, the third arm of the UK intelligence triad has been by far the most expensive. Although suffering some Treasury attention during the 1993–4 Kenneth Clarke period, the Cheltenham-based GCHQ complex has managed to survive two external reports and calls for amalgamation with MI 6. By 1995 it was fully engaged with the SIS Global Tasks agenda, overseeing massive surveillance of international cash flows and sharing with the NSA in the expansion of Echelon. Indeed, one argument put forcefully by the Foreign Office for retaining GCHQ's independent status was a possible loss of influence with the US.[61] With the abandonment of Zircon, Britain's effort at a national satellite capability, in 1987, the link became even closer. The UK made a £500 million timeshare investment in the US Magnum satellite – a state-of-the-art behemoth, with a dish 160 feet in diameter – first launched in 1994.[62]

British and US operatives, along with other UK/USA personnel, are on regular rotation between their respective headquarters at Cheltenham and Maryland. GCHQ has its own offices at Fort Meade's Columbia Annex, on Riverwood Drive, South of Columbia, where the British liaison officer provides target lists to the NSA. A similar arrangement obtains at the NSA's Menwith Hill station in Yorkshire. Even after the considerable relaxation of national data protection and privacy legislation after 9/11, there is still much to be circumvented on both sides of the Atlantic.

A specific clause inserted into the 1993 Intelligence Services Bill prohibited revealing 'information provided by … a territory outside the United Kingdom, where that government does not consent to the disclosure of the information'. Reportedly, some 95 per cent of Sigint data processed at GCHQ is of US origin.[63] It is GCHQ's umbilical links with Fort Meade and the UK/USA global Sigint system that have led to much accusation of 'unfair' commercial advantage in Europe, although this has so far been brushed off by Whitehall. As former Foreign Secretary Sir Geoffrey Howe observed, 'as long as Britain can go on enjoying the best of both worlds, then it's the best thing to do'.

What is clear is that the vast growth of the Internet and global communications in general has secured GCHQ's future, at least for now. A £500 million – now risen to £800 million – expansion plan was agreed in 1998, involving construction of a vast new headquarters. The 176-acre complex, known as 'the doughnut', will provide a self-contained 'city environment', including banks, shops and a hairdresser for some 4,500 staff, and is reputedly the largest Private Finance Initiative project in the UK.[64]

For all the UK intelligence services, the future, uncertain at the end of the Cold War, is a rosy one. On the dark side, however, critics fear that the combination of unaccountability, vastly expanded scope, and methodological stress on quota-based 'challenging output measures' will inevitably lead to indiscriminate snooping and the pursuit of selective legal vendettas. Perhaps little has changed after all.

France

Historically, France has placed a premium on an independent intelligence capability. The two main intelligence arms – the Direction de la Surveillance du Territoire (DST – counter-espionage) and the Direction Générale de la Sécurité Extérieure (DGSE – foreign intelligence) – have been used robustly to advance national goals, usually in opposition to the 'Anglo-Saxons'. And, as with the American and British services, agency 'turf' has been hotly contested. Coordination of French intelligence efforts is provided by the Comité Interministériel du Renseignement, which meets every six months to set agency priorities. Although roughly equivalent to the British JIC, its effectiveness is limited somewhat by the dual nature of Presidential/Prime Ministerial power. This has often given rise to fierce conflict between the services, particularly under periods of (multi-party) *cohabitation*.

Operating from its Paris headquarters – nicknamed La Piscine (the swimming pool) – the DGSE underwent reorganisation in 1991, under the direction of its first civilian head, Claude Silberzahn. With a budget increase of 15 per cent, IT networking was introduced and staff rose from 1,933 in 1989 to 2,402 by 1993. Also included was a new Africa programme.[65] In 1994, the DST also set up a new Sigint unit, targeting cellular phones, fax and the Internet. After some conflict on the management of anti-terrorism actions, a memorandum of understanding permits DST units to operate in conjunction with the DGSE overseas.[66] By virtue of a 1991 law on wiretaps, the regulatory Commission for Monitoring, established at this time, is expressly excluded from examining satellite transmissions.[67]

France's endogenous space programme and enthusiasm for big-spending government projects in general gave an early push to independent satellite intelligence. The Helios programme (a successor to Zenon) was ordered in 1986, at the same time as the British were considering Zircon. Operated in conjunction with the German BND (until funding constraints forced a rethink), the two Helios platforms provide intelligence that is shared with Italy and Spain. In addition to pursuing an independent spy satellite capability, France has also invested heavily in ground stations. There are three sites in France itself – Alluets-le-Roi, near Paris, Domme (Périgord) and Albion (Massif Central). French overseas dominions and territories provide capability for global coverage, with some 15 stations, including New Caledonia (Pacific), Mayotte and Petite Terre (Indian Ocean) and the Kourou Space Centre (French Guyana) – the two latter being shared with the BND.[68] Impressed by US efforts during the 1991 Gulf War, the Mitterand government ordered a Cray supercomputer and a wholesale reorganisation of French Sigint, with the establishment of a new Directorate of Military Intelligence (Direction du Renseignement Militaire – DRM) and Electronic Warfare Brigade (Brigade de Renseignement et de Guerre Electronique – BRGE) set up in 1992–3.

Sigint – the 'business strategy battlefield'

Despite substantial NSA aid in building 'Frenchelon',[69] Sigint in general became the field for bitter trans-Atlantic feuding in the 1990s. While the UK and the US began diverting more resources to economic affairs during the 1990s, commercial intelligence has always been at the unquestioned centre of French policy. A government-led effort to promote business awareness of intelligence issues was launched in 1995, spearheaded by Defence Ministry-sponsored offshoot Intelco, in order to 'occupy the business strategy battlefield in order to keep the Americans out'.[70] The government-sponsored Comité Pour la Compétitivité et la Sécurité Economique (CCSE) held its first meeting on 12 July 1995.

The Thomson/CSF and Airbus Industrie affairs of 1994 represented a new French drive to forge commercial advantage in areas hitherto seen as under US patronage. The NSA's intercepts of alleged bribe offers between Thomson and Brazilian officials were answered by

French intercepts of similar exchanges between the US Raytheon Corporation and aides to Brazilian President Fernando Cardoso. The Brazilian deal was a particularly sensitive issue for the US. Billed as an environmental surveillance system, SIVAM covered aircraft, sensors and mobile radars which could also locate mineral resources and spy on France's major overseas listening post at the Guyana space centre.[71]

Closer to home, on 26 January 1995 the US ambassador to France, Pamela Harriman, was summoned by Interior Minister Charles Pasqua, also head of the DST, demanding the expulsion from Paris of five US diplomats and the CIA chief of station. Also highlighted were the activities of leading US intelligence consultancy Kroll Associates, whose recently opened Paris office was bugged by the DST.[72] The agents were charged with attempting to bribe civil servants to gain information on France's bottom line in the 1993 GATT talks, a charge semi-conceded by the CIA.[73] According to Le Monde, at least 80 CIA agents were operating in France, many under 'non-official cover'.[74] More significant, though, were Pasqua's allegations of CIA spying on France Télécom and its subsidiaries. France Télécom was at the time ahead in the race to develop high-speed data transmission (Asynchronous Transfer Mode – ATM), of crucial importance for the new generation of telecommunications. This was particularly significant in opening new markets, particularly in what France regarded as its own backyard – Francophone Africa. In his first tour of Africa after becoming President, Jacques Chirac condemned 'Anglo Saxons, who dream of pushing France out of Africa without paying a price'.[75] Africa was shaping up as the new battleground. On 27 June 1994, the Clinton administration held its first 'Conference on Africa', intended to spur development, conflict resolution and US investment. In May 1995 Commerce Secretary Ron Brown declared that 'the United States will no longer concede African markets to traditional colonial powers' on a visit to Dakar in Senegal – the old heart of French Africa.[76] The NSA was also expanding its operations, with a listening station in the Ivory Coast capital, Abidjan, jointly operated with the Canadian Communications Security Establishment (CSE), and a refocusing of its activities on Africa in general.[77]

Africa: Operation Turquoise, the Légion Blanc and Carlos the Jackal

In what was viewed as a more direct threat yet by La Piscine and the Quai d'Orsay, the US launched an 'African Crisis Response Initiative' in March 1997, which aimed to provide military assistance, training and support packages to selected African countries. Prime targets were in hitherto Francophone Africa.[78] The main movers behind the initiative were the burgeoning US private sector military consultancies – such as Military Professional Resources (MPRI) – who would shortly set out their stall at a follow-on, classified conference, hosted on 24 June by the Pentagon, on 'The Privatisation of Military Functions in Sub-Saharan Africa'.[79] Present were representatives of the CIA, DIA, oil and mineral interests and, inevitably, the ever-expanding UK– South African firm Executive Outcomes.

The Great Lakes region of Central Africa had become a particular focus of Franco–US intelligence wars – and some far more sanguinary encounters between respective military clients. With the 6 April 1994 assassination – in a still-unexplained missile shoot-down – of French-supported Rwandan Hutu President Habyarimana, an invasion was launched from Uganda by a joint force of Ugandan and rebel Rwandan Patriotic Front (RPF) soldiers.[80] The Tutsi-dominated RPF, led by former Uganda intelligence chief Paul Kagame,[81] enjoyed consistent US Sigint support from the growing DIA presence in East Africa.[82] The US had admitted supplying military aid to the RPF from 1994.[83] Kagame was reportedly given an encrypted Motorola INMARSAT satellite phone, which, however, was tapped into by the DGSE.[84] As the nationwide massacre of Rwandan Tutsis by the more numerous Hutus was unfolding, France itself deployed a 1,000-strong military intervention force, ostensibly to restore order.

While critics accused Operation Turquoise of being aimed primarily at preserving French influence amongst its old Hutu allies, France retaliated with veiled accusations of a US role in the missile attack on Habyarimana.[85] The Rwandan anarchy, however, was only the start of a growing pattern. The *danse macabre* between Great Lakes ethnic conflict and Franco–US rivalry would arise again, in neighbouring Zaïre. By the early 1990s President-for-Life Mobutu Sese Seko, long patronised during the Cold War, was losing favour in Washington.

For proponents of the 'African Renaissance' in the Clinton administration, the egregious kleptocracy of the 'Old Leopard' represented
everything that was wrong with the old order in Africa. Moreover,
the Kinshasa regime's resolute Francophilia represented an unaccept-
able barrier to the increasing interest of US mining corporations in
newly important strategic minerals such as coltan – widely used in
mobile phones. Mobutu's support for UNITA leader Jonas Savimbi
was a further black mark for a US administration seeking to resolve
the enduring conflict (and access further minerals) in neighbouring
Angola.[86] As Mobutu himself stoked the conflict in Rwanda by
backing the former Hutu government forces and expelling ethnic
Tutsis, the US went on to extend a range of military support,
estimated at $100 million, to a Zaïrean rebel force led by former
Marxist Laurent Kabila, backed by a Rwandan/Uganda invasion – the
same alliance which had toppled the Hutu regime in Rwanda.

Appealing to fellow leaders in 'La Francophonie' and to Paris itself,
Mobutu assembled a mercenary force – the Légion Blanc – with the
aid of veteran French mercenary Bob Denard and the Belgian Christian
Tavernier.[87] Aided by the DST, which enjoyed excellent contacts in
the Balkans, Denard recruited seasoned Serb and Ukrainian fighters,
backed by Mig fighters and helicopter gunships, with ammunition
supplied via the Belgian port of Ostend.[88] The DGSE was more
directly involved, supplying field intelligence from French special
forces operating in Eastern Zaïre. They were, however, under strict
instructions to avoid combat.[89] Decisively countering the French
efforts was US intelligence with Sigint support, notably satellite
surveillance of the disposition of Mobutu's forces, which became the
key to success for Kabila. By early 1997, DIA/NSA ground stations
were reported at Fort Portal (Uganda), Kigali (Rwanda) and Congo
Brazzaville[90] – where pro-US President Pascal Lissouba would soon
be ousted, however, in a French-sponsored coup.[91]

As the Franco-US rivalry was unfolding in West and Central
Africa, a further front was opening up in Southern Sudan. And again,
intelligence would provide the key battleground. A 1989 military
coup in Khartoum had brought to power a hard-line Islamist
government under General Omar Bashir. Virulently opposed to the

US though he was, Bashir was largely the front-man for radical cleric Hassan al-Turabi — the 'Islamic Lenin'.[92] Turabi had extensive connections in France and held a Doctorate in Law from the Sorbonne. He was also an avenue through which France hoped to placate the GIA (Armed Islamic Groups) in Algeria. Sudan played host to a network of Islamist terrorist movements — including, as we have seen, Al-Qaida — and began receiving military aid from Iraq and Iran. Washington, in return, began supporting a long-running rebellion in Southern Sudan, with the aid of its new allies in Uganda. Fearing an extension of US influence in any would-be independent Southern Sudanese state, the DGSE opened discussions with the Khartoum regime. In 1993 and 1994, Sudanese intelligence agents were invited to Paris and provided with SPOT satellite intelligence on the disposition of the rebel Sudan Popular Liberation Army (SPLA).[93] Facing government forces aided by Iraqi imagery (Imint) analysts, and a French-provided secure communications net, the SPLA were soon under pressure. More importantly for Paris, however, so was Uganda, which had to divert resources from its efforts to oust French allies in Rwanda and Zaïre.

The DGSE was to see some more tangible return on its arrangements with the Sudanese Mukhabarat. The French oil company Total was given encouragement in its bid for concessions in the disputed South. And in August 1994 French agents seized the notorious terrorist Illych Ramirez Sanchez — 'Carlos the Jackal' — from his exile in Khartoum; he would be tried in Paris for several murders on French soil.[94]

By the decade's end both France and the US began to step back from confrontation in Africa. After seizing Kinshasa on 22 May 1997, Laurent Kabila was soon to fall out with his US and Rwandan sponsors. And the new Bush administration lacked both interest and expertise in African affairs and was content to let what US policy there was be run even more completely by mineral conglomerates and private military consultancies. Washington's 'African Renaissance' had not led to an African Reformation. For France, the setbacks of Rwanda and Zaïre also prompted a rethink. In 1998 incoming Socialist Prime Minister Lionel Jospin, long a critic of Gaullist Africa policies, announced a cutback of French forces on the continent from 7,400 to 5,000 and the closure of some African bases – though the presidency, under Jacques Chirac, would cling as jealously as ever to its troubled stake *outre-mer*.[95]

Germany and the European Union

During the Cold War, the BND had acquired a dubious reputation for collaboration with a range of unsavoury regimes and guerrilla movements. The Nicaraguan Contras, the Angolan UNITA rebels and apartheid-era South Africa were in close liaison, as was Mossad – a relationship which continues to this day. The domestic service – the Bundesamt für Verfassungsschutz (BfV) – was involved in its own dirty war against leftist militants and was also somewhat distrusted by other Western agencies for being penetrated by the East German Stasi. In an intelligence coup which caused some friction with the BND, most of the Stasi files were seized by the CIA in 1989. Although 33 CD-Roms and over 2,000 statistical pages were later returned, suspicion remains that some highly placed Stasi sources remain in place, having been 'turned' by the US. After reunification, investigations were carried out on 2,928 German citizens, resulting in 388 indictments and 245 jail sentences.[96] More recently, conflict has also arisen between Germany and the US over German attempts to cultivate an intelligence relationship with Iran, whose chief of intelligence visited the Federal Republic in 1993.[97]

After reunification in 1990, the BND began extending its activities. The BND operates in some 70 individual countries and has dedicated Sigint capability at two locations, in Schleswig-Holstein and on the Belgian border. Facilities are also shared with France (Kourou and Mayotte), the US (Bad Aibling) and via NATO and the Western European Union (WEU). In a keynote speech of 10 June 2001 Head of Operations Ludwig Mundt outlined new roles in counter-proliferation – taking 20 per cent of resources – and support for Germany's increasing overseas military role. Proliferation is still a sensitive subject for the BND, who were accused of setting up a wholly spurious plutonium smuggling 'sting' which unravelled in a glare of publicity on 10 August 1994.[98] Mundt also stressed 'the human element', which, given Germany's position as a major focus for Al-Qaida, is likely to be increased.[99]

Whilst Germany has been fully active in NATO, the WEU and the EU, its main intelligence partner has always been France. In January 1996 German Foreign Minister Klaus Kinkle – a former head of the BND – acknowledged an informal intelligence agreement on regional 'spheres of influence'. Under the arrangement reached with French Interior Minister Charles Pasqua, the DGSE would have the 'upper hand' in Latin Europe and Africa, with the BND taking the lead in Germanic and Slavic Europe.[100] In 1991, the new Czech Federal Information Service was restructured along BND lines. NATO-wide intelligence pooling has often fallen foul of differing national priorities. In 1998 a French intelligence officer, Pierre-Henri Bunel, was accused of passing on NATO targeting plans to Serbia, with what degree of official sanction remains unclear.

There is the basis for a EU-wide satellite programme under the WEU's satellite processing centre at Torrijon, in Spain. This co-ordinates commercial SPOT imagery with input from French and US sources. The establishment of an EU High Representative for foreign affairs – currently former NATO chief Javier Solana – has also led to the attachment of a two-dozen-strong intelligence cell. This capability is expected to grow, with the possible merger of the WEU with the Council of Ministers' Secretariat.

A further common intelligence track emerged after the Anglo-French declaration on joint military forces at St-Malo in December 1998. Despite public spats, relations between the UK and the French agencies are 'sometimes closer than between the SIS and the CIA', according to one informed source, with ties between the SIS and the DST being 'particularly warm, and they sometimes conduct joint operations on sensitive subjects'.[101] An illustration of this occurred when the DST obligingly arrested MI 6 renegade Richard Tomlinson, who was wholly innocent of any breach of French law.[102]

The gradual extension of pan-EU security structures has taken place in three stages: the Trevi agreements on common data pooling (1976–93), with the Schengen database going online in 1995; the further extension of common measures in the Treaty of Maastricht (1994–9); and the 1999 Treaty of Amsterdam. The embryonic pan-EU police force – Europol – became operational in June 1999. To date there are over 700 measures, some binding and some inter-governmental. Information can be pooled through the secure EU internal security agencies' Bureau de Liaison (BDL) e-mail network, linking Spain, Portugal, Italy, France and Germany. Europe's domestic agencies – the BfV, DST, MI 5 and others – regularly exchange information via the Club of Berne.[103]

Post-9/11 measures

Although briefly threatening to explode into a major pan-EU row at the turn of the millennium, European Parliament and individual country concern over Echelon has receded in the light of 9/11 and the general drive toward a Common Foreign and Security Policy (CFSP). Indeed, many governments look to be joining Echelon rather than attacking it. George Bush's first European visit after becoming President singled out Spain, holder of the EU Presidency, for special attention. Spain soon afterwards announced 'a very promising field of action' in potential information pooling with the UK/USA allies.[104] And on 16 October 2001 the EU responded positively to a list of 47 US requests for common security measures, including the exchange of telecommunications data, the direct exchange of personal data with Europol, common border control policies and a common category of 'inadmissibles' to be refused entry by the US and EU.

On 17 September 2001 the heads of EU intelligence services met at MI 5 headquarters on the invitation of Sir Stephen Lander for a closed-session meeting on anti-terrorist cooperation.[105] And just before Christmas 2001 the EU (Council and European Parliament) rushed through a raft of further measures under the Framework Decision on Combating Terrorism and the Framework Decision on a European Arrest Warrant. The former, which came into effect on 23 June 2002, extended the definition of terrorism to include 'active or passive support' for terrorist organisations; it also introduced the principle that all asylum applications should be vetted by the security services.[106]

On 30 May 2002 the European Parliament passed the Communications Data Protection Directive, authorising police and security service access to all e-mail, phone, fax, Internet and pager records. Long sought by Europe's intelligence agencies, the measure faces a mixed reception from the 15 national governments. Some, like the UK, have enthusiastically jumped on board with the 'snoopers' charter'; others, like Spain, have encountered constitutional difficulties in terms of 'guarantees of secrecy for individual communications' and requirements for court orders. The legislation was watered down somewhat after last-minute pressure from civil liberties groups, with the inclusion of text indicating that data retention must constitute a 'necessary, appropriate and proportionate measure within a democratic society to safeguard national security', and must conform to the tenets of the European Convention on Human Rights and Fundamental Freedoms (ECHR).[107]

If the ECHR has had a positive influence on some aspects of national intelligence practice – notably, in the UK – there is also a sense in which Europe is going down the British road of collective deniability and unaccountable power. The introduction of the European arrest warrant and the fusion of national intelligence databases leave the way open for massive abuse, in the absence of virtually any practical means of redress. To be sure, exceptional cases will still end up in the European Court of Human Rights or in national courts, but in a political climate dominated by 'war on terror' bandwagoning and an organisational climate taken up by 'targets' and bureaucratic empire building, the burden of proof will increasingly fall on the victim.

Notes

1 See Tony Bunyan, 'The War on Freedom and Democracy – an Analysis of the Effects on Civil Liberties and Democratic Culture in the EU', *Statewatch*, September 2002, p. 1.

2 See Mark Hollingsworth and Nick Fielding, *Defending the Realm: MI 5 and the Shayler Affair*, London: Andre Deutsch, 1999, pp. 252–5.

3 See Report on the Profumo Affair, HMSO 1963, CMND 2152, cited in Geoffrey Robertson, *Freedom, the Individual and the Law*, 7th edition, London: Penguin, 1993, p. 183.

4   See Richard Norton-Taylor, 'How the "Hairies" Spied on the Lefties', 'How Agencies Spied on Trade Unions', *Guardian*, 23/24 October 2002.

5   See Hollingsworth and Fielding, *Defending the Realm*, p. 251; David Aaronovitch, *Independent on Sunday*, 9 April 1998.

6   Robertson, *Freedom*, p. 125.

7   *Ibid*, p. 126.

8   *Ibid.*, p. 125.

9   See Robin Ramsay and Stephen Dorril, *Smear: Wilson and the Secret State*, London: Fourth Estate, 1991; see also Seumas Milne, *The Enemy Within: MI 5, Maxwell and the Scargill Affair* (London: Verso, 1994).

10 See Michael Evans, 'MI5 Will Recruit Historian to Reveal Century of Secrets', *The Times*, 8 August 2002.

11 See Hollingsworth and Fielding, *Defending the Realm*, p. 266.

12 *Cm 5360*, January 2002.

13 See 'UK Government Forced to Delay More Surveillance Powers', *Statewatch News Online*, 18 June 2002.

14 Mark Urban, *UK Eyes Alpha*, London: Faber, 1996, p. 237.

15 See 'The Spies' Biggest Secret', *Punch Magazine*, 134 (4–17 July 2001).

16 Urban, 'UK Eyes', pp. 258–9.

17 The two National Audit Office reports, commissioned in 1995, were classified until 2000, when an edited version was released. See also Urban, 'UK Eyes', pp. 254–5.

18 Estimate of former Cabinet Intelligence and Security Committee Office and MI 6 Deputy Sir Gerald Warner: see Stephen Dorril, *MI 6: Fifty Years of Special Operations*, London: Fourth Estate, 2000, p. 799.

19 See John W. Tate, 'Free Speech and National Security: Britain and the United States', spynews@yahoogroups.com, 19 August 2001, p. 20.

20 See Ian Kirby, 'Spies' £1 Billion Secret', *News of the World*, 15 July 2001.

21 For an early history of Control Risks, see John Cooley, *Unholy Wars*, London: Pluto, 1999, p. 95; for notes on the Hakluyt Foundation, set up in 1995, see John Burnes, 'Can They Hack it?' *Lobster*, 42 (Winter 2001), p. 22–3.

22 Urban, *UK Eyes Alpha*, p. 259; Dorril, *MI 6*, p. 761.

23 See Dorril, *MI 6*, p. 761.

24 See Paul Foot and Tim Laxton, 'Not the Scott Report', *Private Eye Special*, November 1994, pp. 14–15; see also *Sunday Business*, 10 November 1998.

25 See 'GCHQ: We Won't Spy for Big Business', thisisgloucestershire.co.uk, 9 October 2001.

26 See Steve Boggan, 'MI 5 Offers to Spy for British Firms', *Independent*, 7 September 2001.

27 See Nick Fielding, 'Did Twitchy MI 5 Spy on Bird Lovers?', *Sunday Times*, 11 March 2001.

28 See Urban, *UK Eyes Alpha*, pp. 120–5.

29 See Gerald James, 'My Experiences, the Scott Inquiry, the British Legal System',

address to the Environmental Law Centre in spynews@yahoogroups.com, 9 May 2001. See also Gerald James, *In the Public Interest*, London: Little Brown, 1995.

30 See Kevin Cahill, *Independent on Sunday*, 26 April 1998.

31 See Private Eye, 'Not the Scott Report', p. 31.

32 See *Guardian*, 23 March 1998.

33 See Dorril, *MI 6*, p. 791.

34 See Tim Judah, 'Banker Hurd to Fund "Butcher of Belgrade"', *Sunday Telegraph*, 27 July 1997; see also Conal Walsh and Philip Willan, 'Hurd Faces Questions on Serbian Deal', *Observer*, 25 August 2002; Ian Traynor, 'Hurd's Telecom Privatisation Unravels', *Guardian*, 30 December 2002.

35 See *Sunday Times*, 8 February 1998; see also Mark Hollingsworth, 'The Hidden Hand', *Guardian*, 30 March 2000.

36 See Joshua Rozenberg, 'Gaddafi's Son Set Up by MI 6, Libel Jury Told', *Daily Telegraph*, 17 April 2002.

37 See *Panorama Special*, BBC, 8 September 1998.

38 See Robert Baer, *See No Evil*, New York: Crown, 2002, p. 88.

39 See 'Britain's Secret Service Rediscovers Its Military Muscle', RB Media/AFI *Intelligence Briefing*, 17 July 2002.

40 See 'New Zealand Said [to Be] Intercepting Bougainville Rebels' Communications', Radio New Zealand International, Wellington, 0800 hrs, 16 February 1998, in *BBC Summary of World Broadcasts*, 17 February 1998.

41 See Michael Ashworth, 'The King's Road Irregulars Versus the Jungle Rebels: "Security Firm" Hired to End Guerrilla War', *The Independent*, 26 February 1997.

42 See Werner Menges, 'Executive Outcomes and Its Tangled Links', *The Namibian* (Windhoek), 7 July 1998.

43 See Nicholas Rufford and Mary Colvin, 'Our Man in Freetown Is the People's Hero', *Sunday Times*, 17 May 1998.

44 See Michael Jones, 'Can Cook Beat the Mercenaries?' *Sunday Times*, 17 May 1998.

45 See Andrew Parker and Jimmy Burns, 'Head of MI 6 to Face Fresh Inquiry by MPs', *Financial Times*, 17 October 1998.

46 HC/FAC *Report*, Vol. 1, paragraph 103 (February 1999).

47 Sir Thomas Legg was Permanent Secretary to the Lord Chancellor's Department, responsible *inter alia* for selecting judges for particularly 'sensitive' trials, including that of Colin Wallace. See John Burnes, 'Joseph K. and the Spooky Launderette', *Lobster*, 36 (Winter 1998/9).

48 See Hollingsworth and Fielding, *Defending the Realm*, p. 246.

49 See Richard Dowden, 'Sierra Leone Locked in Shackles of Corruption', *Guardian* 12 October 2002.

50 See for example, the UK government Green (consultative) Paper, *Private Military Companies: Options for Regulation*, Government Stationary Office HC577, 12 February 2002.

51 See Hollingsworth and Fielding, *Defending the Realm*, p. 137.

52 Urban, *UK Eyes Alpha*, pp. 203–7, 281.

53 See Liam Clarke, 'MOD Gags Press after Army Suspect Is Named on Net', *Sunday Times*, 11 February 2001.

54 See Rosie Cowen and Nick Hopkins, 'Collusion "at Heart" of Finucane Killing', *Guardian*, 14 June 2002.

55 See John Ware, 'We Have Seen Secret Files…', *Sunday Telegraph*, 29 March 1998; 'Time to Come Clean over the Army's Role in the Dirty War', *New Statesman*, 25 April 1998.

56 See John Sparks, 'The Government Created a Monster…' *Sunday Telegraph*, 29 July 2001.

57 See 'Animal Rights Activists Aim to Kill', *Eye Spy* magazine, 1 (2001), pp. 38–41.

58 See Maurice Chittenden and Nicholas Rufford, 'MI 6 "Firm" Spied on Green Groups', *Sunday Times*, 17 June 2001.

59 *Ibid*.

60 The corporate status is somewhat unusual. As a trust rather than a company, Hakluyt enjoys a greater measure of legal privacy. See Burnes, 'Can They Hack it?'. This could represent a prudent anticipation of coming EU legislation on corporate social responsibility.

61 See Dorril, *MI 6*, p. 778.

62 See James Bamford, *Body of Secrets: How America's NSA and Britain's GCHQ Eavesdrop upon the World*, London: Century, 2001, p. 401.

63 Urban, *UK Eyes Alpha*, p. 238.

64 GCHQ's new Director, David Pepper, took office in January 2003, with his PFI as well as IT background apparently weighing heavily in the appointment. The 30-year management deal is now costed at some £1.1 billion. See Richard Norton-Taylor, 'IT Expert Named as New Head of GCHQ', *Guardian*, 1 February 2003.

65 See Peter Klerks, *A Directory of European Intelligence Agencies*, Domestic Security Research Foundation, April 1993, pp. 21–35.

66 See 'DST Takes a Technical Track', *Intelligence Newsletter*, 5 February 1998.

67 See Vincent Jauvert, 'Espionage; How France Listens to the Whole World', *Le Nouvel Observateur*, 5 April 2001.

68 *Ibid*.

69 See *Le Monde du Renseignement*, 16 March 2000; see also Charles Grant, 'Intimate Relations: Can Britain Play a Leading Role in European Defence and Keep Its Special Links to US Intelligence?' *Working Paper – Centre for European Reform*, 15 July 2001.

70 See *Intelligence Newsletter*, 39, 10 June 1996.

71 See Jan Rocha, 'Chancellor Flies into Eye of Storm to Police Amazon Electronically', *Guardian*, 29 December 1995.

72 David Ignatius, 'How a US Lawyer Shook Up "France Inc."', *International Herald Tribune*, 10 January 1996.

73 See Russell Watson, 'Trade Spies: the CIA Takes Off the Gloves', *Newsweek*, 6 March 1995.

74 Robert Dreyfus, 'Help Wanted Spying on Allies', *Mother Jones*, 20, 3 May 1995.

75   See Felix Njoku, 'United States and Africa Begins to Matter to the United States', *PanAfrican News Agency*, 12 March 1996.

76   *Ibid.*

77   See Barbara Starr, 'US Puzzle Palace Seeks New Clues to Combat Old Threats', *Jane's Defence Weekly*, 3 September 1997.

78   Participants included Benin, Mali, Senegal and Tunisia. See US Senate, Subcommittee on International Economic Policy, Export and Trade Promotion, *Statement of Assistant Secretary Thomas E. McNamara, 12 March 1997*, Washington: GPO.

79   See 'Closed Door Meeting in the United States on the Privatisation of African Armies', *La Lettre du Continent*, 4 September 1997; see also 'Mercenary Trades', *Indian Ocean Newsletter*, 14 February 1998.

80   Habyarimana's French-piloted Fokker aircraft was shot down over Kigali airport by a SAM 16 missile. The plane, carrying Rwandan government leaders from both Hutu and Tutsi factions, was returning from a hitherto successful peace conference in Arusha, Tanzania. The aircrew later received an official commendation from the Head of the DGCE.

81   Kagame had been trained in intelligence methods at Fort Leavenworth, Kansas in 1989–90; see Christopher Clapham (ed.), *African Guerrillas*, Bloomington: Indiana University Press, 1998, p. 130.

82   This included a station in Kigali itself. See 'France Versus America in Africa', *Jane's Foreign Report*, 6 March 1997.

83   See Amnesty International, *Rwanda: Ending the Silence*, AFR 47/32/96, 23 September 1997, p. 44.

84   See Jean Guisnel, *Guerres dans la Cyberspace*, Paris: Editions la Découverte, 1995, pp. 186–7.

85   French intelligence leaks claimed that the SAM 16 was delivered to Uganda by the CIA from Iraqi stocks seized after the 1991 Gulf War. See Philip Shenon, 'Fateful Crash in Africa: Link to US Is Denied', *New York Times*, 7 April 1998.

86   See Robert Block, 'US Firms Seek Deals in Central Africa', *Wall Street Journal*, 14 October 1997.

87   See Sean Boyne, 'The White Legion; Mercenaries in Zaïre', *Jane's Intelligence Review*, 1 June 1997.

88   See Jim Lobe, 'War-ravaged Burundi Flooded with Foreign Weapons', *Inter-Press Service*, 8 December 1997.

89   'France Versus America in Africa', *Jane's Foreign Report*, 6 March 1997.

90   See *East African*, 31 March 1997.

91   See Tom Masland, 'An African Big Man in Trouble', *Newsweek*, 15 December 1997.

92   See Patrick Thorne, 'The Rise of the Islamic Lenin', *Casablanca*, London, Autumn 1994.

93   See Peter Moszinski, 'Sudan: How France Captured Carlos', *New African*, October 1994.

94 See Abdel Salam Sidahmed, 'Sudan, France and the Carlos Affair', *Middle East International*, 23 September 1994.

95 See Jacques Michel Tondre, 'French President Takes Dig at US at Giant African Summit', Agence France-Presse, 27 November 1998.

96 See 'German Intelligence Service Experts: Former Stasi Agents Possibly Used by CIA', *BBC Monitoring European*, 27 August 2001; John Hooper, 'Khol Struggles to Protect Stasi Files', *Guardian,* 14 July 2002.

97 See Dorril, *MI 6*, p. 771.

98 See *Intelligence Newsletter*, 13, 57 (August 1994).

99 See Ludwig Mundt, 'Intelligence: the Human Element', International Intelligence History Study Group, *Seventh Annual Meeting*, Hamburg, 8–10 June 2001, intelligence-history.wiso.uni-erlangen.de/meetings.htm.

100 See *Intelligence Newsletter*, 40, 2 (24 June 1996).

101 Grant, 'Intimate Relations', p. 12.

102 See Richard Tomlinson, *The Big Breach*, Edinburgh: Cutting Edge, 2000, pp. 204–11.

103 Grant, 'Intimate Relations', p. 10.

104 See Giles Tremlett, 'Grateful Aznar Oils EU Wheels for President on Missile Shield and Kyoto Pact', *Guardian*, 15 June 2001.

105 See David Leppard, 'Spy Chiefs Agree Plans to Hit bin Laden Cells', *Sunday Times*, 23 September 2001.

106 See Tony Bunyan, 'The War on Freedom'.

107 See Julia Scheers, 'Europe Passes Snoop Measure', *Wired News* (wired.com), 30 May 2002.

CHAPTER 5

RUSSIA

From KGB to FSB
and Back Again?

'*The repudiation of the ideology of Chekism*'
– Vadim Bakatin, *Izvestia*, 2 January 1992

For Russia's security and intelligence services, the end of the old Soviet Union brought the scarcely less shocking dissolution of the Komitet Gosudarstvennoy Bezopasnosti (KGB, Committee for State Security) – the very emblem of Soviet power and its main enforcement muscle. However, a decade on, and with a former KGB man in charge, an organisation not totally dissimilar to the KGB has emerged from the wreckage, again with the ear of the Kremlin and a new mandate for global operations.

As in the old Soviet Union, however, a plethora of intelligence organisations exists, with often overlapping and, indeed, rival functions and attitudes to each other. The major organs concerned with intelligence, as opposed to largely policing matters, are the FSB (Federalnaya Sluzhba Bezopasnosti, Federal Security Service), SVR (Sluzhba Vnesheny Razvedki, Foreign Intelligence Service), FSO (Federalnaya Sluzhba Okrhrany, Federal Protection Service, concerned with the protection of high-ranking state officials), FAPSI (Federal Agency for Government Communications and Information, Russia's equivalent of the NSA, albeit with wider powers), GRU (Glavnoye Razvedyvatelnoye Upravleniye, Main Intelligence Directorate, military intelligence) and GUSP (Glavnoye Upravelenniye Spetsyalnykh Program,

Main Directorate of Special Programmes, attached to the Presidential Office). Amongst the numerous specialist subdivisions of the Russian intelligence community, the State Technical Commission (Gostekh-komissya) undertakes electronic counter-intelligence in conjunction with FAPSI, whilst the once-powerful Presidential Security Service (Sluzhba Bezopasnosti Prezidenta – SBP) has been subordinated to the FSO. The Ministry of Interior Security (MVD) has some localised intelligence functions, but has tended to adopt a more conventional policing and public order role with the advent of Vladimir Putin. Whilst it is charged, along with the FSB, with containing the Chechen war, the FSB remains the senior partner.

The FSB: two coups and a demise exaggerated

Like the Communist Party and the USSR itself, the KGB became a major casualty of the attempted August 1991 coup against then President Mikhail Gorbachev. Gorbachev's options for reforming the KGB – which combined both internal and external intelligence functions in the old Soviet state – were limited. Virtually all the top KGB leadership were implicated, including Gorbachev's own chief body-guard and the coup leader, KGB Chairman Vladimir Kryuchkov.

With Kryuchkov and the other coup plotters in gaol, former MVD chairman and Gorbachev stalwart Vadim Bakatin took over the KGB. Seen as 'by far the most liberal chief of any of Moscow's secret services, before or since',[1] Bakatin set about mass firings of unregenerate KGB 'Chekists' and established five separate state investigations into the coup and other suspected illegal acts. To the horror of remaining hardliners, he also turned over the plans of the extensive surveillance devices implanted in its Moscow embassy to the US ambassador.

Beginning with the transfer of the KGB's military units to the Defence Ministry, Bakatin broke up the monolithic KGB into five separate services and ceded power from the Moscow centre to Boris Yeltsin's Russian Federation and 11 other remaining Union Republics. Yeltsin, however, had largely backed the Bakatin reforms as a way of weakening the position both of Gorbachev as President of the USSR and of the Soviet Union itself. With the formal dissolution of the

Union on 8 December 1991, Bakatin was soon replaced by a succession of Yeltsin appointees whose tenures reflected the increasingly erratic progress of the post-Soviet regime.

The main inheritor of the KGB mantle – eventually reorganised as the FSB – was to undergo six successive name changes and a corresponding number of changes of leadership during the next six years. It initially took over the KGB's Second Chief Directorate (counter-intelligence), Fourth Directorate (transport), Sixth Director-ate (economic counter-intelligence), Seventh Directorate (surveillance) and Operational Technical Directorate.[2] These functions, along with others such as counter-terrorism, were subsequently absorbed in a new Ministry of Security, established alongside an also reorganised Ministry of Internal Affairs by a Yeltsin decree of January 1993. However, the Security Ministry was soon embroiled in the mounting power struggle between Yeltsin and the Russian Duma. Perhaps with an eye to recent history, Yeltsin appears to have had second thoughts about creating a powerful new security arm and in July 1993 sacked the recently appointed chief, Viktor Barranikov. During the armed confrontation with the Duma of 3–4 October, the Security Ministry maintained a studied distance from events, claiming lack of clear legal sanction, and the besieged Duma attempted to reappoint Barranikov as Minister. With matters finally resolved by the Interior Ministry (MVD) forces – who would become Yeltsin's most favoured agency – the Russian President signed a decree on 21 December abolishing the Federation Ministry of Security and creating the Federal Counter-Intelligence Service (FSK).

Whilst publicly promoted as a democratisation measure, the found-ing of the FSK had more to do with Yeltsin's divide-and-rule manage-ment of the state through the manipulation of patronage and parallel power structures. With the loyalist Sergei Stepashin in charge, the FSK lost its organised crime and racketeering briefs to the MVD and certain types of surveillance to FAPSI. In all, staff were reduced by 46 per cent to 77,640 people.[3] More significantly for Yeltsin, the FSK, no longer a ministry, was effectively out of the loop as far as the Duma was concerned and was tasked to report exclusively to the Presidential Office.

Whether such reporting brought a new dimension to Kremlin decision making is unknown. What is clear, however, is that the increasingly degenerating security climate was convincing Yeltsin and his associates that some rebuilding of the FSK was in order. Organised crime networks, posing a political threat as much as any other, were beginning to make an impact in Russia. Former Security Minister Barranikov – himself sacked for corruption – had warned of 'Mafia-like structures' in an open letter given wide media publicity. Foreign intelligence services – notably, MI 6 – were finding rich pickings amongst the vast former Soviet weapons industries and disillusioned former security personnel.[4] Above all, rebel forces in the breakaway region of Chechnya were in open and successful revolt against Moscow's rule. In June 1994, Stepashin announced a new crime-fighting section in the FSK. The organisation also reclaimed the Directorate of Investigations from the General Prosecutor's Office and the anti-terrorist unit from the MVD. In December 1994 the FSK set up a Chechen Directorate, which would grow into one of its biggest operational sections.

Enter the FSB

On 3 April 1995 the President signed a new federal law, 'On the Organs of the Federal Security Service in the Russian Federation'. This changed the FSK into the Federal Security Service (FSB) with some internal reorganisation and greatly increased powers. Under the new law, the FSB was able to enter property and detain suspects, operate abroad in conjunction with the Foreign Intelligence Service (SVR), and establish private companies and train private sector security personnel. This became a growth area for the FSB. By 1998, Russia had some 2,500 banks and 72,000 commercial enterprises with their own security services. The energy giant Gazprom alone employed 20,000 security staff, mostly former or moonlighting FSB or other state security employees.[5] A 'Consultative Council of the Russian FSB' was set up in 1996, with representatives from all the major companies, to regulate the grey-area security sector. As all private surveillance and monitoring equipment requires a state licence, this gained much leverage for the FSB; it could also wield considerable influence on employment prospects. At the high finance level, an Economic Counter-Intelligence Directorate was set up in 1997 to monitor Russian banks, control contacts between Russian defence firms and foreign business, and investigate overseas financial holdings – although, with Yeltsin's inner circle indulging in record capital flight, what success this had is unclear.

Indeed, despite the increasing accumulation of powers, the sheer impoverishment of the Russian economy, with the wages of even senior generals and academicians at starvation level, made widespread corruption a virtual necessity for many. And besides the well-documented slew of human rights abuses in the Chechen conflict, evidence mounted of a return to the methods of the old KGB, with opposition of whatever stripe virtually regarded as treason. In July 1996 newly appointed FSB Director Nikolai Kovalev announced a return to investigation by anonymous tip-off, a procedure abolished by Gorbachev in 1988. Human rights activists, environmentalists and the newly liberalised press all came under increased pressure. In what was widely seen as a revenge case, the FSB in 1995 brought charges against former KGB captain Viktor Orekov, who had spent seven years in a labour camp for warning dissidents of arrest.[6] Other charges were brought against retired Navy captain Alexander Nikitin, who had researched an open-source report on nuclear waste dumping in the Arctic Ocean for the Norwegian environmental group Bellona.[7] And serving naval captain Grigori Pasko, a journalist on the Pacific Fleet newsletter, was arrested in November 1997 for investigating the embezzlement by senior officers of $100 million of Japanese environmental clean-up funding.

The most dramatic set of charges against the FSB came not from dissidents but from one of the most influential figures in Yeltsin's Russia. In March 1998 media tycoon and Yeltsin confidant Boris Berezhovski became involved in the murky investigation of an alleged assassination plot against him by officers within the Directorate of Analysis and Suppression of the Activity of Criminal Organisations (URPO). The allegation had been made by URPO lieutenant-colonel Alexander Litvinenko, who doubled as a bodyguard for Berezhovski. When the named conspirators were cleared by FSB Director Kovalev

– himself sacked by Yeltsin in July 1998, allegedly for taking too close an interest in corruption in FAPSI – Litvinenko gave a press conference repeating the accusations. This was reiterated the following day by Berezhovski, who called the FSB a 'criminal organisation'. After further charges of attempted kidnapping, levelled against Kovalev on Berezhovski's nationwide TV channel ORT in November, Kovalev took – and eventually won – court action against Berezhovski.

The hothouse atmosphere in Yeltsin's Russia had intensified after the elections of 1996. Never one to shirk introducing a further layer of bureaucratic competition into the security structure, in August 1996 Yeltsin appointed presidential runner-up Alexander Lebed as Secretary of the Federation Security Council. Lebed helped establish a new élite unit, the Long Term Programmes Directorate (UPP, later URPO), within the FSB and asked for the retirement of 30 FSB generals – a suggestion which had to be personally denied to senior FSB officials by Prime Minister Chernomyrdin. As well as the plain-speaking Lebed – whose rising popularity with the security services would soon lead to his dismissal – the FSB was in competition with the SBP and the Main Protection Directorate (GUO). Incorporating former KGB functions and personnel, these were set up by Yeltsin after 1993 as a praetorian guard under General Alexander Korzhakov. Functioning with legal immunity, the GUO was transformed into the FSO in 1996 and merged with the SPB. At its peak, the organisation had some 44,000 staff and substantial business interests. It shrank, however, after SPB officers arrested two of Yeltsin's campaign workers with $500,000 in cash on 19 June 1996. Korzhakov was sacked the next day and the department was reduced to 30,000 by 1999, with the SBP cut from 4,000 in 1995 to 900. The URPO, under pressure after the Berezhovski affair, was disbanded in 1999.

Further reforms of May 1997, aimed at cost and staff reductions in the FSB, were intensified as the Russian financial crisis deepened throughout 1998. In some accounts, FSB staff levels fell from 140,000 in 1993 to some 80,000 at the end of 1997.[8] In July and August Yeltsin authorised another restructuring that would bring in the new Department of Economic Security and a Directorate of Information and Computer Security. Military counter-intelligence, responsible amongst other things for nuclear weapons security, was reintroduced to the FSB as a separate element, under its old KGB directorate number, three. The new director, replacing Kovalev on 25 July 1998, was Vladimir Putin.

Putin takes charge

Whilst Putin made an initial impact in the FSB by facing down the Berezhovski/Litvinenko imbroglio, his tenure would be a transitory one. Promoted to Deputy Prime Minister on 9 August 1999, he was replaced by Nikolai Patrushev. If Putin had left little tangible change at the FSB, apart from a 25 per cent across-the-board pay rise and some departmental streamlining, the organisation would take fresh heart from being hitched to a rising star. Indeed, events during September 1999 suggested to some the start of a fresh grab for power by the FSB. A series of bombs, apparently placed at random, exploded in Moscow apartment blocks, killing some 300 people. On 22 September 1999, bags of a powder, claimed by the MVD to be the military explosive Hexogen, and detonating timers were found in an apartment building in the Russian city of Ryazan. In the face of contradictory reports by the police, MVD and local residents, FSB Director Patrushev issued an immediate apology, claiming the discoveries were part of an anti-terrorist exercise 'also taking place in other Russian cities', and that the bags actually contained sugar.

Given the role of the bombings – blamed on Chechen terrorists – in justifying renewed Russian military action in Chechnya, many in Moscow suspected a return to old Soviet *agent provocateur* techniques. This theory was given wide publicity by the now-exiled Alexander Litvinenko in excerpts from a book published in August 2001 under the title *The FSB Blows Up Russia*. Some in the Russian human rights and press community took issue, however, claiming Litvinenko was highly selective with the facts.[9] Given the spate of acknowledged Chechen kidnappings and guerrilla actions throughout the mid-1990s, the Kremlin arguably had ample other justification. And clearly Litvinenko, who sought asylum in Britain in May 2000, like many other former spies would have wanted a good story to tell. The former FSB colonel remains in touch with the also-exiled Boris

Berezhovski, whose feud with Putin and the FSB has continued unabated. Litvinenko's other major claim, that the FSB has retained the KGB's old department of 'wet' – assassination – operations is less controversial. Russian intelligence has taken credit openly for the April 1996 death of renegade Chechen President Dzhokhar Dudayev in an Israeli-style precision missile strike and the 20 March 2002 killing of Saudi-born Chechen guerrilla leader Samer al-Suwailem (Khattab) by means of a letter sprayed with fast-acting neurotoxin. The FSB was quick to contrast its efforts with the continuing US failure to take action against Osama bin Laden.[10]

The FSB took overall charge of the rekindled Chechen war in January 2001, a development immediately marked by the arrest of journalists and a crackdown on information.[11] State harassment of the independent Media Most group further suggests that Putin's KGB reflexes are returning to robust health. In July 2001 the television station NTV was taken over by the state-controlled energy conglomerate Gazprom, which also took a decisive stake in the independent radio station Ekho Moskvy. The daily newspaper *Segodnya* was closed down and senior journalists from the news weekly *Itogi* were forced to leave the publication, while the group's founder, Vladimir Guzinski, fled to Spain after three days in Moscow's Butyrskaya prison. In a press statement officials claimed that 'The FSB has completed the operational work within the framework of the official investigation into the illegal activities of the Most Group,' with favoured *apparachnyi* reportedly being rewarded with DIY home improvement kits and cases of Johnny Walker.[12]

Academic freedom, one of the few enduring legacies of the Glasnost era, is also under threat. On 24 May 2001 the Russian Academy of Sciences issued an 'Action Plan to Prevent Damage to the Russian State in the Spheres of Economic and Scientific Cooperation'. In a direct return to Soviet practice, all academicians were ordered to submit reports on foreign travel, conferences, articles in foreign publications, acceptance of foreign grants and meetings with foreigners. Foreign travellers in Russia, especially visiting students and journalists, were also coming under increased harassment. An American Fulbright Scholar, John Tobin, was arrested in Southern Russia in April 2001, allegedly for dealing in marijuana. While charges of espionage were raised and, after some public embarrassment, dropped again, Tobin claimed he had himself been pressured to spy for Russia.[13]

While rumours that the FSB was truly to assume the KGB mantle by merging with the FSO – or, in some versions, the SVR and FAPSI – were denied in February 2001 by secretary Sergei Ivanov, it clearly remains the senior service of Russian intelligence.[14] With recognised links to 80 countries by the end of 1997 and offices in 18, it clearly rivals the SVR for foreign intelligence gathering, and its growing surveillance and Sigint capabilities are indications of the ambition, at least, to catch up with FAPSI.

The SVR – 'still in the big four'

If spared the many structural makeovers of the FSB, Russian foreign intelligence was badly shaken by the end of the Warsaw Pact and global Soviet alliance system. The KGB First Chief Directorate (known in Russian as the PGU) had a major presence across the US, Canada, Eastern and Western Europe, fellow communist states – Cuba, Vietnam – and 'states of a socialist orientation' such as Ethiopia and South Yemen. The KGB and its Warsaw Pact allies trained security and intelligence personnel of 50 intelligence services in the Third World and maintained large-scale monitoring facilities at Cam Ranh Bay, Vietnam and Lourdes, Cuba. In the immediate aftermath of the 1991 coup, moves were made to sack the KGB personnel working under diplomatic cover and the service briefly became the Central Intelligence Service before settling as the Foreign Intelligence Service (SVR) under former foreign ministry official and long-standing Kremlin insider Yevgeni Primakov.

The SVR was established on a legal basis on 8 July 1992, with a presidential decree of December 1991 ratified by the Russian Duma. With staff reductions of some 40 per cent from a reported strength of 15,000 personnel in the early 1990s[15] and its Elint and cryptography arm taken over by FAPSI, the slimmed-down foreign intelligence service was to concentrate on Humint – always a Russian strong point – and on rebuilding Moscow's position in the former Soviet territories and countries of the Commonwealth of Independent States (CIS). Like its US counterpart, the CIA, it is prohibited from conducting operations on domestic soil.

Of the priority areas for the SVR, the CIS appeared to offer the most potential. Close to Russia geographically, with shared technology and organisational structure and familiar personnel, many former Soviet republics also host substantial minorities of ethnic Russians. With an eye on salvaging what remained of the old all-USSR intelligence structure, Moscow signed an agreement on basic principles of cooperation with the states of Armenia, Belarus, Kazakhstan, Kyrgyzstan, Moldova, Tajikistan, Turkmenistan and Ukraine on 5 April 1992 at Alma Ata. With information sharing on terrorism, organised crime and drug running, the signatories agreed not to mount intelligence operations against each other. Aside from historical factors, Moscow's intense interest in these regions stems from the huge oil and gas potential and the rise of Islamist forces. Here, though, the Kremlin faced some difficulties from the repeated Russian attempts at manipulation of regional politics. Georgia had refused to sign up after Moscow's tolerance of cross-border ethnic dissidents in Abkhazia; and Azerbaijan, with its eyes on Western oil contracts, was similarly wary after Russian support for Armenia on the disputed Ngorno Karabakh region. In 1995, with Georgia now on board, 12 CIS states agreed a further convention on intelligence matters, with crime and terrorism again at the top of the agenda.

Whilst Moscow could expect backing from remaining Soviet-era leaders, such as Azerbaijan's Heydar Aliyev, a former KGB executive and Politburo member, and Saparmurad Niyazov of Turkmenistan, it was hampered by the highly fragmented and volatile regional politics and by heavy Russian involvement – both freelance and from inside the security services – in crime itself.[16] Iran, Turkey and Saudi Arabia are all highly active in Central Asia, as is the Israeli Mossad. In all the former Soviet republics, the familiar combination of corruption and authoritarian rule has proved a fertile ground for insurgent Islamists – many, like Tajikistan's Abdallah Nuri, bankrolled by Gulf-based Islamic charities.[17] With the massive influx of oil money, and the promise of more to come, there has been much temptation for neighbouring powers to contemplate 'regime change' in the region. In March 1995, Azeri President Aliyev was threatened by a coup fronted by Interior Minister Rawshan Javadov. Azerbaijan accused Turkey of being implicated in a complex plot involving oil concessions and the husband of the then Prime Minister, Tansu Ciller.[18] Turkey is viewed as a combination of rival, partner and something of a role model by the SVR. Although suspicion remains of Turkish aid to the Chechens, Moscow has established a working level of cooperation with Turkish foreign intelligence, the MIT, on a joint platform of combating radical Islamists in the region.

As in the Cold War era, Russian foreign intelligence maintains an uneasy relationship with the 'main opponent', the CIA. The US has long maintained cordial links with the Georgian regime of former Soviet Foreign Minister Eduard Shevardnadze, and the March 2002 announcement of the deployment of 160 special forces personnel to train Georgian forces in counter-insurgency[19] became a further cause of friction with Moscow. There is also the matter of the unsolved murder on 8 August 1993 of CIA chief of station in Georgia, Fred Woodruff, by a special-forces-issue customised sniper's bullet. Woodruff reportedly had a confrontation with SVR 'mole' Aldrich Ames in Tblisi shortly before.[20] The arrest of Ames on 21 February 1994 marked a low point in post–Cold War US–Russian intelligence relations. Director of Central Intelligence Robert Gates had visited Russia in October 1992, a visit reciprocated by SVR Director Primakov's US meeting with new DCI Woolsey in June 1993. Washington, however, remained distrustful of Primakov after his diplomatic opposition to the Gulf War in 1991. And a further Russian visit by Woolsey in August 1993 was curtailed after the Woodruff assassination. At the close of the Cold War, some 140 KGB and GRU agents were active in North America, operating under various kinds of cover. This figure declined to around 100 by 1995, but then began to rise, according to some FBI sources.[21] The arrest in May 1996 of two SVR 'illegals' working in Canada and the November 1996 arrest of a CIA agent in Russia threatened relations even further.

Whilst clear advantages are apparent for all sides in the fields of countering crime and weapons proliferation, the same ambivalence exists between the SVR and its counterparts in Western Europe. Relations with Britain's MI 6 remained coloured by a certain Cold War rivalry, compounded by the defection of former KGB archivist Vasili Mitrokhin in 1992.[22] With an official BND representative based in Moscow since 1992, Germany was viewed as a natural intelligence partner during the amicable Yeltsin–Kohl era. Relations continue to be complicated, however, by the extensive Russian criminal diaspora, SVR economic intelligence gathering and historical links with the old East German foreign intelligence service, the HVR – many of whose operatives remain in place. In the mid-1990s, German newspapers alleged that there were 160 Russian agents working in Germany.

FAPSI

In many ways the Russian equivalent of the US National Security Agency and Britain's GCHQ, the Federal Agency of Government Information and Communication (FAPSI) is the most secretive of the security agencies and also, with estimates ranging as high as 120,000 personnel, perhaps the largest.[23] After the Black Sea coup attempt of August 1991, the communications, cryptography and Elint wings of the old KGB – the eighth and twelfth chief directorates, plus a number of other branches – were briefly hived off into the all-Union Government Communications Committee under Gorbachev before being established in their present form as FAPSI by Boris Yeltsin in December 1991. With powers consolidated by an act of the Russian Duma of February 1993, FAPSI is responsible for organising all federal government communications and information, and is in charge of secure communications for large military formations. Although possessing no powers of arrest or detention, FAPSI maintains its own troops for providing base security and setting up mobile field communications. Officers enjoy certain legal immunities, such as immunity from arrest without the presence of a FAPSI representative or the direct order of a public prosecutor.

With a continuation of its global monitoring capability seen as essential to Moscow's maintaining its status as a great power, FAPSI was spared the radical downsizing inflicted on other Russian security and state institutions. The overseas stations in Cuba and Vietnam were kept in operation until 2002. In the volatile atmosphere of Yeltsin's two administrations, the agency, with its unique capabilities for information gathering, soon became a presidential favourite, with Yeltsin receiving a personal daily brief on chosen topics by General Starovotov, the then FAPSI Director.[24]

Although some chaos followed the break-up of the old Soviet Union, FAPSI was gradually able to re-establish contact with its extensive network of facilities and relay stations in the former territories. For many in the successor entity, the CIS, it was a question of recommissioning the existing Russian equipment or having nothing. Accordingly, in May 1992 in Tashkent, 10 CIS heads of government signed an agreement on the security of encryption and established the Government Communications Coordinating Council. In Russia itself, FAPSI was charged with coordinating the central legal database or *sistema* vital for Yeltsin's ongoing struggles with the Duma, where FAPSI runs communication links for both houses. In 1995, FAPSI was officially put in charge of the Russian Federation State Automated System for vote counting and monitoring elections, linking the regional with the central (but effectively powerless) electoral commissions. FAPSI also runs the Regional Information Analysis Centres, located in 58 major regions of Russia, with some 300 substations. These provide local situation updates and analysis of over 1,200 local publications. Communications in the old, control-obsessed Soviet Union took the concept of 'redundancy' very seriously indeed, with each tier of government using its own dedicated network.[25] Whilst those reserved for ministers and deputy ministers have been turned over to the Federal Protection Service, FAPSI retains control of the presidential tier and that linking the centre with the regions. FAPSI has its own secure network – Ishtok – and has taken over at least four other Soviet-era high frequency linkages.[26] The USSR-wide parallel telephone network Kaskad had some 40,000 outposts; now partially privatised, it is leased under FAPSI direction to major oil and gas companies. FAPSI has also inherited the national telephone grid of the old Soviet Communist Party, now hired out as a secure network for business communication.

FAPSI is responsible for the cryptographic security of all government lines, and as the monopoly provider of encrypted communications – state and private sector – is in a strong position to exert commercial leverage. In April 1995 Yeltsin set up a new Federal Centre for the Protection of Economic Information. Supervised by FAPSI, its aim was to access all information flows between the banking sector and overseas operations. Companies and individuals in Russia are not allowed to develop their own computer security systems but must buy those already available, with a licence issued by FAPSI. In similar fashion to the West, private concerns staffed by former officers work closely with their state colleagues. And as in the West, the cross-over of personnel has raised serious issues of corruption. A former FAPSI Financial Director, General Valery Monastyrskiy, was arrested by the FSB in April 1996, charged with embezzling DM20 million in rake-offs from the German Siemens company. In what became something of a Moscow *cause célèbre*, Monastyrskiy countered by charging, not without reason, that the FSB had ulterior motives in seeking to absorb large parts of FAPSI's operations.[27] Clearly, FAPSI's pole position in surveillance and cryptography make it a tempting target for bureau-cratic takeover. In 1996, the then FSB Director Baruskov attempted to dismember FAPSI, and the section running presidential communications was briefly transferred to the Main Protection Directorate, the GUO.

Initially deficient in general purpose computers, FAPSI now claims to be able to match the best available at more specialised levels.[28] However, in the cash-strapped circumstances afflicting the Russian exchequer, keeping up with Fort Meade will inevitably mean an increase in the traditional Russian approach to technological deficit – espionage. Despite the ambitions of the FSB, and possibly the preferences of Putin, this alone could secure the state of FAPSI in something like its present form, at least for now.

Notes

1 See Michael J. Waller, 'Russia's Security Services: a Checklist for Reform', *ISCIP-Perspective*, 8, 1 (September–October 1997).

2 See Gordon Bennett, *The Federal Security Service of the Russian Federation*, RMA

Sandhurst and the Conflict Studies Research Centre, October 2001.

3 *Ibid.*, pp. 14–15.

4 See Mark Urban, *UK Eyes Alpha*, London: Faber, 1996, pp. 221–32.

5 See Bennett, *The Federal Security Service*, p. 29.

6 See *Christian Science Monitor*, 18 September 1995.

7 See Amnesty International, *Torture and Ill Treatment in Russia*, November 1996.

8 See Bennett, *The Federal Security Service*, p. 27.

9 See Yevgenia Borisova, 'Co-author Defends Book on FSB', *Moscow Times*, 4 September 2001.

10 See Mark Franchetti, 'Poisoned Letter Kills Chechen Warlord', *Sunday Times*, 19 May 2002.

11 For extended coverage of information management in the Chechen war, see Glasnost Defence Foundation (Moscow), *passim*, and Alexei Simonov, 'Voina Protiv Zhurnalistov', in Liliya Isakova and Elena Oznobkina (eds.), *Voina v Chechnye: Mezhdunarodnyi Tribunal: II Rabochaya Vstrecha*, Stockholm, 15–16 December 1995 (Moscow: Obshchestvennyi Fond Glasnost, 1996) – Russian/English edition.

12 See *Gazeta* (Moscow), 20 July 2001.

13 See Stanislav Lunev, *NewsMax* (Moscow), 16 July 2001.

14 See Franchetti, 'Putin Resurrects Spectre of KGB', *Sunday Times,* 4 February 2001.

15 See Gordon Bennett, *The SVR: Russia's Intelligence Service*, RMA Sandhurst and the Conflict Studies Research Centre, October, 2001, p. 7.

16 See for example William Webster *et al.* (eds.), *Russian Organised Crime: Global Organised Crime Project*, Washington: CSIS, 1997.

17 A key player here is allegedly the Saudi-based World Muslim League. See Robert Baer, *See No Evil*, New York: Crown, 2002, p. 165.

18 *Ibid.*, p. 228.

19 See Rensselaer Lee and Raphael Perl for CRS, *Terrorism, the Future and US Foreign Policy*, IB95112: 18 April 2002, p. 2.

20 Baer, *See No Evil*, p. 155. The assassins were never found.

21 See 'Russian Spy Presence in the US on the Rise', *Sources – the Security Intelligence News Service*, 26 December 2001.

22 See Dong-Phoung Nguyen, 'Witness Links Spy Suspect to Data on KGB', *St Petersburg Times*, 19 June 2001.

23 See details on: www.agentura.ru/enlish/dosie/fapsi/

24 See Dmytri Makarov, 'Eyes and Ears for the Powers', *Argumenti-i-Facti*, 1997.

25 These are: (1) a special exchange for the president and presidential staff; (2) ministers and first deputy ministers; (3) deputy ministers, heads of directorates; (4) a high frequency inter-city network between the centre and the regions – see Gordon Bennett, 'The Federal Agency of Government Communications and Information', paper for Conflict Studies Research Centre, RMA, Sandhurst (C105–GB), p. 8.

26 *Ibid.*, p. 14.

27 See Makarov, 'Eyes and Ears'.

28 *Ibid.*

CHAPTER 6

ISRAEL

The Living Security Dilemma?

'With blood and fear, we will build us a nation.'
– Vladimir Jabotinski

Unable – and, to date, unwilling – to decide between conquest and reconciliation, the state of Israel spends more GNP per head on intelligence than any other country.[1] Henry Kissinger once condemned 'the illusion that Israel d[oes] not have to conduct a foreign policy, only a defence policy'[2] – to which might be added a similarly illusory pursuit of 'security' at the expense of all else in its domestic affairs. Certainly, Israeli society remains one of the most highly militarised on earth, and this is clearly reflected in its intelligence apparatus. All intelligence personnel – as indeed, with the exception of Arabs and religious Jews, all Israeli citizens – serve a two-year term in the armed forces, with a further period in the reserves. And while this provides for a ready labour pool and expanded range of tactical options, it has also helped promote the use of force as the first resort in any policy decision and, as we shall see, given military capabilities a wholly unpredictable precedence over political intentions.

The main services

Israel has three major intelligence arms: the General Security Service (Sherut ha-Bitachon ha-Kali – Shin Bet, domestic intelligence), the

Institute for Intelligence and Special Tasks (ha-Mossad le-Modi'in ule-Tafkidim Meydahadim – Mossad, foreign intelligence) and the Military Intelligence Service (Agaf ha-Modi'in – Aman). A special division in the Ministry of Defence, the Bureau of Scientific Relations (Leshkat Kesher Madao – Lekem), was established by then Minister Shimon Peres in 1960 to secure scientific intelligence and weapons technology, although this was reorganised, as we shall see, after the 1986 Jonathan Pollard spying affair. There are also a number of army and police covert units – notably the Mista'averim (marauder) – squads operating under deep cover in the occupied territories.

With the conventional domestic/foreign distinction somewhat blurred by Israel's contested geopolitics, there is considerable overlap between these functions in the Israeli military/intelligence apparatus – although turf, as elsewhere, remains a sensitive issue. Signals intelligence is largely a military preserve. A special section – Unit 8200 – performs electronic monitoring and code-breaking tasks, with listening posts on the occupied Golan Heights complementing Israel's own satellite array. Although not formally integrated within the worldwide Echelon surveillance network, Israeli Sigint personnel serve at many levels in the NSA and Pentagon agencies on second-ment. There are likewise US operatives working alongside Unit 8200 personnel, with equipment provided by the NSA. On 27 June 2002 Uzi Landau, Israel's Minister of Interior Security, met with US counterparts to propose a Washington-based joint counter-terrorism office, with classified data shared via a direct secure communications link between Israeli intelligence and the new US Office of Homeland Security.[3]

With an estimated 1,200 full time personnel, Mossad is based in Tel Aviv and divided into eight departments. The Collections Depart-ment is the largest and has lead responsibility for espionage, with field officers in place around the world operating under official and non-official cover. In the year 2000 Mossad began a public recruitment campaign to bring in new or recently retired agents, particularly from Israel's booming dotcom sector.[4] Political Action and Liaison manages contacts with friendly foreign agencies and the many countries with which Israel does not maintain official diplomatic relations. In larger overseas stations, such as Paris, there will normally be separate regional controllers for Collections and Political Liaison. The Special Operations Division – Metsada – takes on covert assassination, sabotage, paramilitary and psyops assignments, in conjunction with the Department of Psychological Warfare (Lohama Psichologit – LAP) which is responsible for briefing friendly journalists and overall media 'spin'. Analysis and publication, including reports, open-source and daily intelligence summaries, is undertaken by the Research Department. This is organised into 15 geographical desks including the US, Canada and Western Europe, Latin America, former Soviet territories, China, Africa, the Maghreb (Algeria, Morocco, Tunisia), Libya, Iraq, Jordan, Syria, Saudi Arabia, the Gulf and Iran. A dedicated section covers ongoing developments in nuclear weapons and weapons of mass destruction in general. The development of Mossad's own technological base – notably, in computers – is the task of the Technology Department. This too has been making recent efforts at recruitment from the private sector.

The identity of the Mossad director was traditionally a state secret, but in March 1996 the government announced the appointment of Major General Danny Yatom as a replacement for Shvtai Shavit. Yatom was replaced by former commando General Meir Dagon, a close colleague of Ariel Sharon, on 30 October 2002.[5]

The domestic service, Shin Bet, is divided organisationally into three operational departments and five for operational support. Arab Affairs is responsible for anti-terrorist operations, counter-subversion and maintaining an index on Arab militants. Special detachments, known as Henza, work with Aman Mista'averim units under cover in the West Bank, Gaza and some neighbouring countries. The Department of Non-Arab Affairs has a broad counter-intelligence role, penetrating foreign agencies and diplomatic missions and vetting incoming immigrants, whilst the Protective Security Department oversees industry, government and defence installations and the El-Al national airline.

The military service – Aman – has some 7,000 personnel and is responsible for the comprehensive national intelligence estimates, daily intelligence reports, risk assessment and overall Sigint. It is the largest and in some ways the senior service of Israeli intelligence. Like Mossad and Shin Bet, Aman conducts covert operations, notably via the Dudevan (cherry) undercover units, specialising in assassinations in the occupied territories.

The toll of targeted killings

While assassination has been a sanctioned Israeli intelligence practice since the Mandate days, its use has escalated during the first (1987–93) and current Intifada or Palestinian uprising. In 1992, Israel assassinated former Hizbollah leader Sheikh Abbas al-Mussawi in an air attack on his convoy. It also abducted two other Hizbollah leaders, Sheikh Abdel-Karim Obeid and Mustapha el-Dirrani in 1989 and 1994. On 30 August 2001 Popular Front for the Liberation of Palestine (PFLP) leader Abu Ali Mustapha Zabri was killed in a missile strike on his West Bank offices. Most assassinations, however, rely on the close proximity of Palestinian informers. In November 2000 Israeli agents planted a bomb in the headrest of a car used by Hamas activist Ibrahim Odeh. His cousin had been on the Mossad payroll. In some accounts, Israel carried out at least 60 'targeted killings' in the period September 2000 to August 2001[6] – out of a total of 583 conflict-related Palestinian deaths in the same period.[7]

The course of these missions has not always run smoothly, however. The failed attempt to poison Hamas leader Khaled Meshal in Amman on 25 September 1997 – reportedly at the express order of then Prime Minister, Binyamin Netanyahu – put unprecedented public pressure on Mossad chief Danny Yatom. Yatom had been forced to fly to the Jordanian capital in person to deliver the antidote.[8] A favoured method within Israeli-controlled territories is the booby-trapped cellular phone. Islamic Jihad leader Iyad Harden was blown up in this way in May 2001. This tactic has been widely used by Israel, since virtually all the mobile phone traffic in the territories is routed through Israeli companies. The most famous such incident concerned Palestinian bombmaker Yahya Ayyash – 'the Engineer' – and took place on 5 January 1996. On finding out Ayyash's mobile number, Shin Bet arranged for a fault signal to be transmitted. In the repair shop, a small explosive charge was placed behind the earpiece, which was detonated when an Israeli informer later dialled him up. Caretaker Prime Minister Shimon Peres was widely praised by the Israeli right for authorising the mission. However, the spiral of revenge bombings over the succeeding months probably lost him the election.[9]

The uncertain results of raising assassination to an acknowledged tool of state policy have drawn criticism from close allies in the US, where executive order 12333 remains − at least notionally − still in force. 'It is apparent that the assassination campaign is neither effective nor moral,' claimed a retired senior CIA operative, Vincent Cannistraro, in the *Washington Post*. The Mussawi killing had led to an intensified Hizbollah effort under his replacement, Hassan Nasrallah, which resulted in the deaths of 'more than 100 innocents' worldwide and the expulsion of Israeli forces from Southern Lebanon. Likewise, the 1995 assassination of Islamic Jihad leader Fathi Shikaki promoted a new leadership which had 'stabilised Islamic Jihad' and engaged 'a new round of deadly suicide bombings inside Israel'. Noting that, 'The targets are selected and validated by a small clique composed of the Prime Minister, the military Chief of Staff and the internal security agency, Shin Bet', the CIA's former head of counter-terrorism concludes that 'Targeted killings may satisfy a bloodlust … but are ineffective in achieving their stated objective of deterring terrorism.'[10]

Perhaps the most notorious incident in Shin Bet's recent history concerns not commissioning assassinations but failing to prevent one. On 4 November 1995 right-wing Israeli extremist Yigal Amir managed to penetrate the supposedly 'sterile' security protection zone and fatally shoot Israeli Prime Minister Yitzhak Rabin. Less than four months before, an internal Shin Bet assessment by then head of VIP protection Haggai Tal had considered the effects of the Oslo peace process on the Israeli right wing. In Tal's view, Rabin's increasing support at the right's expense could well provide ' a catalyst for action' for the 'same 1,000 people demonstrating all over the place'. Arguing for a range of protective measures at public meetings, including a weapons ban, the report observed that 'the possibility that a political assassination could be perpetrated in Israel looks far more realistic today than in the past'.[11]

A clue to the 'abject failure' of one of the world's supposedly leading security agencies to protect their own Prime Minister in their own country can be found in the post-assassination inquiry of the Shamgar Commission. Whilst deliberating for four months and calling all relevant witnesses, this resulted in more obfuscation than fundamental reassessment Though the head of Shin Bet, Carmi Gillon, resigned, he was soon employed again in government service and is now (somewhat controversially) ambassador to Denmark.[12] Other senior operatives were found lucrative private sector jobs or reassigned to other parts of government with full privileges. The author of the critical 10 July report, Haggai Tal, however, faced career blight after a perhaps too-honest testimony. The only dismissal in Shin Bet befell the most junior operative, responsible for physical proximity protection. His immediate chief, Yoram Rubin, is now head of security at an Israeli foreign mission. Questions which were not seriously raised concerned Shin Bet's reluctance to consider native Israelis a security threat – despite the growing and obvious fanaticism of the 'same 1,000 people' – and the open carrying of arms at demonstrations.

Further controversy surrounds a Shin Bet assessment of the risks of then opposition leader Ariel Sharon's proposed visit to the Temple Mount in June 2000. The view that Shin Bet 'had no professional or principled objection'[13] to an action which sparked the second Intifada casts further doubts on the organisation's competence, if not culpability. Shin Bet has taken a belated interest in the right-wing threat, particularly after the gruesome July 2001 killing of a West Bank family by the openly racist Kach organisation, one of two Jewish groups proscribed on the State Department's list of 'foreign terrorist organisations'.[14] However, given the high proportion of settler families in the security forces, the full rigour of Israeli interrogation methodology – including the *tahqiq* (sustained shaking) and electroshock treatments – not to mention assassinations, disappearances and collective punishment, seems unlikely to apply.[15]

Structure and oversight

The pivotal policy forum for Israeli intelligence is known as the Va–adat Rashei Hasherutim, or Va–adat for short. Based on the intelligence service heads (Mossad, Aman, Shin Bet) and the Inspector General of Police, Va-adat also brings together the Director General of the Foreign Ministry, the Director of the Research and Political Planning Centre and the Prime Minister's principal political and military advisers on anti-terrorism.

While the head of Aman reports to the Minister of Defence, the heads of Mossad and Shin Bet report directly to the Prime Minister. After many allegations of torture and unauthorised killing, the Israeli parliament has introduced oversight measures. On 11 February 2002, the head of Shin Bet was ordered to be publicly named, a five-year term of office was imposed and the organisation was brought under the supervision of a committee of cabinet ministers. Control of Mossad, however, remains entirely at the discretion of the Prime Minister, who can authorise operations and appoint and sack its director at will. In the past, this has led to accusations that the organisation was verging on a personal hit squad.[16] On 25 February 1998 five Mossad agents were arrested in Switzerland, having attempted to bug the Berne apartments of visiting Hizbollah representatives. As one Israeli agent had also been involved in the failed Jordan poisoning, there was speculation that Mossad was planning a similar fate for the 'two men involved in assisting Hizbollah in the acquisition of non-conventional weaponry'.[17] The Berne episode led finally to the resignation of Mossad Director Danny Yatom, who was replaced by Ephraim Halevi on 2 March.[18] But the start of Halevi's tenure was inauspicious. On 13 March three Mossad agents were obliged to beat a hasty retreat to Israel after another bungled bugging operation on Islamist activists, this time in London.[19]

Mossad's global reach

On 16 August 2001 the Israeli newspaper *Ha'aretz* reported that Israel has signed intelligence cooperation agreements with 39 countries, including China and India. *Ha'artez* noted that 'the agreements oblige the signatory states to work together in the investigatory operations where a leakage takes place to a third party' and permits joint operations with the Israelis.[20] Israel's close relations with the People's

Republic have been a sore point with the US, which has protested the exchange of classified technical information, particularly the sale of advanced avionics from the jointly developed and largely US-funded Lavi fighter. Although marked by a deafening silence in official US comment, China's acquisition of nuclear weapons technology acknowledged to be based on US designs must surely raise similar issues. According to Senate investigators, China's scientists began acquiring warhead miniaturisation and neutron bomb technology in the early 1980s – at the height of the Pollard affair (see below). These were precisely the technologies sought (and acquired) by Israel.[21]

One of Israel's closest intelligence links is with Turkey. With relations established in the 1950s via the informal Trident network (Israel, Iran, Turkey), Mossad has gained extensive coverage of Turkey's neighbours Iran, Iraq and Syria, in addition to a further avenue into NATO. Israel and Turkey signed a formal strategic cooperation agreement in April 1996 that provided for joint air patrols and Israeli-manned listening posts on the Iraqi, Syrian and Iranian borders.[22]

One focus was the Kurdish Workers Party (PKK) leader, Abdullah Ocalan, whose Damascus living quarters were destroyed in an unexplained bomb blast in May 1996. Other bombs had exploded in Istanbul, apparently accidentally, killing what were believed to be Turkish death squads operating jointly with Mossad in a further anti-PKK operation.[23] In the summer of 1998 Syria bowed to Israeli and Turkish pressure and expelled Ocalan, who was then tracked by Mossad in an increasingly desperate odyssey around Iran, Russia, Italy and Kenya before being seized by Turkish intelligence in Nairobi.

In Europe, while the biggest Mossad station is located in Paris, it is with the German BND that relations have traditionally been closest. In July 1996 BND head Bernd Schmidbauer was able to negotiate a ceasefire and prisoner exchange between Israel and Hizbollah after intensive shuttle diplomacy between Beirut, Damascus, Tehran and Tel Aviv. The BND also assists with more covert contacts with Iran, whose intelligence minister, Ali Fallahian, paid a controversial visit to Bonn in 1993.

Other countries with close Mossad links include Sri Lanka, where Israel has trained some 112 commandos in anti-terrorist tactics, and

Singapore, where a small Sigint post is maintained with a further training mission. The latter has also been involved in training for the Burmese SLORC intelligence agencies, with whom the Singapore government has maintained friendly relations (see Chapter 7).[24] Central and South-east Asia have also seen an increasing focus. On a visit to New Delhi in January 2001 Foreign Minister-designate Shimon Peres announced that Israel was prepared to cooperate with India to fight terrorism. Weeks earlier, an Israeli counter-terrorist team, including Aman specialists, reported on Kashmir and other contested areas, bringing to bear Israel's own experience on the Lebanese border. In March, Israel sold India its advanced Green Pine radar system and other military equipment in deals approaching $2 billion.[25]

The US connection: codenamed Jumbo

By far the most significant Israeli intelligence partner is the United States. The CIA has long valued its relations with Mossad as a means of tapping otherwise inaccessible sources in the Middle East and, particularly, Russia; Mossad also assists its coverage in regions, like Africa, where the Agency's own assets are thinly spread. Central and Latin America have provided a further area for productive division of labour, particularly during the Contra years of the Reagan administration, when unwelcome publicity was a constraining factor on the CIA. Recently, however, the spotlight has fallen on Israel's intelligence activities within the US borders.

In October 1995 two reports from the US Defense Department and one from the General Accounting Office (GAO) highlighted Israel's espionage activities within the US and illegal transfer of avionics technology to China. The Defense Investigative Service circulated a warning to US contractors that Israel was 'aggressively' probing US military and intelligence secrets. It cited six separate incidents, including the theft of advanced radar and computer technologies, 'repeated' bribery of Pentagon officials and the 'placing [of] Israeli nationals in key industries'.[26] The following GAO report was more specific about Israeli intelligence interests, including artillery tubes manufacture, stealth technology and aircraft communications systems. 'Country A' (identified as Israel in the *Washington Times*) 'conducts the most aggressive intelligence operation against the US of any US ally.'[27]

Controversy immediately surrounded the description of Israel by the Investigative Service as a 'non-traditional adversary' in the intelligence world that was using 'strong ethnic ties' in suborning US citizens. As the 9/11 investigations demonstrated, US intelligence procedures contain strong (and laudable) strictures against any form of 'racial profiling'. However, the strong reaction of the Israeli lobbying organisation, the Anti-Defamation League (ADL), also served to highlight the sheer extent of the routine intelligence gathering and perception management by Israeli intelligence in the US. On 25 April 2002 the San Francisco Superior Court awarded $150,000 damages in an action against the ADL led by former Congressman Pete McCloskey. McCloskey, in his capacity as an attorney, represented one of three civil lawsuits filed against the ADL in 1993. Police and FBI raids on ADL offices had revealed a database of 10,000 files on individuals across the US, most of which had been obtained illegally from police and FBI sources and state driver's licence data. A high-ranking San Francisco police officer was charged with obtaining the illegal data, which investigators believed was obtained in collusion with the CIA. In the McCloskey case, two of the plaintiffs, who were themselves Jewish, were targeted for speaking out against Israeli policies toward the Palestinians. A third was an anti-apartheid activist whose personal details were passed on to the then white-supremacist government in South Africa. And in a further judgement of 31 March 2001, $10.5 million in damages was awarded to two US citizens of Evergreen, Colorado who were falsely labelled as anti-Semites.[28]

According to former Mossad agent Victor Ostrovski, the ADL/Mossad relationship operates like 'the Moon Church for the Korean CIA ... it does specific jobs to gather information when asked for it'.[29] The possible activities of private Israeli companies, such as Comverse Infosys – who run a nationwide US wiretapping franchise for the FBI under the Communications Assistance for Law Enforcement (CALEA) legislation of 1994 – have been the subject of 'a highly classified investigation'.[30] And amongst the 60 Israeli citizens picked up after 9/11,[31] six were employed by another Israeli firm, Amdocs, which administers call records and billing data for the bulk of US phone companies. To be sure, some of this might be subject to at least tacit US sanction, 'a cosy subcontracting arrangement that allows the FBI to monitor those it can't by law, by letting the Israelis do it',[32] as one correspondent in the Comverse controversy observed. However, there have been other instances where Israeli espionage has gone beyond even the exceptional indulgence Washington has been prepared to grant its principal Middle Eastern ally.

The arrest of US Naval Intelligence official Jonathan Jay Pollard in November 1985 caused acute embarrassment to both Israel and the extremely pro-Israel Reagan administration. Pollard had used his sensitive position as a civilian analyst in the Navy's Field Operations Intelligence Office to supply over 1,800 classified documents – an estimated 500,000 pages – over a four-year period. The flow of information had become so large that a special department was established within Lekem to channel the output – codenamed Jumbo – to eager recipients throughout the Israeli intelligence community. Prominent Jumbo items were US diplomatic codes, NSA intercepts covering the Middle East, details of Soviet weapons systems and nuclear targeting data on the then Soviet Union. Israel had earlier requested – and been denied – 'real time access' to advanced US KH-11 satellite imagery and the establishment of a receiving station in Tel Aviv. Instead, the KH-11 data was sequestered by Pollard and trans-mitted back to Israel via its Washington embassy. Through these means, Israel was able to secure a nuclear strike option against the southern Soviet Union for its medium-range Jericho missiles and a 'one-way' airborne capability against Moscow. In order to maximise its political leverage from the Pollard data, sections were 'sanitised' by Lekem and presented to the KGB. Whilst Pollard's Aman handler, nuclear targeting expert Colonel Aviem Sella, fled back to Israel under a US indictment, there has been no real move on either side to pursue extradition. Pollard himself remains in jail. Energetic efforts to secure his release by then Prime Minister Netanyahu at the Wye River conference in 1996 were resisted by the US, with CIA chief George Tenet and senior aides reportedly threatening resignation.[33]

By both sides, the Pollard affair was glossed over as soon as decently possible. For Israel, though, the acquisition of the KH-11 data and advanced information on nuclear weapons miniaturisation would help complete the transition from a 'threshold' state to a fully comprehensive nuclear power. [34] The ill-fated invasion of Lebanon in 1982 was a further consequence of the Pollard data, which enabled Israeli forces to accurately target the Syrian airforce and missile systems.

The dilemmas of 'security'

Theorists of international relations have a stock phrase for a recurring syndrome in world politics – the 'security dilemma', defined in one reading as 'a situation in which the security of one state requires the insecurity of others'.[35] Perhaps to a greater extent than anywhere else at the present time, Israel remains the embodiment of this hoary dilemma, with both disputed borders internationally and a captive population within. The closest recent comparison, apartheid South Africa, managed to transcend the conflict spiral by dint of inter-national pressure, a creative opposition and – as we shall see – the not-insignificant momentum for change from within the security establish-ment itself. In the Israeli case, the undoubted skills of its military and intelligence apparatus have only served to vitiate any serious choice making, by providing an always-available option to prevail militarily. Not coincidentally, apartheid South Africa was a close Israeli ally for many years. The lessons of its transformation must surely point to the possibilities for such a 'third way' for Israel. Given the seemingly bottomless indulgence of the world's only superpower for Israel's present course, however, at present writing this seems unlikely.

Notes

1 See Ajaz Akram, 'A Comparative Analysis of the Structure and Functions of Intelligence Community in Israel and India', *Defence Journal*, December 1999.

2 See Henry Kissinger, *The Years of Upheaval*, London: Weidenfeld, 1982, p. 621.

3 See Tony Geraghty and David Leigh, 'The Name of the Game is Assassination', *Guardian*, 19 December 2001.

4 See Anthony C. Lobaido, 'Who Wants to Be a Mossad Agent?' *Worldnetdaily*, 18 February 2001.

5 See Steven Farrell, 'Ex-commando Takes Charge of Mossad', *Times*, 31 October 2002.

6 See Jack Kelly, 'We're Going to Get Them', *USA Today*, 21 August 2001.

7 See 'Top Palestinian Intelligence Officer Killed in Mysterious Car Bomb', Agence France-Presse, 2 September 2001.

8 See Alan Cowell, 'The Daring Attack Which Blew Up in Israel's Face', *New York Times*, 15 October 1997.

9 See John Simpson, 'An Eye for an Eye for an Earpiece', *Sunday Telegraph*, 29 September 1996.

10 See Vincent Cannistraro, 'Assassinating Israel's Adversaries Is Wrong and Also Dumb', *Washington Post*, 31 August 2001.

11 See Yossi Melman, 'Nothing Succeeds like Abject Failure', *Ha'aretz*, 19 October 2002.

12 Gillon was accused by human rights groups of sanctioning torture. See Amnesty International, 'Amnesty International Calls upon Denmark to Fulfil Its Obligations under the UN Convention against Torture', amnesty.usa.org/news, 20 August 2001.

13 *Ibid*.

14 See Uzi Mahnaimi, 'Army Moles Hunt Israeli Troops Linked to Terror', *Sunday Times*, 22 July 2001.

15 See *Submissions to the Israel Supreme Court by the Public Committee against Torture in Israel* (AR 58-026-191-5), 28 May 1998. In some reports, the Israeli Attorney General was said to be considering 'easier-fitting hand-shackles' and a 'less offensive-smelling head sack'.

16 See Ze'ev Segal, 'A Law for the Mossad', *Ha'aretz*, 1 October 2002.

17 *IINS News Service*, 'What Was the Mossad Mission in Switzerland?', 4 March 1998.

18 See Martin Seiff, 'New Chief to Inherit Deeply Troubled Agency', *Washington Times*, 2 March 1998.

19 See 'Israeli Agents Said to Flee London after Bungled UK Spying Mission', Reuters, 14 March 1998.

20 See 'Israel Signs Agreements with 39 Countries', Arabicnews.com, 17 August 2001.

21 The extent of China's nuclear development was revealed in 1995 by a 'walk-in' agent who provided 'design information' on five US nuclear warheads – see Walter Pincus, 'Planted Document Sows Seeds of Doubt', *Washington Post*, 28 May 1999. For background, see Shirley Kan, 'China: Suspected Acquisition of US Nuclear Weapons Secrets', CRS *Report* RL30143 (Washington: CRS/Library of Congress, 20 December 2000).

22 See Robert Olsen, 'The Turkey Israel Agreement and the Kurdish Question', *Middle East International*, 526 (24 May 1996).

23 See Victor Ostrovski, 'Capture of Kurdish Leader Ocalan Recalls Israeli Collaboration with Both Turkey, Kurds', *Washington Report on Middle East Affairs*, April/May 1999.

24 See Andrew Selth, *Burma's Intelligence Apparatus*, The Burma Project (soros.org, July 2000), pp. 5–6 .

25 See Ed Blanche, 'Mutual Threat of Islamic Militancy Allies India and Israel', *Jane's*

Terrorism and Security Monitor, 14 August 2001.

26 See R. Jeffrey Smith, 'Defense Memo Warned of Israeli Spying', *Washington Post*, 30 January 1996.

27 See Shawn L. Twing, 'Pentagon, GAO Report Israeli Espionage and Illegal Technology Retransfer', *Washington Report on Middle East Affairs*, April 1996.

28 See Barbara Ferguson, 'ADL Found Guilty of Spying by California Court', <u>Arabnews.com</u>, 25 April 2002.

29 Victor Ostrovski, 'A Brief History of Mossad Influence on American Policy', Public Talk, 2 September 1995, <u>archive.com/cntrl</u>.

30 See Carl Cameron, 'Comverse, CALEA, Israel and the Terror Investigation', *Fox News Special Report*, 13 December 2001.

31 See Ben Fenton, 'US Arrests 200 Young Israelis in Spying Investigation', *Daily Telegraph*, 7 March 2002.

32 See reader feedback from 14 December 2001 in *Fox News Special Report*, 13 December 2001.

33 See Richard Best for CRS, *Intelligence Issues for Congress*, IB10012: 7 December 2001, p. 12.

34 Still the best account (in a somewhat restricted field) of the Israel/US nuclear relationship is Seymour Hersh, *The Samson Option*, London: Faber and Faber, 1991.

35 See, for example, Jack L. Snyder, 'Perceptions of the Security Dilemma in 1914', in Robert Jervis (ed.), *Psychology and Deterrence*, Baltimore, MD: Johns Hopkins University Press, 1985, p. 154.

CHAPTER 7

INTELLIGENCE
IN THE
SOUTH
The Growth of the Virtual State

'I know who is about to betray me before the traitor does himself.'
– Saddam Hussein

Intelligence services in the South share globally in techniques, organisational practice and, sometimes, personnel. They also have a common proclivity to use 'sources and methods' as a mandate for bureaucratic empire building and extra-legal interference in public life. The Cold War era placed intelligence conflict in the front line, with the commensurate end–and–means justification accepted without question. What has changed since the Cold War ended is the growing influence of the private sector. Throughout much of Africa, large corporations are increasingly turning to private firms, often employing ex-government personnel, to conduct a full range of security-related activities, from commercial espionage to fully constituted private armies. In the Middle East and South Asia, by contrast, we see a *virtual* privatisation of intelligence. Here we find intelligence formations within what are ostensibly state structures; in some cases, these have become self-serving corporate enterprises. In this chapter we consider a sample range of intelligence activities in what, out of habit, is still referred to as the Third World. This is a sector that, like so many other emergent features of the 'knowledge economy', seems fated to get bigger.

The Middle East – the 'hidden hand' syndrome

The sadly enduring character of much of Middle Eastern politics has
been well summarised by one seasoned observer. Here, 'relations
between states and the societies they rule remain, in the great majority of cases, dominated by patterns of authoritarianism, characterised
by élite theft of on average 30 per cent of state income, and an
ideological resort to demagogy of a nationalist and/or religious
character'.[1] If anything, the end of the Cold War has quickened these
tendencies, as insecure regimes scramble to re-tool their armaments
in the absence of even the equivocal restraints of superpower
competition. Given the volatile mixture of vast wealth, oil, arms,
repressive government and foreign meddling, intelligence agencies in
the region have a unique scope for action. This has long impacted on
the way politics are perceived. Sanctioned by embedded Islamic
traditions of *taqiya* or concealment and dissimulation (the product of
centuries of foreign and sectarian rule), the wide circulation of
ancient forgeries such as the *Protocols of the Elders of Zion* and the more
modern efforts of such as Lyndon LaRouche,[2] virtually all media and
government and the now oft-cited 'Arab street' subscribe to one or
other variant of conspiracy. In fact, given the personal and clan-based
nature of rule in the region, a great deal of Middle East politics *is*
conspiracy, for all practical purposes – with intelligence, as ever,
playing the central role.

Syria – the rise of the Mukhabarat state

Since Syrian independence, control of the intelligence services –
notably, the French-modelled Deuxième Bureau – has been crucial to
the grip on power of a long procession of military rulers. Since the
successful coup of Air Force General Hafiz al-Assad in 1970, overall
intelligence coordination has centred on the Presidential Security
Council, which reports directly to the executive. Traditionally headed
by an Air Force officer, the Council also provides for monitoring the
diplomatic community in Damascus through its Foreign Liaison Office,
and generally has the last word in inter-agency turf clashes.

Of the estimated 15 other separate intelligence organs, many have overlapping, indeed, competitive remits that flourish or decline with the careers of their respective government patrons.[3] Syria's four main intelligence services have functioned as instruments of presidential control and are directly subordinate to the President. Whether new-comer Bashar al-Assad is able to retain the iron grip exercised by his father Hafiz remains to be seen. The General Security Directorate (Idarat al-Amn al-A'mm) is the main civilian agency. This is divided into three branches covering general intelligence matters, foreign intelligence and Palestinian affairs. It oversees the civilian police and frontier guards and has primary responsibility for surveillance of the Ba'ath Party, government bureaucracy and the population in general.

With limited autonomy within the GSD, the Political Security Directorate (Idarat al-Amn al-Syasi), is responsible for monitoring organised political activity. This involves surveillance of registered parties and publications, or, indeed, virtually any social gathering at all – its suppression of the (politico/cultural) 'discussion clubs' after Bashar's short-lived liberal honeymoon is a recent example.[4] The movements of all foreigners in Syria automatically come under scrutiny. The Political Directorate also monitors all print and other media under the auspices of the Internal Security Department, whilst the External Security Department has a regional surveillance brief, covering Arab, refugee (largely displaced Palestinian) and Israeli affairs.

Within regimes that have always been led or dominated by the military, Military Intelligence (MI, Shu'bat al-Mukhabarat al-Askariya) has played an indispensable – and usually pre-eminent – role in the Syrian intelligence apparatus. The successor to the Deuxième Bureau, the MI combines conventional strategic and tactical intelligence functions with the critical role of ensuring the leadership's physical security and the loyalty of the armed forces. It has a wide brief for covert action abroad and monitoring the regime's many overseas dissidents. Support is also provided to a variety of militant groups such as the Hizbollah and the Kurdish PKK (we have seen that the PKK leader Abdullah Ocalan was expelled from Damascus after intense pressure from Turkey). The MI has overall charge in Lebanon, where it has largely become the dominant voice in policy. As throughout Syria, clan and sectarian loyalties count for much. The current head of Military Intelligence, General Hassan Khalil, is, like his predecessor, a member of the minority Alawite sect, while his Deputy – reputedly the real power figure – General Assaf Shawkat, also an Alawite, is married to Bashar Assad's elder sister.[5]

While smaller than the MI, Air Force Intelligence (AFI, Idarat al-Mukhabarat al-Jawiya) is perhaps the élite element in the Syrian intelligence empire. With offices in the presidential palace, it was headed for nearly thirty years by Assad confidant General Muhammed al-Khouli. Al-Khouli was moved out in 1987 after the widely publicised arrest of Syrian agent Nizar Hindawi for the attempted bombing of an El-Al airliner at London's Heathrow in April 1986. Hindawi's controller, AFI deputy chief Haitham Sayid, was placed on an international arrest warrant and the incident caused Britain to break off diplomatic relations. AFI officers are frequently placed in Syrian embassies and overseas branch offices of the national airline. Further light on the agency's international role emerged in declassified files of the East German Stasi. Amongst a range of terrorist actions uncovered was the 1983 bombing of the French Cultural Centre in West Berlin.[6]

As well as taking a leading role in covert actions overseas, Air Force Intelligence has frequently taken charge of the domestic crackdown on militant Islamists. The suppression of the Muslim Brotherhood in the 1970s and early 1980s was coordinated by the AFI, as was the more recent manhunt for members of the Islamic Liberation Party (Hizb al-Tahir) in December 1999. The present AFI head, General Ibrahim Houwaiji – al-Khouli's nephew – is an Alawite and member of the Ba'ath Party central committee.

While Syria and Syrian-occupied Lebanon have provided sanctuary for a range of international militant groups and guerrilla factions, special mention should be made of the Popular Front for the Liberation of Palestine–General Command (PFLP–GC). Founded as a PFLP breakaway in 1968 by Ramallah-born former Syrian army captain Ahmad Jibril, the 1,000-strong PFLP–GC has a range of military assets – including artillery and some tanks – a powerful radio station, Sawt al-Quds (Voice of Jerusalem) operating from Damascus and bases in North Lebanon and Syria. Although maintaining a covert network abroad and an influential presence in South Beirut and the Beka'a Valley, it has little public following in Palestine proper, being almost entirely a Syrian construct. Yet it has functioned significantly as an arms and training conduit for other, more demotically based groups – such as Hamas and Hizbollah – and, from Syria's perspective, successfully maintained the regime's profile as a player in Palestinian affairs and the Middle East power struggle in general.

Ahmad Jibril's activities internationally – including bombings and hijackings in the 1970s and, in the view of many, masterminding the destruction of PanAm flight 103 over Lockerbie, Scotland, in December 1988[7] – helped forge long-standing alliances with Iran's Pasdaran Revolutionary Guards and Libyan intelligence – who, fortuitously (and fortunately for Syria), had temporarily assumed the funding of the organisation at the time of Lockerbie. The PFLP–GC's European network was also able to take over from Syrian state intelligence for a time after the expulsions that followed the Hindawi affair. Perhaps of the greatest value to Syria, however, has been the PFLP–GC's ability to put effective pressure – sometimes acting as a conventional military formation – on other Palestinian factions and the mainstream PLO of Yasser Arafat. Thus, although President Hafiz al-Assad was happy to expel a range of known terrorist figures, including Carlos the Jackal, to improve his international standing at the end of the Cold War and the 1991 Madrid peace conference, calls for a clampdown on Jibril and the PFLP–GC were resisted.

The assassinations of several officials of Arafat's Fatah movement in Lebanon during the early 1990s were (according to Fatah sources) carried out by Jibril's henchmen. In April 1995, according to one report, PLFP–GC agents were on the verge of assassinating Arafat himself, after infiltrating his security detail. Unfortunately for Jibril, the group had itself been penetrated by Egyptian intelligence, which promptly informed the PLO leader of the plot.[8] In March 1999, members of the PFLP–GC, and other Syrian-dominated Palestinian factions – Fatah-Uprising and Sa'iqa – attacked offices of the Democratic Front for the Liberation of Palestine (DFLP) in Syria and Lebanon, killing one member of the group and injuring several others.

PFLP–GC militants were also active in Jordan. In May 1996, Jordanian
intelligence uncovered a plot by the PFLP–GC and Fatah–Uprising to
assassinate (then) Crown Prince Hassan and then Prime Minister Abd
al-Karim al-Kabariti, as well as to bomb Israeli and American targets in
the kingdom.[9] In May 1998, Jordanian police again rounded up many
PFLP–GC militants after the country was rocked by a month of
terrorist strikes, including bombings of an American school, a police
compound, and the four-star Al-Quds Hotel in Amman.

Facing growing health problems in late 1998, Hafiz Assad apparently
transferred operational management of the regime's Lebanon assets –
including the PFLP–GC – from Vice-President Abdul Halim Khaddam
to his (Assad's) surviving eldest son and heir apparent, Bashar. With
the major Lebanese-based guerrilla organisation – Hizbollah – less
susceptible to Syrian influence after the Israeli withdrawal from its
South Lebanon strongholds in June 2000, the PFLP–GC became the
main focus of Syria's efforts in the region. Whilst the PFLP–GC was
put on hold during the late 1999 period of Israeli–Syrian negotiations
in Shepherdstown, West Virginia, it was back in business after the
breakdown of talks in early 2000.

As Syria oversaw a major rearmament of the PFLP–GC in this
period, the group was reorganised under Jibril's son, Jihad, in order to
conduct operations independently of Hizbollah and other Lebanon-
based factions. Israel attacked in May 2000, by bombing the Sultan
Yacoub Beka'a Valley base, destroying ten tanks and killing three
PFLP–GC guerrillas. On 7 May 2001 Israel seized 40 tonnes of arms
aboard a ship – the *Santorini* – claimed by the PFLP–GC. And on 20
May 2002 Jihad Jibril was killed when a bomb under the driver's seat
of his Peugeot sedan was detonated by remote control while he drove
through the Mazraa district of West Beirut. Although Israel has denied
a hand in the assassination – claimed by a previously unknown group
calling itself the 'Movement of Lebanese Nationalists' – few in the
region believe that the PFLP–GC's military operations chief died at
the hands of a localised Lebanese faction.

Shortly after the killing, the PFLP–GC seized two suspects, including Jihad Jibril's Palestinian driver, who were handed over to Syrian
Military Intelligence. The subsequent media blackout on the affair

certainly suggests a wider conspiracy.[10] If the Mossad was indeed responsible, it is likely that Israeli agents have penetrated the PFLP-GC with the undoubted facility brought to bear in operations elsewhere. As with the Iraq-based Abu Nidal organisation – the Fatah Revolutionary Council – which was sponsored by Syria during 1983–7, the main focus of the PFLP–GC's activities has been the mainstream PLO – which has also been Israel's principal target for disruption.[11]

Syria – like Iraq – has earned the soubriquet 'Mukhabarat state'. Over its 30-year reign, the Assad regime promoted an intelligence world of competing fiefdoms as a matter of policy. Only the President himself was able to view the whole picture. With the presidency of the somewhat unlikely figure of younger son Bashar, a London-educated ophthalmologist much in the shadow of now-deceased elder brother Basil, the secret services would seem to be even more indispensable.

Iraq – 'a sort of frenzy'

In a statement that effectively sums up the ideal type of fascism, Saddam Hussein once observed, 'I must whip them [Iraq] into a sort of frenzy or emotional mobilisation so that they will be ready for whatever may happen.'[12] Like Syria's, the regime in Iraq was founded on the Ba'ath (Renaissance) Party. An essentially conspiratorial organisational structure from the beginning, the rule of Saddam Hussein was based on clan and tribal networks compounded by vicious rivalries and a climate of constant crisis unmatched even in the Middle East. Saddam's own rise to power – gaining the vice-presidency in 1968 and finally the leadership itself over the 1973–8 period – left a trail of violence and assassinations. As Saddam and his leading henchmen emerged solely through the Ba'ath Party, the relationship between the latter and the Iraqi armed forces, including the intelligence agencies, always was ambivalent.

In some estimates, the total staff level of intelligence and security agencies was some 30,000, with a further 70,000 troops assigned to leadership protection.[13] The National Security Council, meeting on a weekly basis, brought together all the major players from the military and intelligence services. Chaired by Saddam's younger son (and heir-apparent), Qusay, it oversaw the Special Security Committee. Set up in 1996 and with a staff of some 2,000, the Committee's main task was to prevent the uncovering of Iraq's weapons of mass destruction (WMD) by the United Nations UNSCOM weapons inspectors. Qusay was also prominent in the three mutually controlling Protection Units responsible for Saddam's personal safety.

The main overall body was the General Intelligence Directorate of the Iraqi Intelligence Service (IIS, or Jihaz al-Mukhabarat al-Amma). With a staff of some 4,000, the Mukhabarat began as the Special Apparatus (Jihaz al-Khas) of the Ba'ath Party; in the mid-1960s it became Saddam's personal power base, and it absorbed the existing state internal security department after the coup of July 1968. Further shake-ups followed in 1973 and 1982 as Saddam consolidated his hold on power. In June 1995 Saddam dismissed the then head, Sab'awi Ibrahim al-Hassan (Saddam's stepbrother), after the failed coup attempt by former Military Intelligence chief Wafic Samarai (see Chapter 3). Al-Hassan's replacement was Brigadier Majid Hassan al-Majid.

Of the 28 separate directorates of the Mukhabarat, the most important were the Private Office (Directorate 1), responsible for overall coordination, and the Political Bureau. This incorporated both domestic and foreign intelligence functions centred on the Secret Service (D4), which had offices covering Arab states, Africa, Europe, Iran, Turkey, South Asia, former Soviet territories and North and South America.[14] D4 agents also operated inside government departments, Ba'ath Party associations, unions and organisations. It had a presence in Iraqi embassies worldwide and, as we have seen, achieved a widespread infiltration of the Iraqi opposition. Operating in parallel and in competition with D4 was D9, Secret Operations, a highly reclusive directorate specialising in assassinations – notably of dissidents overseas. In true Iraqi fashion, this work was paralleled once again by D14, Special Operations, the branch thought to be responsible for planning the attempted assassination of former President Bush in Kuwait in April 1993. These efforts led to the subsequent cruise missile strike on the Mansour district Mukhabarat headquarters in

Baghdad on 26 June. D14, believed to be the largest directorate, was charged with joint operations with the Iranian opposition forces of the Mujahidin Kalq (MKO), whose cross-border guerrilla operations varied directly with the overall state of relations with Tehran. The MKO also had its own dedicated department in the Mukhabarat, D18. Other departments with a regional brief included D23 (Southern Iraq/Shi'ite opposition groups), D24 (Northern Iraq/Kurdish opposition, with offices in Kirkuk) and D25 (Western Iraq, charged with recruitment and infiltration in Syria and Jordan).

Lines of control and responsibility were deliberately blurred across the military and civilian agencies, with Military Intelligence itself (Al-Istikhabarat al-Iskariya) maintaining branches for foreign intelligence gathering, internal (armed forces) security and covert operations (the Special Branch). A major covert role was also undertaken by Unit 999, which maintained a six-battalion regional structure in parallel with the Mukhabarat. A special monitoring unit, the Military Security Service (Al Amn al-Iskaria) sought out the ever-present threat of dissidence within the armed forces, whilst any immediate threats to Saddam and the inner leadership were taken on by the 5,000-strong Special Security Service (Al-Amn al-Khas), viewed as, 'the most feared Ba'athist organ of repression'.[15] Although a prime target during and after the 1991 Gulf War, Iraq maintained a sophisticated Sigint/Elint capability under the Al-Hadi Project 858. With a staff of 800, Al-Hadi had its headquarters at Al Rasheda, 20 kilometres north of Baghdad, and five regional collection stations. All domestic communications traffic was monitored and Al-Hadi claimed to be able to locate clandestine radio broadcasts within 30 seconds of transmission. Priority targets also included US/NATO communications from Incirlik airbase in eastern Turkey, the Iraqi opposition (INA/INC) and the Kurdish PKK and KDP. In late 1995, Iraq banned direct-dial international telephone calls, with traffic being routed through an operator-controlled exchange at Al Rasheda. Calls were monitored in three daily shifts by a team including Mukhabarat, Istikhabarat and Amn al-Khas personnel.[16]

The success rate of Iraqi intelligence – foreign and domestic – was formidable. Prior to September 1990, a global network of arms dealers, financial front companies and scientific and technical experts succeeded in creating a sophisticated military capability, notably in the realm of advanced technologies and WMD. As revealed in US Congressional hearings and the British Scott Report on the 'arms to Iraq' affair, arms and manufacturing firms such as Matrix Churchill were simply bought out by Iraqi middlemen, and technology transfers were often wittingly aided by governments and private companies in the West.[17] Involvement in terrorist actions – both globally and in the Middle East – also featured heavily. As in other Middle Eastern contexts, the fragmented Palestinian diaspora was a favoured instrument. Perhaps the major player here was former PLO Baghdad envoy Sabri al-Banna, known as Abu Nidal. Operating through a variety of *nommes de guerre* such as Black June, the Fatah Revolutionary Council carried out a swath of bombings and assassinations – including the killing of a Jordanian diplomat in Beirut in 1994 – at Iraq's behest. Also useful as a gun for hire – before moving to Damascus after a temporary rift with Baghdad at the height of Saddam's rapprochement with the Reagan administration – Abu Nidal's main function for the Mukhabarat was the intimidation of other Palestinian factions, and in particular, the mainstream PLO. The sheer scope of these operations, and the number of senior PLO personnel killed in incidents in London, Paris, Madrid, Brussels, Rome and Kuwait, led many to suspect some degree of collusion between Abu Nidal and Mossad.[18]

The internal record of Iraqi intelligence was substantial. Aside from the Wafic Samarai coup attempt of 1995, major threats to the regime included the defection of Saddam's daughters and sons-in-law, General Hussein Kamal (head of the covert WMD procurement programme) and Colonel Saddam Kamal al-Majid, to Jordan in August 1995. The most significant incident was the coup attempt of June 1996 by General Ata Samawal, former head of Saddam's personal communications. In round-ups across Iraq and Kurdistan, some 400 officers were executed and many others disappeared. In a follow-up move, at least 96 INC activists were executed by the Mukhabarat after Iraqi forces seized Irbil in the August/September period. And in December 1996 mass arrests and executions took place across Iraq after the failed assassination attempt on Saddam's eldest son, Uday, outside a Baghdad nightclub – an act claimed by Shi'ite radicals of the SAIRI.

Despite having a widespread and well-organised overseas presence, Iraq's record of direct involvement in terrorism declined outside the Middle East. In Congressional hearings of February 2002, CIA analysts gave the view that Iraqi intelligence efforts internationally were focused chiefly on weapons acquisition and penetration of the INA/INC opposition.[19] After 9/11 there were several determined US efforts to prove possible Iraqi links with Al-Qaida, if not with the WTC bombing itself. In early 2002, Deputy US Defense Secretary and leading Washington hawk Paul Wolfowitz dispatched former CIA Director James Woolsey to Britain with a copy of the fingerprints of convicted 1993 World Trade Center bomber Ramzi Yousef to prove that this was the same person as an Iraqi who had studied at Swansea University. Unfortunately, the prints did not match up.[20]

Speculation then focused on Prague, where known bin Laden associates were reported living in 1998.[21] The Czech capital, as well as hosting the transmitters of Radio Liberty/Radio Free Iraq, was also a centre for Baghdad's European operations and efforts at weapons/technology procurement from the former Eastern bloc countries. However, Baghdad's point man in Prague at the time, Iraqi consul and Mukhabarat officer Jabir Salim, was a long- term MI 6 informant[22] who defected to Britain in January 1999 with 'his wife, seven children and 60 cases of documents and possessions'.[23] A more likely interface was Sudan, where Iraqi intelligence indeed maintained a large presence prior to 1996 – during the period when bin Laden had made Khartoum the centre of his network. Again, though, such contacts as may well have taken place were, in the view of most Western analysts, routine rather than 'institutional'. A leaked UK Defence Intelligence Staff report of 12 January 2003 observed, 'While there have been contacts between Al-Qaida and the [Saddam] regime in the past, it is assessed that any fledgling relationship foundered due to mistrust and incompatible ideology.'[24] US claims of such 'institutional' links between Iraq and Al-Qaida led to some friction between the gung-ho Pentagon and the more sceptical CIA and the British.[25] Prime Minister Tony Blair flatly denied a Saddam role in 9/11 when speaking in Parliament on 5 February 2003.

Palestine

Following the Oslo accords of 1993–4 the stage seemed to be set for a long-delayed final settlement on the Middle East and the establishment of an interim Palestine National Authority (PNA) The follow-on Israel–Palestine interim agreement of autumn 1995 also involved bringing the multitude of PLO militias into some sort of recognisable formal structure – not least in order to clear the way for funding from the EU and others. The agreement provided for the training of some 30,000 security personnel and intelligence sharing with Israel in conjunction with the CIA.

Initially, the PNA was to have 9,000 police in Gaza and Jericho and a further 12,000 on the West Bank, organised in four divisions: civil, public order, rapid-response and intelligence. While the Palestine police were fairly conventional, with training from EU forces and joint patrols with the Israelis, the role of the nine or more other intelligence services would remain controversial. While some existed largely at the personal direction of prominent leaders, the major multi-function bodies were the General Intelligence Service (GIS), the Preventative Security Service (PSS), the Presidential Guard, the Fatah-based Force 17, and the Special Security Force (SSF). With 2,000 agents in the West Bank, led by Jibril Rajoub, and a further 2,000 in Gaza, headed by Mohammed Dharlan, the PSS was considered the principal intelligence and security arm.

The first year of the interim agreement was to record some successes in cooperation between Palestinian intelligence agencies – particularly the PSS – and Israel's Shin Bet,[26] but this *entente* came under intense pressure after the November 1995 assassination of Israeli Prime Minister Yitzhak Rabin. As the caretaker Peres government became vulnerable to hardliners opposed to any cooperation with the PNA, like-minded Hamas extremists on the Palestinian side mounted a relentless bombing campaign that the PSS seemed unable to stop. The PNA had requested up to $1 billion for security services at a series of pre-election summits on 28–29 March, but with the triumph of Netanyahu in May 1996 prospects for peace looked even slimmer.

The reluctance of the Netanyahu government to countenance any sort of cooperation was overcome by intervention from the perhaps unexpected quarter of the CIA. While Netanyahu was reluctant even to meet with Arafat or resume negotiations on the stalled three-phase Israeli withdrawal agreed at Oslo, talks were finally convened which resulted in the January 1997 Hebron Agreement.[27] Pressure from an increasingly exasperated Clinton administration led on to the Wye River Memorandum, signed on 23 October 1998. This provided for a Trilateral Security Committee composed of Israeli, Palestinian and US representatives to coordinate anti-terrorist efforts. Reportedly, it was the CIA itself which suggested a more formal role as a means of out-manoeuvring the intransigent position of Netanyahu and the hardline Likud cabinet.[28] We have seen that the CIA was also instrumental in blocking Israeli efforts to secure the release of convicted Israeli spy, former US Naval Intelligence analyst Jonathan Pollard, with DCI George Tenet threatening resignation.[29] Under the Wye River agreement, the CIA was to provide equipment and training to the PNA and open offices in Gaza, Hebron and Nablus.[30] While the Agency's prominent role and welcome from the PLO was perhaps surprising from a guerrilla organisation long allied to Moscow, contacts have extended back many years. In the early 1980s, then Beirut Chief of Station Robert Ames was in direct contact with Yasser Arafat on the 1982 Reagan Plan for a Middle East settlement, and helped facilitate the PLO evacuation to Tunis after the Israeli invasion. In recognition of this possibly life-saving relationship, the PLO chairman was keen to encourage more CIA participation, personally guiding Tenet around Nablus and Ramallah. Indeed, Tenet, in a press release, claimed that 'for many years the CIA has been working with the Israeli government and the Palestinians'.[31]

If the election of Ehud Barak in place of the intransigent Netanyahu raised hopes, notably in Washington, of renewed movement on the peace process, these were again to founder. Fresh security agreements were signed at Sharm el-Sheikh in October 2000, and on 15 June 2001 Tenet made his most ambitious mediation yet in brokering a ceasefire. The parties pledged 'specific, concrete and realistic security steps' including weekly meetings of the joint security committee and 'US-supplied video conferencing systems ... provided to senior level

Israeli and Palestinian officials to facilitate frequent dialogue'. The PNA promised to 'stop any Palestinian officials from inciting, aiding, abetting or conducting' attacks on Israeli targets 'including settlers' and to 'undertake pre-emptive operations against terrorists'. Israel, for its part, agreed not to 'conduct proactive security operations in areas controlled by the PA', to 'adopt additional non-lethal measures' to deal with demonstrations, and to 'seek to minimise the dangers to the lives and property of Palestinian civilians' in conflict areas.[32]

Overall, the Tenet Plan, with its stress on regular intelligence exchange, the withdrawal of Israeli troops and 'joint standard operating procedures', represented a worthy effort by the CIA to play honest broker. Like its predecessors, however, it would soon unravel. The sheer number of security forces encouraged internecine rivalry and non-cooperation. Leader such as Jibril Rajoub and Mohammed Dharlan were also clan chiefs running personal fiefdoms and jockeying for political power – a state of affairs encouraged by Arafat as a means to sustain his tight personal rule. The relations between the security bodies and the terrorists they were supposedly fighting were ambivalent. PNA security forces had themselves emerged from militias and many were linked by clan or tribal loyalties. Indeed, the terrorists themselves were often split, with foreign-based leaderships taking a harder line than the rank and file in the territories. Hamas is a case in point, with the leadership in Damascus under strong pressure from Syria.[33] Moreover, the heavy-handed Israeli occupation and, notably, the extensive use of assassinations meant that militant organisations – Hamas and Hizbollah in particular – were assured of continuing support at street level.

With the total breakdown of Israel–Palestine relations in the autumn of 2001, and – as we have seen – apparent efforts by the Sharon government to destroy the PNA altogether, Arafat bowed to pressure from both his own ranks and the Bush administration to reform the security apparatus.[34] For the first time, a Minister of the Interior was appointed, a role previously filled by Arafat himself. General Abd al-Yahya was appointed to oversee a reformed security force. Pared down from its existing 35,000 level, the new body was to have three main divisions: Presidential Security, General Security and

Internal Security, with the declared aim of avoiding overlap. The PSS, meanwhile, was divided between a largely intact Gaza branch under Mohammed Dharlan and a shattered West Bank branch under Jibril Rajoub. On 2 April 2002 Israeli forces physically demolished Rajoub's headquarters – built with US funding – with the PSS chief himself barely escaping alive courtesy of protection from the CIA. Tenet was again tasked to visit the region to get reform up and running.

India and Pakistan – the democratic deficit

With a history of conflict stretching back over fifty years, intelligence services on the sub-continent were heavily involved with both the respective Cold War antagonists – Pakistan with the US, India with Russia – and the regional rivalries between Russia and China and Iran and Afghanistan. As the world's first Islamic state, Pakistan has also looked to the Middle East for support and become likewise increasingly caught up in the ongoing strife of the region. While full-scale warfare has erupted on three occasions – and threatened on many others, notably in early 2002 – the main arena of India–Pakistan struggle has been the covert one. This has involved not only the sponsorship of domestic subversion by dissident minorities – Sikhs, Assamese, Bengalis – but also large-scale counter-intelligence, propaganda and the pursuit of weapons technology internationally, notably in the high-tech and nuclear sphere. If many of the missions of the respective agencies are similar, however, the contrast has been marked between their larger role in society. This section considers the impact of this institutional asymmetry, beginning with a look at the Pakistan intelligence body often in the news, the Inter-Services Intelligence or ISI.

Pakistan: the Bhutto inheritance

Originally formed to coordinate conventional military intelligence in Kashmir after the 1948 war, the ISI has gradually expanded its activities throughout Pakistan to the point of seeming indispensable. Combining personnel from the three armed services (who also maintain separate arms for tactical intelligence), the ISI comes under the Ministry of Defence while Pakistan's other main service – the Intelligence Bureau (IB) – is controlled by the Ministry of the Interior. The ISI is headed by a Director General who is generally a serving army lieutenant general, assisted by three deputies for political, external and administrative affairs. Organisationally, there are eight major departments, covering open-source and Humint (Joint Intelligence Bureau, JIB), counter-intelligence (JCIB), signals and Elint (JSIB), covert warfare in Kashmir and Afghanistan (Joint Intelligence North, JIN), weapons procurement and overseas operations (Joint Intelligence Miscellaneous, JIM), administration (JIX), technical research (JIT) and the 'Special Wing', charged with international liaison.[35]

The spread of the ISI's empire from conventional military intelligence gathering to becoming major power brokers stems from the central role of the armed forces in Pakistan's public life. Used by a succession of military dictators as a personal power base, the ISI underwent massive expansion after the 1971 Bangladesh War as a means of extending covert support to Sikh and Kashmiri militants fighting India. The decision by civilian ruler Zulfikar Ali Bhutto (1971–5) to develop nuclear weapons gave the ISI an increasingly international role in acquiring denied technologies and channelling the massive influx of funds from Libya and elsewhere for the 'Islamic bomb'. The 1979 Iranian revolution and Soviet invasion of Afghanistan led to further expansion, with the ISI taking the lead in supporting the Afghan Mujahidin and cracking down on domestic unrest amongst Pakistan's Shi'a minority on the orders of Bhutto's successor, Zia ul Haq.[36] Buoyant with US and Saudi cash and generous CIA technical support, the ISI was to continue growing after the Soviet withdrawal and the August 1988 death of Zia.[37] By this time, both the foreign and domestic efforts of the ISI were coloured by the fundamentalist Islam favoured by Zia and promoted by his appointees in the ISI leadership. In Afghanistan, aid was channelled overwhelmingly towards the hardline forces of Gulbuddin Hekmatyar, whilst inside Pakistan efforts focused on disrupting, by virtually any means, Bhutto's Pakistan Peoples Party (PPP) and other opponents of the regime such as the Mojahir Quami Movement (MQM). The province of Sindh, power base of the Bhuttos, came in for particular attention from the ISI, even after the election of Benazir Bhutto as Prime Minister in December 1988.

The issue of who controls the ISI came to a head during Benazir's first administration. Theoretically directly responsible to the Prime Minister, the ISI Director General – usually a serving officer – has in practice taken orders from the Army Chief of Staff. The efforts to rein in the ISI by appointing a retired officer (and Bhutto supporter) as its head in place of the fundamentalist General Hamid Gul led to Ms Bhutto's dismissal, after heavy army pressure, in August 1990.

As well as maintaining a low-intensity conflict against the PPP within Pakistan, the ISI had earlier assassinated Benazir's brother, Shah Nawaz Bhutto, in France in 1985 and posed a continuing threat to the Prime Minister herself. The ISI's more or less undisguised partisan role was to have unpredictable consequences for later relations between the intelligence agency and the Bhutto family. Following Benazir's re-election in 1993, the PPP leadership sought to appoint their own candidates in what effectively had become an independent ISI fiefdom, Afghanistan.

As we have seen, of the six major resistance groupings operating out of Peshawar during the 1980s, the ISI favoured the Hezb-e-Islami of Gulbuddin Hekmatyar. Closely allied with another ISI favourite Jama'at-e-Islami (JEI) in Pakistan itself, Hezb-e fought a series of inconclusive battles with erstwhile allies Burhannudin Rabbani and Ahmed Shah Massoud for control of Kabul after the 1992 defeat of President Najibullah.[38] With the capital in ruins and no overall government control, a new force arose from the rubble: the Taliban.

The invention of the Taliban

As their name (*Talib* – religious student) suggests, the Taliban originated in the many *madrassas* catering for the estimated two million refugees living along Pakistan's Afghan border. Trapped by the continuing warfare in Afghanistan itself, a radicalised generation arose, drawing inspiration from Pushtun nationalism and the Wahabi-influenced religious politics of the Jamiat-e-Ulema Islam (JUI). Sidelined during the first terms of Benazir Bhutto and Nawaz Sharif, the

JUI was to enter government for the first time in 1993 as part of the PPP coalition, with JUI leader Maulana Faisal Rahman chairing the Standing Committee for Foreign Affairs of Pakistan's National Assembly. With Rahman fundraising on a large scale from the Gulf states and Saudi Arabia, thousands of Pushtun fighters began streaming across the border,[39] encouraged by the JUI, and secured a string of victories against the Afghan warlords. Pakistan's Interior Minister – and controller of the IB – Naseerullah Barbar, was determined to open up the lucrative trade routes (and, as we have seen, possible oil and gas transit routes) to Central Asia with the support of Bhutto's financial backers in the powerful 'trucking Mafia', and also to wrest Afghan policy from Bhutto's opponents in the ISI. Accordingly, the Interior Ministry began a massive logistical support programme for the Taliban, coordinated with other PPP-run civilian ministries in public works, Pakistan Telecom and the Civil Aviation Authority.[40]

With the Taliban seizing much of Afghanistan during 1995–6 and becoming the favoured client of the ISI's biggest overseas backers, Saudi Arabia – not to mention the international oil companies – the ISI itself decided to change sides, whilst hoping to secure a position for its erstwhile allies, Hezb-e, in a future Islamist coalition. Agreement on Afghanistan, however, had not lessened the almost visceral phobia induced in the ISI by the Bhuttos and the PPP. In September 1996 Benazir's surviving brother, Murtaza Bhutto, was assassinated – under circumstances widely attributed to an ISI contract killing. The act was used by Farooq Legari, Pakistan's President and a Bhutto opponent, to level charges against Benazir's husband, Asif Zidari, and to force the Prime Minister's own dismissal in November. With Benazir again out of office, the ISI was back in control.

Control, however, was proving to be a somewhat relative concept. The Islamist mass movements such as the JEI and the JUI, promoted by then Army Commander Pervez Musharraf and ISI chief Mahmoud Ahmed (who had set up a special task force in the ISI), were by this time beginning to run their own agenda. The sectarian anti-Shi'ite grouping Sipha Sahaba, succoured by the Taliban as part of their ongoing struggle with Afghani Shi'ism, were mounting a savage assassination campaign in Sindh and Karachi, focusing on doctors and other Shi'ite professionals. Militants from frontier *madrassas* were demanding Taliban-style measures throughout Sindh and elsewhere and taking inspiration, and, indeed, instruction, from the Taliban themselves.[41]

As well as sharing Islamist and pan-Pushtun nationalist goals with the Taliban, the largely Pushtun ISI leadership needed the training and logistics facilities built for the Mujahidin in Afghanistan and militants fighting in Kashmir. Whilst originally a struggle for independence by the indigenous Jammu and Kashmir Liberation Front (JKLF), the Kashmir conflict had become increasingly dominated by the multinational 'Arab Afghans', backed, as in Afghanistan, by the ISI.[42] Under intense US and Indian pressure, Islamabad had moved many of the militant bases away from the Kashmir border and turned over training and funding facilities to private organisations such as the JUI and Islamic charities. Amongst the prominent foreigners encouraged to take on this role was, as we have seen, Osama bin Laden. The struggle in Kashmir had become crucial to the ISI's justification of its support for the Taliban, whose excesses were alienating many in Pakistan and, increasingly, old allies in the CIA. Even before the Taliban, the links between terrorist bombings, 'Arab Afghans' and the ISI had become highly damaging to Pakistan's international standing. In March 1993, a series of bombings took place in Calcutta and Bombay, killing over 300 people. With public landmarks such as the Stock Exchange and Air India buildings among the targets, parallels were clear with the contemporaneous attacks on the New York World Trade Center.[43] At the trial, many of the 189 defendants were found to be Afghan veterans with alleged links to the ISI.[44]

The US embassy bombings of 1998 put the ISI in an awkward position. Reluctant to finger the Taliban leaders directly, it cooperated to the extent of allowing FBI agents limited access to militants in Peshawar and North West Frontier Province (NWFP), whilst urging the Taliban to expel bin Laden. It also provided the (faulty) intelligence for the US cruise missile strikes on Afghanistan.[45] The 12 October 1999 coup of Army Chief of Staff Pervez Musharraf at first seemed like good news for the ISI. Its head, General Mahmoud Ahmed, was a close associate who had served on the mid-1990s task force in Sindh. As 9/11 would demonstrate, however, even a hardline Islamist leader could be out of the loop. Mahmoud was visiting Washington DC at the time. Musharraf, suddenly propelled to international respectability as a US ally, moved swiftly to replace him with General Ehans ul-Haq – 'a professional who obeys orders'[46] – while reducing the ISI's 15,000 staff level by 40 per cent. However, the reported disbandment of units in the JIN division may not have occurred without a struggle. On 13 December an assault on the Indian Parliament was claimed by longstanding Kashmiri ISI clients Lashkar-e-Taibar and Jaish-e-Mohammed, both classed as foreign terrorist organisations by the US State Department. Jaish has also claimed responsibility for the death of US journalist Daniel Pearl.

Whether or not – as often claimed by Indian analysts – Pakistan has drawn up a 'grand strategy' to break India up into its ethnic constituents,[47] there is certainly much evidence of *ad hoc* support for ethnic separatists in Assam and the Punjab ('Khalistan') as well as the acknowledged backing of militants in Kashmir. Moreover, it is clear that an influential group of ISI officers, 'more Taliban than the Taliban', were using the legitimacy conveyed (in the eyes of Pakistanis) by the Kashmir struggle to advance an international Islamist agenda, including the merger of Afghanistan, Pakistan and Kashmir in General Zia's old dream of a Sunni Muslim Caliphate standing on equal terms with Shi'a Iran and Hindu India.

India

The Indian agencies have historically avoided the central position taken by the ISI in public life and looked more to UK and US practice. Central coordination for intelligence is provided by the Joint Intelligence Committee (JIC), which has its own secretariat located in the Cabinet Office. It reports to the National Security Council, established in 1990, which includes the principal ministers and is chaired by the Prime Minister. Foreign and domestic intelligence is divided between the Research and Analysis wing (RAW) and the Intelligence Bureau (like its historical twin in Pakistan, the IB). RAW is the most secretive organisation. Whilst much more of a conventional foreign intelligence service than the ISI, its precise command structure remains undisclosed and it avoids direct parliamentary accountability and reports directly to the Prime Minister. With cross-ministerial linkages, it has a wide brief encompassing military and political intelligence and economic affairs. Inevitably, much attention is focused on Pakistan. In some reports, over 30,000 agents are active in Pakistan and Bangladesh, while RAW's Special Service Bureau runs 40 training camps for anti-government militants. A particular focus of RAW has been Indian communities in Canada and the United States, which have been fertile recruiting grounds for Sikh militants.

The Ministry of Defence historically had its own intelligence arm – the Directorate of Military Intelligence (DGMI) – as did the other services. They remained dependent to a large degree, however, on RAW and the IB. Then mounting dissatisfaction with the quality of product – particularly after Pakistan's military incursion into the Kargil Valley of 1999 – led to the setting up of a new Defence Intelligence Agency in March 2002. Modelled on the US, the DIA brings together the three services under a rotating leadership.[48] Unlike the DGMI, the DIA will have an international anti-terrorist mandate. A further area of responsibility is Sigint, which has been a significant growth area. In February 2002, India announced a programme of four high-resolution satellites to be in place by 2004. The indigenously developed Technology Experimental Satellite (TES) is claimed to have a one-metre resolution, the only satellite with this capability outside the US.[49]

Burma – opposition and micro-management

In a country that has been under some form of military rule since 1962, the intelligence services of Burma (renamed Myanmar in 1989 by the military junta) perform both a conventional information-gathering role – particularly regarding the numerous armed insurgencies in the regions – and that of a secret police in micro-managing opponents of the regime.[50]

When the ruling Burma Socialist Programme Party (BSPP) was shaken by the general current of opposition to one-party regimes of the late 1980s, the military seized power in 1988, as the State Law and

Order Restoration Council (SLORC), with the declared aim of preparing the way for free elections. Clearly, the securing of much-needed outside investment was a major factor here, as was the combination of pressures from some 17 ethnic insurgent groups and a mass, urban-based opposition. With the unexpected landslide victory in May 1990 of the National League for Democracy (NLD) – led by Aung San Suu Kyi, daughter of Burma's independence leader – the SLORC swiftly moved to suspend the results and placed Aung San under the house arrest which has not been totally eased at the time of writing.[51] After an internal purge, on 15 November 1997 the SLORC reconstituted itself as the State Peace and Development Council (SPDC) without, however, any noticeable moves toward relinquishing power or other policy changes, except in the realm of increased military expenditure.[52]

Along with the army itself – its loyalty subject to doubt in the 1990 elections – the intelligence services provide the backbone of the regime. Officially the National Intelligence Bureau (NIB) is the senior coordinating body, but effective power rests with the Directorate of Defence Services Intelligence (DDSI), headed by regime strongman Khin Nyunt. General Nyunt is also Director General of the NIB and First Secretary of the SPDC. Under a committee of some 25 loyalist military officers, the DDSI is divided into individual bureaux covering areas of intelligence interest, regional branches and local 'intelligence companies', often attached to military units, spread around the country. Also answering to the NIB are the ostensibly civilian Special Investigation Department (SID) and Bureau of Special Investigations (BSI). A further intelligence organ, the Office of Strategic Studies (OSS) was established by Khin Nyunt in 1994. Divided into five departments (covering international affairs, narcotics, security, ethnic affairs and technology), the main focus of the OSS seems to be monitoring opposition parties – notably Aung San Suu Kyi's NLD – and Burma's extensive exile diaspora.

With intelligence absorbing a significant but undisclosed proportion of Burma's annual budget and a network of informants numbering hundreds of thousands, the rise of pro-democracy activism and of the NLD in particular came as a profound shock to the SLORC. As well as the somewhat Orwellian change of title, the junta mounted an extensive propaganda campaign and ever more intensive surveillance. In 1993, the regime founded its own mass organisation – the Union Solidarity and Development Association (USDA), under the patronage of Khin Nyunt and senior general Thwan She – to rally support. Membership – compulsory for some sections of the population, such as government employees – has extended to some 11 million people aged 15 and over. As well as being bussed to mass rallies, members are encouraged to report on social deviance and 'disloyalty'.

Burma's principal outside backer, the People's Republic of China, has provided a wide range of Sigint and communications equipment, reportedly in exchange for base facilities on offshore islands in the Andaman Sea, as part of a $3 billion military credits programme.[53] Singapore, one of Burma's largest outside investors, has also provided Sigint and encryption technology along with training packages, as has Israel, one of the keenest outside observers of the Association of South-East Asian Nations (ASEAN). The Israeli aid programme has also extended to special forces training and training for an élite bodyguard.[54]

Like its authoritarian counterparts elsewhere in South-East Asia, however, the SPDC has discovered that the spread of information technology is the keenest of two-edged swords. The SLORC established the Defence Services Computer Directorate in the early 1990s to oversee a wide range of military and civilian interception and monitor the spread of computers in private hands. In September 1996 it enacted the Computer Science Development Law, banning the use of IT because it was 'undermining State security, law and order, national unity, the national economy or national culture'. Sentences range from seven to 15 years in prison, whilst 20-year terms have been handed out for illegal possession of a fax machine.[55] The widespread belief that all telephones are routinely tapped received dramatic confirmation when the DDSI broke off a live telephone interview with Aung San by the BBC World Service, while it was still on air.[56] The regime's preoccupation with portrayals of its international image, and the major intelligence effort made to counter this, was demonstrated in a publication of 1990. In *Skyful of Lies: BBC, VOA – Their Broadcasts and Rebuttals to Disinformation,* the regime reproduced over

265 pages of transcripts of news broadcasts by the BBC and Voice of America, together with critical comment. While there is a clear capability to monitor open-source transmissions, attempts at jamming have been less successful. The transmissions of Karen Patriotic Youth Radio and other rebel stations and the Burmese-language Democratic Voice of Burma, broadcast by Radio Norway, continue to be received in Burma. The regime makes it known, however, that it has dossiers on the staff involved in BBC and VOA Burmese transmissions, together with information about their families.

The black economy

One major factor sustaining Burma's vast intelligence apparatus is the clandestine nature of much of the Burmese economy. Drug production, illegal logging, and rake-offs from arms and oil and gas contracts (Unocal again)[57] have created a parallel 'black' economic sector underpinning the powerful personal fiefdoms of military and intelligence chiefs. Indeed, Burma's largest official business enterprise – the Union of Myanmar Economic Holdings (UMEH) – is jointly owned by the Ministry of Defence and individual senior military personnel.[58] Military expenditure doubled (to 44 per cent) as a proportion of government spending during the 1990s[59] and the SPDC's refusal to publish a yearbook of economic statistics for 1998/9 suggests a reluctance to reveal how much of this is derived from drug money. According to US State Department estimates, extra-legal economic activity is at least as large as the declared economy, if not larger.[60]

As the coordinating hub for the intelligence agencies of the three armed services, and controlling body for all other intelligence activities, the DDSI bears comparison with the ISI of Pakistan. Like the latter, it takes a close interest in opposition within the armed forces themselves and has a direct line to the ruling junta, bypassing regional military commanders. In a further parallel, the DDSI has access to sources of income independent of government in Burma's vast illegal heroin trade.[61] Of the major ethnic guerrilla armies, many – such as the United Wa State Army (UWSA) and the Myanmar National Democratic Alliance Army (MNDAA) – have reached mutually profitable ceasefire arrangements with the SPDC[62] allowing the trade to continue undiminished. And while it took the wholly unprecedented events of 9/11 and similarly unparalleled US pressure to begin prising the ISI from its dominant position in Pakistan, pressure for regime change in Burma – as the junta and the DDSI are well aware – will come from below.

South Africa – the democratic chance

The transition of South Africa's intelligence services from secret police force/hit squad to a measure of flawed but functional democratic accountability is one of the more remarkable tales of modern times, given both the network's well-earned reputation of unstinting support for apartheid and its clandestine nature. Many of its more notorious sections were established by hardline President P. W. Botha in the 1980s, and a steep need-to-know gradient shielded its activities even from government ministers. As one observer notes, '[incoming President] De Klerk's control over his "inherited" intelligence and security community … was intrinsically weak from the beginning'.[63] If this had advantages in the negotiating latitude allowed reformists such as then Defence Minister Roelf Meyer, it also made the transition to democracy more close-run than was realised at the time.

Three Acts of Parliament established the intelligence services of the new South Africa. The Intelligence Services Act and the Strategic Intelligence Act of 2 December 1994 established a National Intelligence Agency (NIA) for domestic intelligence, the South African Secret Service (SASS) for foreign intelligence and the National Defence Force Intelligence Division for military intelligence. The National Intelligence coordinating committee was also established at this time, bringing together the heads of the respective services reporting to the Cabinet. Critical steps have been taken to resolve the fate of the many covert police and army units. Most have been disbanded or, as with the Special Forces Reconnaissance, incorporated into the new South African National Defence Force (SANDF); Special Forces have been brought under the control of the Chief of Staff, Army (rather than Chief of Staff, Intelligence). Oversight by an Inspector General is also provided for under the Intelligence Services Control Act of 1995.

Much of the new policy framework emerged out of informal discussions between the existing National Intelligence Service (NIS) and the African National Congress (ANC) Department of Intelligence and Security (ANC–DIS) in March–July 1993. This dialogue was taken up more officially in discussions of the Sub-Council on Intelligence of the Transitional Executive Council (TEC), formed in November 1993 to oversee the transition to elections and the transfer of power, as well as in negotiations on the Interim Constitution. The ground for an earlier accord had been laid by secret discussions between M. J. M. (Mike) Louw (then NIS Deputy Director General, now Director General of the SASS), Thabo Mbeki (now President) and Jacob Zuma (former ANC intelligence chief) in Switzerland in early 1990. The involvement of significant sections of the security establishment, also including NIS Director General Neil Barnard and Chief of Operations Maritz Spaarwater, was to ease the transformation of the intelligence structures under democratic government, although, as we shall see, it was not without its opponents.[64]

During the transition of power, a Joint Coordinating Intelligence Committee (JCIC) was added to the Transitional Executive Council, as an ANC/NIS compromise on day-to-day managerial control. With discussions now including the so-called 'homelands' intelligence services of Transkei, Venda and Bophuthatswana, the JCIC eventually gave way to the Heads of Combined Services Committee, in turn the basis for the National Intelligence Coordinating Committee (NICOC). Finally, the new Cabinet Committee on Security and Intelligence replaced the apartheid-era Cabinet Committee on Security Affairs, first chaired by Executive Deputy President de Klerk. The JCIC was authorised to oversee the coordination of the intelligence services, to investigate the activities of any service that appeared to contravene its mandate, and to provide intelligence information to the TEC and its other sub-councils. The Sub-Council on Intelligence became the forum where discussions on the future structure of intelligence were carried out within the interim Government of National Unity. This was especially important because the future scope and focus of South Africa's intelligence community was not covered in the Interim Constitution, unlike the military and police, which were.

A 'big tent' approach – the new structures, control and accountability
With the fund of goodwill accumulated by the Government of
National Unity, the hopes that the emerging intelligence and security
structures would provide an international example for 'best practice'
were not entirely misplaced. Drawing on experience from Australian
and Canadian oversight models, rather than the secretive British system,
'the watchwords must be control, accountability and supervision',
observed Mike Louw, appointed Director General of the new SASS.
'Too many people equate us with other secret organisations. We need
to establish our own identity.'[65] The existing structures were the
former State Security Council and its National Intelligence Committee, the National Intelligence Service, the Military Intelligence
Division (of the South African Defence Force, including the
Directorates of Military Intelligence and Special Tasks), and the
Crime Combating and Investigation Division (of the South African
Police). Of the several replacement schemes considered, the one
chosen was, perhaps surprisingly, the most inclusive.

Of the approximately 4,000 personnel included in the new civilian
structures, 2,130 came from the NIS, 910 from the ANC–DIS, 304
from Bophutatswana, 233 from Transkei, 76 from Venda, and the
remainder from the Pan-Africanist Security Service (PASS). The NIS
was disbanded on 1 January 1995. Under section 3(1) of the
Intelligence Services Act, the NIA was established, taking in former
members of the NIS, ANC–DIS, the Pan-Africanist and homelands
services, and some smaller bodies, with some dispersal to the new
South African Police Service. The foreign intelligence-gathering
department of the NIS was reconstituted as the SASS, although the
respective heads of the NIA and the SASS are obliged to consult on
some aspects of operations.

While the inclusion of much of the NIS in the new structures was
in accord with the overall conciliatory ethos of the post-apartheid
regime, there were also practical considerations. The strong contribution of some (certainly not all) NIS leaders to the peace process
was clearly a factor. More concretely, the NIS possessed assets and
capabilities that the ANC would not want to lose, including sources
on both the white right wing and extremists in other parties such as

the Inkatha Freedom Party (IFP), technological capabilities, and greater
professional training. Left unstated was concern for the massive
database also developed on the Pan-Africanist Congress (PAC), South
African Communist Party (SACP) and the ANC itself, accumulated
through years of sometimes highly successful penetration.[66]

The wisdom of seeking an inclusive 'big tent' approach to erstwhile
opponents was seen to be justified, not simply on the pragmatic
grounds of avoiding numbers of disgruntled former agents peddling
their wares, but by the virulence of the hardcore opposition which
had remained unreconciled as a highly dangerous 'Third Force' (of
which more below).

The new head of the NIA was the former deputy head of the
ANC–DIS, Sizakele Sigxashe, while the head of the SASS was the
former Director General of the NIS, Mike Louw; many of the former
NIS department heads have retained their positions in the interim.
The NIA is composed of seven chief directorates: domestic collection,
research, counter-espionage, security, corporate resources, technology,
and the intelligence academy, while the SASS is structured along
similar lines for foreign operations.[67] The structure was left intact
through agreement between the NIS and ANC prior to the 1994
elections, to maintain continuity. Similarly, the principle of 'effective
management' was established in the hope of avoiding excessive politi-
cisation of the upper tiers of leadership while meeting affirmative
action concerns. It is estimated that the total personnel complement in
the civilian services is around 4,000; the overall 1995 budget for these
services, initially reported as R283 million (approximately US$70
million), was increased by Parliament in 1995 to R400 million
(US$100 million).[68]

Under the National Strategic Intelligence Act, the NIA was mandated to 'gather, correlate, evaluate ... domestic intelligence ... to fulfil
the national counter-intelligence responsibilities ... and to gather
departmental intelligence at the request of any department of State'.[69]
The NIA was not to have powers of arrest, but rather to 'supply
intelligence' for action by the South African Police Service (SAPS).
The priority targets were identified as drug syndicates, organised crime,
the conflict in KwaZulu–Natal, and 'taxi violence' amongst rival

gangs. For the police intelligence structures, moving from the old South African Police Security Branch and its later incarnations into the new SAPS–NCIS (National Criminal Intelligence Service) required reductions in the NCIS from an estimated 3,000 personnel to a much smaller staff of 400, supplemented by an extra 100 security personnel from the ANC. For the intelligence services, as with the defence services and the police, a provision forbids members to 'publicly display or express support for or associate himself or herself with a political party, organisation, movement or body'.[70]

The foreign service, SASS, was designed to fulfil a conventional intelligence mission 'in relation to external threats' but 'excluding foreign military intelligence', with a comprehensive oversight system to restrain excesses like those of its freewheeling predecessor.[71] Under apartheid, it was Military Intelligence which often played the leading role both internally and externally. In June 1993 Deputy Intelligence Minister Joe Nhlanhla set out revised guidelines for the new and somewhat leaner National Defence Force Intelligence Division or, more usually, Military Intelligence (MI). The primary focus was on tactical acquisition in support of given military objectives, with strategic intelligence by and large left to the civilian agencies. The internal counter-insurgency activities routinely undertaken in the 1970–80s were also prohibited 'unless mandated by the constitution'.[72] Here, though, the new regime was faced with a genuine quandary. While it may seek to avoid partisan civilian operations, it remains true that, as one analyst observes, 'An unemotional analysis would indicate that support for the SAPS in internal law and order duties will remain a semi-permanent task of the SANDF for many years to come.'[73] Whether this will lead to 'mission creep' in the manner of the old order remains to be seen.

Coordination of intelligence activities is overseen by the National Intelligence Coordinating Committee (NICOC), which replaced the Joint Coordinating Intelligence Committee. NICOC reports to the President through the Cabinet Committee on Security and Intelligence, and comprises the National Intelligence Coordinator, the Director General of each service (including the heads of SAPS-NCIS and MI). For accountability purposes, the civilian services are directly responsible to the Office of the State President, through the Minister of Intelligence (originally combined with the Ministry of Justice). At the same time, the Intelligence Services Control Act created the position of Inspector General for the services, to whom the Director General of each service is accountable. The Office of the Inspector General includes an investigation arm, a legal section and an information resource centre. With a promised full access to budgetary and classified information, the office was set up to work in conjunction with the parliamentary Joint Standing Committee on Intelligence, which was modelled on the Canadian Security Intelligence Review Committee in its functions.[74] The Committee is composed of 18 members appointed by the President, and is proportionally representative of the various parties in Parliament.

There has been some disquiet, however, around the issue of civilian control. While the post was established in 1995, the first incumbent, Lewis Skweyiya, declined to take up the post, claiming that it was insufficiently funded. The office was then unfilled from 1996 until the appointment of former Truth Commission member Fazel Randera in June 2000. His tenure, however, only lasted six months. While he cited 'personal reasons' for resignation, funding was believed to be once again at issue.[75] Tensions also existed between Randera and Intelligence Minister Lindiwe Sisulu, a former ANC intelligence analyst trained in the Soviet Union. In some accounts, the six-year hiatus is a significant pointer to ANC attitudes toward an official oversight role. The elevation of the Intelligence Ministry to Cabinet rank gives some indication of the importance placed on intelligence by the ANC government, as also does a clause in the enabling law empowering a presidential veto on the release of any information gathered by the Inspector General and restricting the scope of the parliamentary committee on intelligence to receive reports.

War in the shadows – the apartheid legacy

The transformation of South Africa's vast and secretive security apparatus was and is not without its problems. Prominent here is the issue of strategic culture. The old NIS was developed along Western lines and became a key player in the destabilisation and counter-insurgency operations against the liberation movements, drawing on the British experience in Malaya and the US practice in Vietnam and elsewhere. The ANC–DIS and PAC Security Service were trained and to some extent modelled on the practice of the KGB and on Cuban, Libyan and East German models. The issue of a non-political service, therefore, has a resonance perhaps uncomfortable for both sides. Recognising this, the 1994 Intelligence White Paper contained specific strictures against 'active measures', 'covert action' and 'disinformation' in the South African political process and further stated that 'measures designed to deliberately interfere with ... the internal workings of parties and organisations engaged in lawful activity within South Africa, must be expressly forbidden'.[76]

As evidence uncovered during the Truth and Reconciliation Commission and the Goldstone Inquiry on political violence in KwaZulu–Natal was to reveal, such concerns were timely.[77] The long period of struggle during the presidencies of P. W. Botha and F. W. de Klerk was marked by increasingly desperate measures under the so-called 'Total National Strategy' and 'Total Counter-revolutionary Strategy' and by a proliferation of covert intelligence units operating quasi-independently of even government control. At the formal apex of government was the State Security Council with its own intelligence arm, Strategic Communications (STRATCOM), able to draw on a variety of units. Also mounting covert actions were the army's Directorate of Military Intelligence and the police Security Branch. Increasingly worried by negative publicity, then Minister of Law and Order Adriaan Vlok suggested to President P. W. Botha the formation of a 'special capability unit existing independently of the police and the Defence Force'.[78] The 'Third Force', as it became known, would be unacknowledged, covertly and independently financed, and able to draw upon the diverse pool of trained manpower from South Africa's numerous regional wars.

Although a variety of semi-freelance units sprung up during this period – such as Witdoeke (Western Cape vigilantes), Uma Afrika (Eastern Cape vigilantes), and the Black Cats gang in Ermelo[79] – the main arms of the Third Force were the unit C1/10 of the SAP Security Branch and the Civil Cooperation Bureau (CCB) set up by the Directorate of Military Intelligence. Based at Vlakplaas police barracks outside Pretoria, C1/10 became known within the apartheid security establishment as the 'security arm of the National Party'. It rarely made any determination of targets on its own but acted under the direction of the commanders of the Security Branch in cooperation with STRATCOM. Acting through Military Intelligence front companies and using weapons provided by the SAP Security Branch, C1/10 soon constituted the core of a hit squad that assisted the ANC's rivals, the Inkatha Freedom Party. After evidence of these atrocities began to surface in 1990, then-President De Klerk ordered the unit suspended. However, Vlakplaas was not finally closed down until the eve of the 1994 elections, while C1/10 members continued their activities from within the Security Branch or in cooperation with Military Intelligence for some years after.

The most secretive covert unit of all was the CCB. Formed in 1986 out of defecting Rhodesian special forces under the original designation 'Barnacle', it was to be a fully independent covert unit available not only for current purposes, but for use if the tide of reform from more 'enlightened' National Party leaders became irresistible. Thus, while intelligence was shared amongst the other agencies, the 'Barnacle'/CCB units also began to build up their own networks and front organisations in order to reduce their reliance on other actors. Units were not accountable to local or regional police or Security Branch structures, nor to the army commanders; they reported only to the Army Chief of Staff. As the anodyne name suggests, the Civil Cooperation Bureau was designed from the outset for built-in deniability *vis-à-vis* the established police and army security structures. While funded initially from the army's Special Defence Fund, the major revenue source was to be front companies and commercial operations. This would descend by the early 1990s into outright criminality, involving narcotics dealing, diamond smuggling, prostitution, extortion, fraud and weapons trafficking.

The Third Force

Set up by Major-General Abraham Joubert, the General Officer Commanding Special Forces, with the authorisation of Minister of

Defence Magnus Malan (who later claimed no knowledge of the unit prior to November 1989) and army chief General Jannie Geldenhuys, the CCB was structured along quasi-corporate lines. Its first 'Chairman' (1987–90) was Joubert himself. A 'Managing Director' was operational head (the first being Special Forces Colonel Pieter 'Joe' Verster) overseeing six regional commands, each disguised as a commercial company. These were responsible for (within shifting parameters), Europe, Zimbabwe, Swaziland, South West Africa (soon to be Namibia), Mozambique, Botswana, Lesotho, Malawi, Zaïre, Zambia, and the internal regions. Each region was composed of individual 'cells', run by a 'coordinator' and operated with anywhere from five to twenty full-time operatives. CCB personnel invariably adopted false identities both within and outside the unit. 'Informal members' would be used, including criminals and former policemen, often completely unaware of the identity of their taskmaster.

While the overall size of the CCB never exceeded 250–300 full-time personnel, its activities were highly disruptive. They included media 'psyops' in Europe – including the planting of the story that the ANC was aiding the Irish Republican Army (IRA)[80] – armed attacks on the 1989 Namibian elections, and hundreds of assassination attempts on apartheid's opponents. Notable here were the 1989 bombing of the Early Learning Centre in Athlone, the attempted murder of Gavin Evans, the attempted murder of ANC lawyer Dullah Omar (later Minister of Justice), and – their most bizarre operation – the planting of an ape foetus at the residence of Archbishop Desmond Tutu.

With the momentum for reform within South Africa becoming irresistible by the early 1990s, a tide of revelations began emerging about the activities of the CCB and its cohorts in the Third Force. Amidst the torrent of apparently orchestrated political violence in KwaZulu–Natal, evidence of collusion between the IFP and security forces – the 1991 'Inkathagate' scandal – led to the roles of C1/10 and the CCB being further exposed in the Goldstone Commission hearings of 1992–4.[81] A serving member of C1/10 anonymously testified that hit squad activities, the training and arming of IFP hit squads, illegal killings, fraud, forgery, bombings and other acts of public violence were being planned and/or carried out at Vlakplaas and through a

number of army units and departments. This information was first
made public by the Commission on 18 March 1994. While the investigation had proved that hit squads were operating in South Africa with
the complicity of the security forces ('evidence of the existence of a
Third Force' in South Africa), it was unable to prove a direct line of
command to the political leadership in Pretoria. Concrete evidence
was not to come until the trial (it finished in October 1996) of former
C1/10 commander Colonel Eugene de Kock on over 100 indictments of murder, extortion and inciting violence. The assignment of
guilt and command responsibility would become a matter of public
debate during the hearings of the Truth and Reconciliation Commission after 1995.

Perhaps as disturbing as the bloodstained record of the Third Force
itself was the evidence that many of the units and personnel involved
had become divorced from any sort of control and simply gone
'underground'. Thus, while the CCB was technically 'disbanded' on
31 July 1990, many of its members had joined the secret Directorate
of Covert Collection (DCC) branch of Military Intelligence, the
police Security Branch, the army Special Forces or the private sector.
This was confirmed during a raid by the Goldstone Commission on a
Military Intelligence building in Pretoria in 1992, in which the
existence of the DCC was discovered. President de Klerk claimed no
knowledge of the unit, and ordered it disbanded immediately. Similarly,
allegations have been made that the STRATCOM intelligence wing
of the old State Security Council, officially disbanded in 1991, was
never actually dismantled but taken quietly into the police Crime
Combating and Investigation Service, and redesignated 'Trewits' for
Teenrevolusionere Strategie ('Counter-Revolutionary Strategy'). In
press interviews with former agents, it was claimed that three generals
– including Basie Smit (former commander of the police Security
Branch) and Johann le Roux (former head of the NIS and then
Deputy Minister for National Intelligence) – determined at the time
of the National Peace Accord that it was necessary for STRATCOM
to disappear from the record but continue to operate covertly.[82]

Allegations that the remnants of Trewits might still be operating, in
collusion with elements of the Third Force and right-wing extremists,

surfaced again in 1995 in response to a series of assassinations of local police officials, massacres and bombings.[83] Closer to home for the new intelligence establishment was the death of NIA Chief Director (Security) Muziwendoda Mdluli on 2 October 1995. Found shot in his car, it was thought that he had run foul of the mercenary group which took over the Comoros Islands in the autumn of 1995. This group – led by the ubiquitous French mercenary Bob Denard – was linked to Third Force units in South Africa.[84] The continuing violence in KwaZulu–Natal was unfolding against a background of mutual suspicion between the NIA and the Police Service, who accused the intelligence agency of illegal surveillance of its senior officials.[85]And in March 1996 President Mandela publicly stated his concern that 'the South African Police Service is being infiltrated by agents provocateurs – powerful elements in this country who are planning to overthrow the government'.[86]

Life in the private sector

Whilst Mandela was not alone in fearing the continued presence of unreformed apartheid hardliners in the security services, most former personnel of the compromised covert units – the CCB in particular – were finding employment elsewhere.[87] True to its founding principles of autonomy, 'the Organisation' as the CCB was known to insiders, had began to diversify into the private sector from the outset, under 'Plan Blue' for generating funds anonymously. Set up in 1989, the Pretoria-based military consulting firm Executive Outcomes was one of several CCB front companies which underwent considerable expansion during the transfer of power. With an influx of recently demobilised personnel, the company linked up with a network of mineral, diamond and air transport companies providing services from construction to mobile field hospitals.[88] Its core business, however, was military assistance, ranging from security details to combat-ready private armies. With established military and intelligence links in Africa and the UK – where it was registered in 1993 – and a global network of partnerships with such firms as the British Sandline, it had soon picked up a portfolio of blue-chip clients in the oil and diamond businesses, including De Beers and Rio Tinto Zinc.[89] In an ironic twist, one of the biggest Executive Outcomes contracts was to provide security for Gulf/Chevron oil facilities in Angola against the UNITA guerrillas of former South African and US client Jonas Savimbi. The Gulf contract was closely followed by an approach from De Beers to oust Savimbi from diamond fields in Angola's Luanda Norte province and the firm was soon providing general military assistance to the Angolan government forces of apartheid's old enemy, the MPLA.[90]

By the mid-1990s, some thirty governments had approached Executive Outcomes for its services, including Algeria, Turkey, and Sri Lanka – all fighting bloody civil insurgencies – and others, notably Nigeria, Botswana, Ethiopia, Qatar, Yemen and Bahrain.[91] Perhaps its highest-profile operation was in Sierra Leone. In April 1995 Freetown's military ruler, Captain Valentine Strasser, was convinced by the mercenary firm's close associates, Branch Energy, to engage Executive Outcomes, apparently after reading about them in *Soldier of Fortune* magazine. Branch Energy's diamond concessions were under attack from the Revolutionary United Front of ex-army corporal Fodhay Sankho, in collusion with the Liberian guerrilla forces of Charles Taylor. Over an 18-month period, Executive Outcomes succeeded in wresting back most of the country, in exchange for a $1.5 million monthly pay-out from the contested diamond fields.[92] Then, however, mounting publicity surrounding the Sierra Leone operation – later, as we have seen, to involve UK associates Sandline – led the South African government in April 1997 to issue an order prohibiting private companies from providing military services to other countries without government approval.[93] And on 1 January 1999 the firm officially 'ceased operations'.

With the demobilisation of apartheid-era forces from all sides, and the recruitment of perhaps more than six private security employees for every SAPS officer in South Africa,[94] it is clear that fertile ground exists for destabilisation on a massive scale. There has been some discussion of placing a clause in the Constitution prohibiting South African citizens from becoming mercenaries. Whether or not this happens, the re-cast intelligence services of the 'rainbow nation' will not be short of work to do.

Notes

1 See Fred Halliday, *Nation and Religion in the Middle East*, London: Saqui, 2000, p. 214.

2 For a wide-ranging, if somewhat partisan, account of the role of conspiracy theory in the Middle East, see Daniel Pipes, *The Hidden Hand*, London: Macmillan, 1996.

3 See Andrew Rathmell, *Syria's Intelligence Services: Origin and Development*, which can be read at: www.ci-ce-ct.com/article.

4 Prominent civil rights and pro-democracy activists, such as Syrian MPs Mamoun al-Homsi and Riyad Sayf, received five-year sentences, as did Riyad al-Turk, the chairman of the Syrian Communist Party Political Bureau. Well-known economist Aref Dalila was sentenced to ten years and Walid al-Bunni, a doctor and human rights campaigner, was given three. See 'Last of the Damascus Ten Are Sentenced', *Middle East Intelligence Bulletin*, 4, 9 (September 2002).

5 See 'Syria's Intelligence Services: a Primer', *Middle East Intelligence Bulletin*, 2, 6 (July 2000).

6 See Daniel Pipes, *Syria beyond the Peace Process*, Washington DC: Washington Institute for Near East Policy, 1996, p. 115.

7 See 'Closing in on the Pan Am Bombers', *US News and World Report*, 22 May 1989. See also Gary Gambill, 'The Lockerbie Bombing Trial: Is Libya Being Framed?' *Middle East Intelligence Bulletin*, June 2000; Ian Ferguson, 'The Lockerbie Bombing Trial: New Problems in the Prosecution's Case', *Middle East Intelligence Bulletin*, September 2000.

8 See *The Intelligence Newsletter*, 14 November 1996.

9 *Sawt al-Mar'a* (Amman), 24 July 1996.

10 See Gary Gambill, 'Sponsoring Terrorism: Syria and the PFLP–GC', *Middle East Intelligence Bulletin*, 4, 9 (September 2002). See also *Al-Nahar* (Beirut), 25 May 2002.

11 Some have carried this argument to its logical conclusion. See for example, Patrick Seale, *Abu Nidal: A Gun for Hire*, New York: Random House, 1992.

12 Saddam in conversation with Saudi US Ambassador Prince Bandar bin Sultan, 5 April 1990, cited in Bob Woodward, *The Commanders*, New York: Simon and Schuster, 1991, p. 202.

13 See Federation of American Scientists Intelligence Resource Program, 'Iraqi Intelligence Agencies', www.fas.org/irp/world/Iraq/summary.htm. See also Ibrahim al-Marashi, 'Iraq's Security and Intelligence Network – a Guide and Analysis', *Middle East Review of International Affairs*, 6, 3 (September 2002) – this piece was somewhat controversially recycled as an 'intelligence report' by the Downing Street Press Office on 5 February 2003. See Brian Whitaker and Michael White, 'UK War Dossier a Sham, Say Experts', *Guardian*, 7 February 2003.

14 See Sean Boyne, 'Inside Iraq's Intelligence Services' – Parts I and II, *Jane's Intelligence Review*, 9, 7/8 (July and August 1997).

15 See *National Security Newsletter*, 9, 'Agency Profile: Iraqi Intelligence', 19 December 1998.

16 See Federation of American Scientists Intelligence Resource Program, www.fas. org/irp/world/Iraq/summary.htm, Al Hadi Project (Project 858).

17 For a good overview, see Paul Foot and Tim Laxton, *Not the Scott Report – Thatcher, Major, Saddam and the Merchants of Death,* Private Eye Special, November 1994.

18 See Seale, *Abu Nidal*; see also Peter Beaumont, 'Abu Nidal Sows Chaos from the Grave', *The Observer*, 25 August 2002; Christopher Hitchens, 'The Terrorist I Knew', *ibid*. In early August 2002 Abu Nidal was reported dead in his Baghdad villa with four gunshot wounds in the head; the Iraqi police said it was suicide. He remains, amongst others, a strong suspect for the Lockerbie bombing of 1988.

19 See James Risen, 'Iraqi Terror Hasn't Hit US in Years, CIA Says', *International Herald Tribune*, 6 February 2002.

20 See Con Coughlin, 'Powell Will Struggle to Link Saddam with Al-Qaida Terrorism', *Sunday Telegraph*, 2 February 2003.

21 These were Khalid Shaikh Mohammed and Shawki Istambouli, brother of the assassin of Anwar Sadat. Both were on the FBI wanted list and involved in Egyptian Gama'at al-Islami; see Robert Baer, *See No Evil*, New York: Crown, 2002, p. 270.

22 Apparently, professional pique of the Czech intelligence service BIS led to the 'outing' of allegedly gay MI 6 Prague station chief Christopher Hurrenn on this occasion. See Michael Smith, 'Fate of Iraqi Mole Led to Spy Clash', *Electronic Telegraph*, 4 February 1999.

23 See Kieran Williams, *Security Intelligence Services and the New Democracies*, London: Palgrave, 2001, pp. 108–9.

24 See 'Powell's Evidence against Saddam: Does It Add Up?', *Guardian*, 6 February 2003.

25 See Richard Norton-Taylor, 'Britain Disputes Terror Link to Police Murder', *Guardian*, 6 February 2003.

26 See Olivier Schmidt, 'Palestine: Intelligence Eating Up the Budget', *Intelligence Newsletter*, 36 (29 April 1996): 68.

27 See Graham Usher, 'Netanyahu's "Concession" – an Offer Too Far', *Middle East International*, 564 (5 December 1997).

28 See Steve Posner, 'The Spy at Wye', *Washington Post*, 27 October 1998.

29 See Walter Pincus, 'Tenet Said He Might Quit over Pollard Release', *Washington Post*, 11 November 1998.

30 See *AFIO Weekly Intelligence Notes*, No. 05–99 (3 February 1999).

31 See George J. Tenet, 'What New Role for the CIA?', in *CIA Public Affairs Staff*, Washington DC: 1998.

32 See 'Original Text of Tenet Ceasefire Plan', *Ha'aretz*, 15 June 2001.

33 See, for example, Gary Gambill, 'Sponsoring Terrorism: Syria and Hamas', *Middle East Intelligence Bulletin*, 4, 1 (October 2002).

34 See Edward Cody, 'Even from Palestinians, Arafat Faces Demands for Reform', *International Herald Tribune*, 14 May 2002.

35 See B. Raman, 'Pakistan's Inter-Services Intelligence', South Asia Analysis Group, Working Paper No. 287 (1 August 2001), pp. 5–6.

36 It has been alleged by retired Chief of Army Staff General Mirza Aslam Beg that the ISI's controversial Internal Political Division was established by Zia in 1975, principally to campaign against the PPP; see Raman, 'Pakistan's Inter-Services Intelligence'.

37 Zia's still mysterious plane crash also resulted in the deaths of former ISI chief Akhtar Rahman Khan, eight other Pakistani generals and US ambassador Arnold Raphael; see John Cooley, *Unholy Wars*, London: Pluto, 2001, pp. 229–30.

38 See Ahmed Rashid, *Taliban*, London: Penguin, 2001, p. 26.

39 In some estimates, 12,000 had crossed the border by December 1994; *ibid.*, pp. 28–9.

40 See Mariana Barbar, 'The Battle for Economic Gains in Afghanistan', *The News*, 15 January 1996.

41 See Raman, 'Pakistan's Inter-Services Intelligence', pp. 12–13.

42 See Cooley, *Unholy Wars*, p. 234.

43 See Human Rights Watch, *India: Arms and Abuses in Indian Punjab and Kashmir*, Washington DC: Human Rights Watch, September 1994, p. 18.

44 See Agence France-Press, Bombay, 14 July 1994.

45 See Edward Luce, 'Pakistan Ears and Eyes Are Key to Search for bin Laden', *Financial Times*, 2 October 2001.

46 See 'Wild Card Spies', *Businessweek*, 29 October 2001.

47 See Major-General Ashok Krishna, 'The Inter-Services Intelligence of Pakistan', *IPCS*, Article 191 (25 May 1999).

48 See *Hindustan Times*, 'Defense Intelligence Agency Becomes Operational', 6 March 2002.

49 See Reseal H. Laskar, 'India to Launch New Series of Spy Satellites', *IANS* (New Delhi), 13 February 2002.

50 When gatherings of more than three people are monitored and it is obligatory to report the movements of any foreigners, the figure of 1,000 political prisoners is clearly much understated. Amnesty International has reported the presence of 20 known detention centres throughout Burma. See Amnesty International, *No Law at All: Human Rights Repression under Military Rule*, London, 1992 and *Myanmar: Renewed Repression*, London, 1996.

51 The League secured 392 seats out of the 485 (52.9 per cent) in the projected assembly – see Robert H. Taylor, 'Military Politics and the Prospects for Democratisation in Myanmar', *Asian Affairs*, 29 (1 February 1998).

52 For a good overview, see Andrew Selth, *Burma/Myanmar: How Strong Is the Military Regime?*, International Crisis Group (IGC) Report No. 11, Bangkok/Brussels: IGC, December 2000.

53 These include Hainiggyi and Great Coco islands off the Andaman coast, Ramtree and Zadetki islands off the Southern coast, and possibly others, with agreements finalised in 1997 – see William Ashton, 'Chinese Bases in Burma – Fact or Fiction?', *Jane's Intelligence Review*, 7, 2 (February 1995): 84–7; Rowan Callick, 'China and Burma Strengthen Ties with Military Agreement', *Australian Financial Review*, 24 January 1997, p. 12.

54 See Selth, *Burma/Myanmar: How Strong*, pp. 13–14; William Ashton, 'Israel, Myanmar

Develop Military Pact', *Jane's Intelligence Review*, March 2000.

55 Selth, *Burma/Myanmar: How Strong*, p. 20.

56 See 'Suu Kyi Interview Pulled Off Air', *Bangkok Post*, 30 May 1996.

57 For an account of the lengthy court cases filed against UNOCAL by representatives of Burmese minorities and the Federation of Burma Trade Unions, see www.unocal.com/ myanmar/suit.htm.

58 See Mary Callahan, 'Cracks in the Edifice? – Military–Society Relations in Burma since 1988', in Morten B. Pedersen *et al.* (eds.), *Burma: Strong Regime, Weak State?*, Adelaide: Crawford House, 2000, p. 48.

59 See Defence Intelligence Organisation (Australia), *Defence Economic Trends in the Asia Pacific 1999*, Canberra: DIO, 2000.

60 See US Embassy Rangoon, *Foreign Economic Trends Report: Burma 1997*, Washington DC: GPO, 1998.

61 See Desmond Ball, *Burma and Drugs: the Regime's Complicity in the Global Drug Trade*, Strategic and Defence Studies Centre, Working Paper No. 336 (July 1999), Canberra: Australian National University.

62 Anthony Davis and Bruce Hawke, 'Burma, the Country That Won't Kick the Habit', *Jane's Intelligence Review*, March 1998.

63 Robert D'A. Henderson, 'South African Intelligence under De Klerk', *International Journal of Intelligence and Counter-Intelligence*, 8, 1 (Spring 1995): 51–89.

64 For a full discussion of this process, see Allister Sparks, *Tomorrow Is Another Country*, London, 1994, pp. 54–6, 109–19. There have been indications that as far back as 1986 the NIS had arranged meetings between the ANC and NP, as well as participating in their own secretive talks with ANC–DIS. In addition, former Minister of Law and Order Hernius Kriel reportedly stated in early 1995 that he had held secret meetings with Nelson Mandela and other senior ANC leaders in 1985 while they were still in prison.

65 See Rex Gibson, 'Memoirs of an Invisible Man', *Star International Weekly* (Johannesburg) 26 January–1 February 1995.

66 There is evidence that many of the NIS files detailing informers in the ANC were destroyed prior to integration, in order to avoid a witch-hunt. See Ronnie Kasrils, *Armed and Dangerous: My Underground Struggle against Apartheid*, Oxford: Heinemann, 1993, pp. 261–7.

67 See Sharon Chetty, 'Meeting the Government's Needs Is Sigxashe's Aim', *The Star and SA Times*, 20 December 1995.

68 See 'Warning against Intelligence Cuts', *The Star International Weekly* (Johannesburg), 1–7 June 1995.

69 See National Strategic Intelligence Act, s2 (1) (a/b/c). The NIA is required (1) to identify any threat or potential threat to the security of the Republic or its people; and (2) to supply intelligence regarding any such threat to NICOC, and inform the President of any such threat.

70 See South African Police Service Act, s46 (1)/(2), although this does not preclude membership in a political party.

71 See National Strategic Intelligence Act (1994), s2 (2) (a/b/c).

72 See Joe Nhlanhla, 'The Transformation of Military Intelligence and Special Forces: towards an Accountable and Transparent Military Culture', *South African Defence Review*, 12 (1993): 38.

73 See Jakkie Cilliers, Institute for Defence Policy, *SAPA Report*, 22 May 1996, pp. 18–19.

74 See Kevin O'Brien, 'South Africa's Evolving Intelligence and Security Structures', *International Journal of Intelligence and Counter Intelligence*, 9, 2 (Summer 1996): 187–232, especially 200–4.

75 See 'Resignation of Intelligence Inspector General Poses Question Whether ANC Wants This Watchdog', *Southern Africa Report*, 20, 5 (1 February 2002).

76 The 'Basic Principles and Guidelines of National Intelligence' document states that no intelligence or security service/organisation shall be allowed to carry out any operations or activities that are intended to undermine, promote or influence any South African political party or organisation at the expense of another by means of any acts ('active measures' or 'covert action') or by means of disinformation. White Paper, 1994, *Annexure B*, s5.3.

77 See *Reports of the Commission of Inquiry Regarding the Prevention of Public Violence and Intimidation* (R. J. Goldstone, Chairman) on the illegal importation, distribution and use of firearms, ammunition and explosives by the SAP, SADF, ANC and IFP (5 October 1993); on security force involvement and alleged misconduct by the SAP (26 November 1993); Fourth Interim Report on hit squads and the SAP Internal Stability Division (6 December 1993); on attacks on members of the SAP, Self-Defence and Protection Units of the IFP or ANC, and the murder of IFP members (21 April 1994). See the report of 18 March 1994 detailing 'Third Force activities' and criminal political violence of the ANC, IFP, and elements within the SAP and KwaZulu Police in KwaZulu–Natal in particular.

78 See Patrick Laurence, 'SA's Third Force Soon in the Dock', *The Star International Weekly* (Johannesburg), 30 December 1994, p. 15. See also: John Battersby, 'A Secret Network to Preserve White Power', *Christian Science Monitor*, 24 August 1992; Paul Taylor, 'S. Africa's Past Horrors Pose Questions about Future Justice', *Washington Post*, 4 March 1995.

79 See Herbert M. Howe, 'The South African Defence Force and Political Reform', *Journal of Modern African Studies*, 32, 1 (1994): 33–8.

80 Eben Barlow, later of mercenary firm Executive Outcomes, was head of the CCB's European (Region 6) operations responsible for this long-running British tabloid favourite. See Wayne Madsen, *Genocide and Covert Activities in Africa 1993–1999* (Lewiston, NY: Edwin Mellen, 1999), p. 171. See also Jeremy Harding, 'The Mellow Mercenaries', *The Guardian*, 8 March 1997.

81 See Allister Sparks, 'Answers Are Needed about NP's Secret Operations', *The Star International Weekly* (Johannesburg), 29 June–5 July 1995.

82 See 'Intelligence Officer Says He Knew about STRATCOM', *Weekly Mail and Guardian*, 21 July 1995; 'The Secrets of STRATCOM', *Weekly Mail and Guardian*,

23 June 1995; Anne Everleth, 'STRATCOM Never Died, Says Ex-cop', *Weekly Mail and Guardian*, 18 August 1995.

83 See *The Star* (Cape Town), 31 January 1995; *Weekly Mail and Guardian* (Pretoria), 3–9 February 1995; *The Citizen* (Johannesburg), 9 February 1995.

84 See Madsen, *Genocide*, pp. 254–5.

85 See Ministry of Intelligence Services, *Background on the Report to NICOC on the Investigation into Allegations of Illegal Electronic Interception and Physical Surveillance Directed against the Senior Management of SAPS*, 22 February 1996; see also, 'No Conclusive Evidence That NIA Bugged Police: Sisulu', *SAPA Report*, 29 March 1996.

86 See 'Police Being Infiltrated by "Provocateurs", Mandela Says', *SAPA Report*, 21 March 1996.

87 See Howard W. French, 'Now for Hire: South Africa's Out-of-Work Commandos', *New York Times*, 24 May 1995; Phillip van Niekerk, 'African Soldiers-for-Rent Just Businessmen at Heart', *The Globe and Mail*, 21 September 1995.

88 For a detailed account of Executive Outcomes' numerous associates, grouped at one stage under the corporate umbrella of the Pretoria-based Strategic Resources Corporation, see Yves Goulet, 'Executive Outcomes: Mixing Business with Bullets', *Jane's Intelligence Review*, 9, 9 (1 September 1997) – interestingly enough, *Jane's* was forced to retract much of this article under legal pressure and, perhaps, pressure from other sources.

89 See Kirsten Sellars, 'Old Dogs of War Learn New Tricks', *New Statesman*, 25 April 1997.

90 See Michael Ashworth, 'The King's Road Irregulars versus the Jungle Rebels: "Security Firm" Hired to End Guerrilla War', *The Independent*, 25 February 1997.

91 See David Isenberg, *Soldier of Fortune Ltd*, Washington DC: Centre of Defense Information monograph, November 1997.

92 Madsen, *Genocide*, pp. 379–81.

93 See Goulet, 'Executive Outcomes'.

94 See O'Brien, 'South Africa's Evolving Intelligence and Security Structures', p. 229.

CHAPTER 8

CONCLUDING PERSPECTIVES
Knowledge, Power and Accountability

If the end of the Cold War proved a mixed blessing for many of the world's intelligence services, the advent of the new 'war on terrorism', pursued globally post–9/11, also has a distinct downside. To be sure, pursestrings are opening and long-neglected skills in analysis and human intelligence are being rushed back online. Neither is money an object for Signals and technical intelligence generally, and operational restrictions are being brushed aside in ways unknown since the 1950s. Certainly, intelligence officials have the ear of governments as never before. However, the shock of the Twin Towers has also posed some hard questions for intelligence agencies – notably in the US. The sorry saga of missed leads and passed bucks surrounding the hijackers is a major – and still unresolved – issue for the US intelligence community.[1] Moreover, there are wider questions of past intelligence involvement with terrorists – glaringly, in Afghanistan – and government sponsors – most egregiously, Pakistan and Saudi Arabia – that have come back to haunt the cheerleaders of the new crusade. Perhaps the greatest intelligence issue of them all, though, remains largely sidelined in the scramble for ever more draconian powers and a definitive technical fix: whether the cause of civil society – understood as terror's antithesis – can be advanced without recognising the threat posed to sound intelligence by uncritical secrecy and unqualified power.

The new Iron Triangle

In summing up what is probably the mainstream view of evolution in international politics, US academic Kenneth Waltz observes that 'competition produces a tendency toward sameness of the competitors'.[2] Sociologist Max Weber highlighted the role of bureaucratic rationalisation in the growth of the modern state nearly 100 years ago. Today, the headlong growth of IT and global communications has added a further momentum to the process of international socialisation, under the shadow of a new orthodoxy – globalisation. The organisational doctrines of the Harvard Business School – the so-called 'Washington consensus' on economic organisation – have become the template for social action across the board. The stress on quantification – expressed in targets, quotas and numerical measures of value – is uniquely suited to the digital organisation of information that technology is now providing. Military establishments have long provided the crucible for this process, its chemistry visible in the unchecked development of security establishments and secret services.

Clearly, in avowedly totalitarian states – North Korea, shall we say – the dangers to individual liberty are not only manifest but indeed actively promoted by the respective security organs, as an integral part of their grip on public life. For democracies, the public stance is one of denial. This is, however, increasingly shrouded in massive government 'spin'. As John Wadham of the UK-based civil rights group Liberty observes, 'Those caught up in the snare of our draconian terrorist legislation are now all presumed guilty. We must not risk a situation where the possibility of a fair trial is so eroded that we cannot safely acquit the innocent and convict the guilty.'[3] For democracies and dictators alike, though, the methodologies and technical means at issue are essentially the same in a globalised world.

As journalist Tony Collins observes in a series for the *Guardian*, 'suppliers of advanced computer systems want to sell their products. Government wants ever more sophisticated surveillance technologies

.... The growth of the surveillance state is nothing but a classic example of the power of marketing.'[4] It might also be understood as the intensification of a long-present sociological trend, identified by C. Wright Mills in the 1960s, for a 'power élite' to emerge in the now normal passage from government to consultancy to corporation and back again. For the balance between accountability and effectiveness in intelligence services, this well-trodden career path also represents an incremental erosion of any sort of public control, even before the current crisis has given the new 'iron triangle' a quantum boost. The resignation of Henry Kissinger as chairman of the US 9/11 inquiry provides a classic, if unintentionally humorous, example. After two weeks' tenure, the former US Secretary of State realised that even his legendary skills in *realpolitik* would be unable to bridge the gap between objective analysis and close business links with governments who, to put it mildly, allowed the plotters a certain indulgence.[5]

Intelligence and accountability – bucking the trend?

There have, to be sure, been developments which constitute a more positive trend in the relations between states and their intelligence services. Australia and Canada have shown it is possible to combine efficient intelligence gathering with democratic accountability and emerge with enhanced capabilities across the board. For Australia, a series of scandals that were centred around the 11 November 1975 removal of the Gough Whitlam government in a 'constitutional coup' – abetted by the CIA and the Australian (domestic) Secret Intelligence Organisation, ASIO – led to widespread reform.[6] In 1986, Australia set up the office of Inspector General of Intelligence and Security (IGIS), to provide government oversight of intelligence operations. Normally a retired civil servant, the Inspector is charged with reviewing activities throughout the Australian Secret Intelligence Service (ASIS, the foreign agency), the Defence Signals Directorate (DSD, the Sigint body) and a reformed ASIO. He has powers to demand all documents and compel any officer to divulge information. In addition to compiling a detailed annual report and audit, subject to parliamentary scrutiny, the IGIS can react directly to complaints from members of the public in ensuring that intelligence agencies are acting legally and 'with propriety ' – sadly, not a term readily associated with Canberra's close UK/USA allies in Washington and Whitehall. In 1995, oversight was further strengthened by the findings of the Samuels Commission.[7] The ASIS annual report notes that 'ASIS is not a police or law enforcement agency. It does not have paramilitary responsibilities and does not employ force or lethal means carrying out the tasks set for it.'[8]

In Canada, too, the secretive model inherited from the British was scrapped in favour of external oversight by the Security Intelligence Review Committee (SIRC), established in 1984. Here, a similarly empowered Inspector General was put in place, reporting to the Solicitor General (the chief Canadian law officer). While appointed by the Prime Minister, the five-member SIRC enjoys executive independence as a branch of the Canadian Privy Council. SIRC members, which usually include representatives of opposition parties, are able to access all information held by the Canadian Security Intelligence Service (CSIS), review ministerial directives and inspect warrant files. A particular function – in glaring contrast to UK practice – is that of reviewing complaints from people refused federal employment on security grounds. In addition to the SIRC, the intelligence community is also subject to audits by the Auditor General, reviews of data holdings by the Privacy Commissioner, requests for access to documents through the Access to Information and Privacy Acts and examination by the Human Rights Commission.[9]

In both Australia and Canada, stress has been placed on tightly drawn mandates for operations and a conspicuous avoidance of open-ended definitions of 'terrorism' and 'subversion' which have often given rise to abuse in the UK. For Britain, if the Terrorism Act 2000 (which came into force in February 2001) served to enshrine a range of powers of surveillance and detention hitherto found in the supposedly temporary act of 1975, these were further entrenched by the Anti-terrorism, Crime and Security Act of 15 December 2001, its 126 clauses rushed through to extend further the powers of the police to investigate, arrest and detain. It created new offences allowing courts to deal with terrorist activities which occurred outside UK national borders. While claiming on the day of the Bill's Parliamentary presentation that the powers were measured, reasonable and necessary, Home Secretary Blunkett issued a Human Rights Derogation Order, thereby partially withdrawing from the European Convention on Human Rights (ECHR) because (Article 5) it guarantees the right to liberty and prohibits detention without trial. It was the issue of indefinite detention without charge that raised major opposition. A person reasonably suspected of being an international terrorist could be detained indefinitely and without charge. It was to cover 'dozens of foreign' people, the Home Secretary claimed, who could not be prosecuted for insufficiency or inadmissibility of evidence, nor could they be deported if they faced either torture or death overseas. As of January 2003, 238 people have been arrested under the Terrorism Act of 2000, with 208 detained after 11 September 2001. Only 15 of these have since been brought to trial.[10]

The moves toward greater EU integration in security matters, evident before 9/11, have become a stampede. Increasingly lost in the search for ever more inclusive databases (and greater budgets) has been the distinction between active terrorism and legitimate protest. Already, a raft of EU-wide *acquis* (acquired legislation) has targeted asylum seekers, protest 'troublemakers' and third country nationals for scrutiny, arrest and detention. Under projected legislation, some could even be denied protection under the ECHR.[11]

As EU governments and security services rush to close ranks around the 'Anti-terrorism roadmap' – notably, the 'Framework' measures of June 2002 – some instances remain of more rigorous concern for oversight and civil liberties amongst individual EU states. Since the landmark 1987 ECHR decision, all EU citizens must enjoy some right of redress against security and intelligence services. This was reaffirmed by the European Court in 2001: 'The Court, being aware of the danger such a law poses of undermining or even destroying democracy on the ground of defending it, affirms that the Contracting States may not, in the name of the struggle against terrorism, adopt what measures they deem appropriate.'[12] In the Netherlands, for example, surveillance wiretaps must be approved by four ministers and complaints can be taken up by a parliamentary ombudsman, while in Germany oversight is provided by four parliamentary bodies loosely coordinated by the bi-partisan Bundestag Control Commission. In addition, special investigative committees can be formed at the request of a quarter of deputies, as happened in the case of the 1994 plutonium 'sting'.

In the US, once a pioneer of oversight legislation, the tendency seems to have been reversed. Whilst the system of Congressional monitoring and the landmark Freedom of Information Act remain in place, the shock of 9/11 has produced an all too predictable and so far unchecked rush of legal authoritarianism. The USA-Patriot Act bestowed a range of new and sweeping powers on Federal agencies, which found further expression in the Office of Homeland Security. Set up in late 2002, and likened by the President to the National Security Act of 1947 – which established the CIA – the OHS takes 22 Federal agencies under its ($37.5 billion) wing, including the US Customs, Secret Service, Immigration and Naturalisation Service and Coast Guard. If the implications of combining law enforcement, necessarily restricted to the observation of legal norms, with the functions of intelligence – extra-legal by definition – have raised civil liberties concerns, these have become manifest realities in the launch of the Information Awareness Office (IAO) – a new intelligence-gathering body hived off from the Pentagon. Headed, as we have seen, by former National Security Advisor Admiral John Poindexter, the IAO ambitiously aims to locate potential terrorists by identifying an electronic footprint for virtually every US resident.

With an initial budget of $10 million (and potential $200 million in the pipeline), a quasi-masonic, eye-and-pyramid logo and a motto declaring *Scienta est Potentia* ('Knowledge is Power') the IAO has seemingly popped straight from the worst nightmares of conspiracy theorists everywhere. And for once they're not wrong. The theory behind Total Information Awareness is that terrorists exhibit recognisable behaviour patterns, which can be discerned by data-mining the totality of an individual's recorded lifetime activities. These range from ATM receipts, web use, insurance/medical/financial records and parking tickets to movement data recorded on closed-circuit television and police speed cameras, accessed through emerging facial recognition software. Whilst the aim of a truly unified personal database on a cosmic scale has outraged US civil libertarians – reversing, by default, the legal 'presumption of innocence' – glaring flaws in the concept itself have caused similar consternation amongst more politically aware US scientists. One such flaw, the assumption that a distinct 'terrorist personality' can be identified, smacks of the worst excesses of 1950s behaviourism – a doctrine long favoured by the CIA in its notorious 'mind control' programmes[13] and since widely discredited. Another flaw is that the successful identification of behavioural regularities and associations sufficient to provide intelligence indicators itself depends crucially on there being sound data to begin with. Given the vast scale of the enterprise, the possibilities of mistaken identities and false trails amongst the terabytes of corruptible records and input errors could well mean data gridlock and less efficient intelligence than is presently available. And as the presumption of innocence has already been effectively dumped in the cases of the 1,200 non-US suspects still interned after 9/11, the prospect of huge numbers of wholly innocent names feeding through a self-generating blacklist is very real.

Looking to the future

What, then, of the future? As the Australian and Canadian cases have shown, it is perfectly feasible to combine successful intelligence with public accountability. And, as we have seen from South Africa, the most unregenerate of services can be made to yield to political will. In a well-regarded study of the Canadian system, Lustgarten and Leigh have identified eight features of constructive intelligence oversight on the pattern established by the SIRC:[14]

• independence from the executive;

• the power to initiate inquiries;

• a non-partisan membership which reflects the political spectrum;

• extensive access to information;

- the ability to maintain confidentiality;

- institutional expertise;

- adequate support staff; and

- the capacity to mobilise public opinion.

Given these priorities, our assessment of global intelligence identifies two sorts of 'rogue agency' against which a war on (state) terrorism might be declared. One might hope to see straightforwardly 'roguish' agencies in the service of outright dictatorships abolished, along with their regimes. Here, Western and other governments can clearly do much more in linking trade, aid and diplomatic contacts with the observance of such international law as does exist – the UN Convention on Human Rights, for example, and the Torture Convention. The second sort present a more diffuse danger to civil society, a highly dangerous toxin brewed from headline-driven politics, bureaucratic empire building and blind technological momentum. Here, oversight can make a difference – but only if agencies are prevented from being 'self-tasking' in the way they still are in the UK and are rapidly becoming in the EU and America. A clear distinction also needs to be upheld between intelligence and law enforcement. The granting of extra-legal powers of surveillance and lethal force to bodies which, by definition, can never stand in open court will inevitably involve abuses. Effective oversight must be the first priority, rather than a reluctant afterthought. For parliaments, legislators and civil society as a whole, *scientia* is indeed the essence of *potentia* – and more so now than ever before.

Notes

1 See, for example, Eleanor Hill and the Congressional Joint Enquiry Staff, *The Intelligence Community's Knowledge of the September 11 Hijackers Prior to September 11 2001* – found at the (invaluable) Federation of American Scientists website: www.fas.org/congress/2002_hr/092002hill.html.

2 See Kenneth Waltz, *Theory of International Politics*, Reading, Massachusetts: Addison and Wesley, 1979, p. 127.

3 See Richard Norton-Taylor, 'Spin "Endangering Terror Trials"', *Guardian*, 18 January 2003.

4 See Tony Collins, 'Mandarins and Technocrats', in 'Big Brother, the Secret State and the Assault on Privacy', Part II, *Guardian* Special Report, 14 September 2002.

5 See Julian Borger, 'Henry's Revenge', *Guardian*, 29 November 2002; see also, 'Kissinger Resigns as Chairman of Inquiry into September 11 Attacks', *Guardian*, 14 December 2002.

6 *Inter alia*, Whitlam was ousted the day before a major debate on the CIA's role in Australia was scheduled in the Australian Parliament. See James A. Nathan, 'Dateline Australia: America's Foreign Watergate?' *Foreign Policy,* 49 (Winter 1982): 168–85.

7 This reinforced the oversight role of the renamed Cabinet National Security Committee. See Ian Dugeon, 'Does Covert Intelligence Have a Future?', ADSC paper at conference on 'Optimising Open-Source Information', Canberra, 7–8 October 1998.

8 See Australian Secret Intelligence Service (ASIS), www.asis.gov.au/asiscorpinfo.html, August 2001, p. 5.

9 See Government of Canada, Privy Council Office, 'The Canadian Security and Intelligence Community', www.pco-bcp.gc.ca/, December 2001, pp. 9–10.

10 See Daniel McGrory, 'Europe's Police Round Up Terror Suspects', *The Times*, 19 December 2002.

11 Countries, including the UK, are lobbying for the terms 'or inhuman and degrading treatment or punishment' to be removed from Article 3 of the Convention. See Tony Bunyan, 'The War on Freedom and Democracy – an Analysis of the Effects on Civil Liberties and Democratic Culture in the EU', *Statewatch*, September 2002, p. 13.

12 See Philip Thomas, 'Legislative Responses to Terrorism', *Guardian*, 11 September 2002.

13 For a good overview of this highly under-researched field, see Armen Victorian, *The Mind Controllers*, London: Vision, 1999.

14 See Lawrence Lustgarten and Ian Leigh, *In from the Cold: National Security and Parliamentary Democracy*, Oxford: Oxford University Press, 1994, pp. 461–2.

HOW TO RESEARCH YOUR INTELLIGENCE AGENCY

A Citizen's Guide

This appendix has three parts, namely:

1. Sources of information on intelligence in general and by country;

2. Use of freedom of information and data protection legislation; and

3. The prosecution of torturers.

1. Sources of information on intelligence in general and by country

Most intelligence agencies now have websites on which they give the public their version of events and their organisational structure. The result is that there are thousands of websites covering intelligence, agencies, methods, etcetera.

The starting point for any analysis of intelligence agencies should be one or more of the websites listed below. They specialise in providing links to several hundred if not thousands of websites relating to intelligence agencies.

◆ **The Canadian Association for Security and Intelligence Studies** (CASIS) is a non-partisan, voluntary association established in 1985. Its principal purpose is to provide informed debate in Canada on security and intelligence issues. Membership is open and currently includes academics, concerned citizens, government officials, journalists, lawyers, students and former intelligence officers. Its website (**www.sfu.ca/igs/CASIS**) provides 7,500 links. Of particular interest are the links under Associations, Centres and Foundations:

- Intelligence Organisations By Country;
- Intelligence Organisations – International;
- Intelligence Reform;
- Intelligence Threats and Assessments;
- Global Security Threats;
- National Security Threats;
- Intelligence Topics; and
- Online Intelligence Resources.

◆ **www.kimsoft.com/kim-spy.htm** is another good jumping-off point, particularly with respect to Canada.

◆ **Federation of American Scientists**
www.fas.org/
FAS Intelligence Resource Program:
www.fas.org/irp/intelwww.html
Address
Federation of American Scientists
1717 K Street, NW, Suite 209
Washington, DC 20036
Contact
Steven Aftergood
Tel (202) 454-4691
fax (202) 675-1010
email saftergood@fas.org

The Intelligence Resource Program provides in-depth information on agencies around the world and many other reports and resources.

Originally the Federation of Atomic Scientists (whose first members worked on the Manhattan Project), the Federation of American Scientists is dedicated to ending the arms race and avoiding the use of nuclear weapons. Its involvement in a number of peace and security projects is reflected by the broad issue coverage of its website.

FAS publishes *Secrecy News* which 'provides informal coverage of new developments in secrecy, security and intelligence policies, as well as links to new acquisitions on our website'. It is published two or three times a week, or as events warrant.

◆ **www.cryptome.com** is worth a regular visit. It is the only regular 'anti-secrecy' website. As it states,

> Cryptome welcomes documents for publication that are prohibited by governments worldwide, in particular material on freedom of expression, privacy, cryptology, dual-use technologies, national security, intelligence, and blast protection – open, secret and classified documents – but not limited to those.

Documents are removed from this site only by order served directly by a US court having jurisdiction. No court order has ever been served; any order will be published here or elsewhere if gagged by order. Bluffs will be published if comical but otherwise ignored.

Contact/Address
Cryptome Administrator: John Young
251 West 89th Street
New York NY 10024
Tel: (US) 212-873-8700
Fax: (US) 212-787-6102
E-mail: jya@pipeline.com

◆ **Loyola University, www.loyola.edu/dept/politics/intel.html** focuses on Strategic Intelligence, Military Intelligence and Economic Intelligence. It has links to US intelligence and military intelligence websites, plus a brand-new international intelligence centre. This is a huge collection.

◆ **www.globalsecurity.org/index.html**, a private site created and mantained by John Pike, provides a selection of official and unofficial resources on intelligence policy, structure, function, organisation and operations. It has a world intelligence guide.

◆ **www.intelbrief.com** bills itself as 'A portal to all the intelligence of the internet. Organising over 2,000 intelligence sources and news feeds into a site of actionable information.'

◆ **http://mprofaca.cro.net/** is a massive website on intelligence matters maintained by Mario Profaca, a Croatian journalist.

◆ **http://www.intelforum.org/resources.html** also has extensive links.

◆ **http://www.agentura.ru/english/** is a website devoted to intelligence agencies in Russia.

◆ **www.futurewar.net** focuses on Information Warfare and has a large collection of articles and links related to this subject.

Useful publications covering intelligence matters

◆ **www.intelligenceonline.com** is a French-based online service.
Address
142 rue Montmartre
F-75002 Paris
Tel: + 33 1 44 88 26 10
Fax: + 33 1 44 88 26 15
E-mail: info@indigo-net.com

◆ The ***Quarterly Journal of Intelligence and National Security*** (**http://www.frankcass.com/jnls/ins.htm**), British-based, is now in its 17th volume.

◆ The *International Journal of Intelligence and Counterintelligence* is American-based (www.frankcass.com/jnls/ins).

◆ *The Lobster* (**www.lobster-magazine.co.uk**) is a left-wing magazine which focuses on intelligence and is edited and published twice a year by Robin Ramsay.
Email: editor@lobster-magazine.co.uk

Organisations studying intelligence agencies

◆ The **Geneva Centre for the Democratic Control of Armed Forces** (**www.dcaf.ch**), which has backing from the Swiss and other governments, publishes a useful series of working papers on the accountability of the intelligence agencies, particularly in the USA and in Western and Central Europe. Of special interest is No. 103 (January 2003): Peter Gill, 'Democratic and Parliamentary Accountability of Intelligence Services after September 11th'.

◆ The **Project on Justice in Times of Transition of Harvard University** (**www.ksg.harvard.edu/justiceproject/Index.htm**) has also produced some interesting working papers on internal security reform, covering *inter alia* South Africa and Peru.

◆ The **Helsinki Foundation for Human Rights of Poland** (**http://www.hfhrpol.waw.pl/Secserv/**) had a project to promote oversight and accountability of security services in the newly emergent countries of Eastern and Central Europe. The website contains a useful section on 'Links to official government websites on secret services and related agencies'.

◆ The **CIA's Center for Intelligence Studies** (**www.odci.gov/csi/studies.html**) is also active in this field, of course, publishing the quarterly *Studies in Intelligence*.

◆ The **International Intelligence History Association** was established in 1993 to promote scholarly research on intelligence organisations and their impact on historical development and international relations. Annual meetings provide a forum for academic exchange, and the *Journal of Intelligence History*, published by the IIHA, informs members and the broader public on scholarly research in this field.

> *Contact/Address*
> Dr Sigurd Hess
> IIHA Executive Director
> Mathildestrasse 9
> 53359 Rheinbach
> Germany
> Tel.: +49-2225-706 124 or 125
> Email: SigurdHess@compuserve.com

◆ The **UK Political Studies Association** (**www.reading.ac.uk/ SecInt**) also has a specialist Security and Intelligence Studies Group.

◆ **http://intellit.muskingum.edu/** has the best bibliography of printed materials on the subject, including books and articles: *The Literature of Intelligence: a Bibliography of Materials, with Essays, Reviews, and Comments* by J. Ransom Clark, Vice-President for Administration, Muskingum College, New Concord, USA.

Civil liberty organisations which focus on intelligence

Because of the relationship of civil liberties to intelligence agencies, several civil liberty organisations have focused on this area. In the USA there are two main organisations:

◆ The **Center for National Security Studies** (**http://www. gwu.edu/~cnss/**), a non-governmental advocacy and research organisation, was founded in 1974 to work for control of the FBI and CIA and to prevent violations of civil liberties in the US. The Center is the only non-profit human rights and civil liberties organisation in the

USA with a core mission to prevent claims of national security from eroding civil liberties or constitutional procedures.

Address
Center for National Security Studies
1120 19th Street, NW
8th Floor
Washington DC 20036
Tel (202) 721-5650
Fax (202) 530-0128 (fax)
email cnss@gwu.edu

◆ The **American Civil Liberties Union (ACLU) (www.aclu. org/NationalSecurity/NationalSecurityMain.cfm)**, the major civil liberty organisation in the USA, monitors intelligence activities in the USA to the extent that they impact Americans. It has also done work on the Echelon project.

Address
American Civil Liberties Union
125 Broad Street
18th Floor
New York
NY 10004

In the United Kingdom the equivalent of the ACLU is
◆ **Liberty (http://www.liberty-human-rights.org.uk/issues/ security-services.html)**, which has been involved in several lawsuits involving intelligence.

Address
Liberty
21 Tabard Street
London SE1 4LA
Tel: 020 7403 3888
Fax: 020 7407 5354
Email info@liberty-human-rights.org.uk

◆ **Statewatch** (**www.statewatch.org**) is the nearest European equivalent to the Center for National Security Studies and fulfils a similar role in the United Kingdom and the rest of Europe. It also focuses on European institutions and legislation emerging from the various European institutions. In addition to its informative website, it publishes a newsletter, *Statewatch Bulletin*.

> *Address*
> Statewatch
> PO Box 1516
> London N16 0EW
> Phone: 0208 802 1882
> Fax: 0208 880 1727
> E-mail: office@statewatch.org

◆ **Amnesty International** (**www.amnesty.org**) and **Human Rights Watch** (**www.hrw.org**), the two main international human rights organisations, in their various and numerous reports cover the activities of intelligence agencies insofar as they impact on human rights.

2. Use of freedom of information and data protection legislation

Many countries now have Freedom of Information (FOI) Acts that give citizens the right to request documentation about either themselves or government organs and actions. There are usually many exemptions that allow these bodies to withhold information. Nevertheless, the use of this legislation can be a useful aid to those seeking to investigate particular events or incidents. The extent of CIA involvement in the overthrow of Allende in Chile and in various other areas was exposed by the use of the FOI Act.

Data protection legislation exists also in many countries, theoretically protecting people from unlawful gathering of information on them. Under the provisions of some of these laws citizens may apply to see files held on them. There have already been several legal actions in the United Kingdom where people have tried to obtain their files from the security services using the Data Protection Act.

♦ **http://europa.eu.int/comm/internal_market/en/dataprot/links.htm** is a website maintained by the European Union, with a list of Data Protection Commissioners around the world.

♦ **www.fas.org/foia** gives access to the Project on Government Secrecy supported for many years by the Federation of American Scientists in the US, where FOI activism first flourished.

♦ **www.aclu.org/library/foia.html** is ACLU's detailed online guide to getting US documents.

♦ **http://foi.missouri.edu/laws.html**, website of the Freedom of Information Center, offers an exhaustive guide.

♦ **Freedominfo.org**, first port of call to find out about FOI around the world, is the organisation spawned by the **National Security Archives**, another source for documents released under the FOI Acts in the USA. It is particularly strong on the Third World and its website hosts the compendium *Freedom of Information and Access to Government Records Around the World* by David Banisar of Privacy International.

> *Address*
> **Freedominfo.org**
> Suite 701
> Gelman Library
> The George Washington Library
> 2130 H Street NW
> Washington DC 20037
> Email email@freedominfo.org

♦ **Privacy International (PI)** (**www.privacyinternational.org**) is a human rights group formed in 1990 as a watchdog on surveillance by governments and corporations. Based in London, PI has an office in Washington DC and has conducted campaigns throughout the world on issues ranging from wiretapping and national security to ID cards, video surveillance, data matching, police information systems and freedom of information and expression. Its website contains country reports on data protection and FOI.

Addresses
Privacy International London Headquarters
2nd Floor, Lancaster House,
33 Islington High Street,
London N1 9LH
Tel: 07947 778247

Privacy International Washington Office
1718 Connecticut Ave, NW Suite 200
Washington DC 20009
Tel: 1-202-483-1217
Fax: 1-202-483-1248

◆ **EPIC** (**www.epic.org**) is a public interest research centre in Washington DC established in 1994 to focus public attention on emerging civil liberties issues and to protect privacy, the First Amendment and constitutional values. It works very closely with Privacy International.

Address
EPIC
1718 Connecticut Ave NW Suite 200
Washington, DC 20009
Email info@epic.org

◆ *Privacy and Human Rights* (**2002 edition**), published by EPIC and Privacy International, reviews the state of privacy in over fifty countries around the world. It outlines legal protections for privacy and new challenges to these, and summarises important issues and events relating to privacy and surveillance. It examines the impact of government proposals after 11 September 2001 on privacy and civil liberties. The report documents many new anti-terrorism and security measures and identifies key trends, including increased communications surveillance, weakening of data protection regimes, and increased profiling and identification of individuals.

◆ **Article 19** (**www.article19.org**) is a London-based NGO that monitors, lobbies and litigates on behalf of freedom of expression. It also campaigns for the right to access information held by governments, public authorities and private bodies or companies. Article 19 has posted a Model Freedom of Information Law on its site. It has also published a *Survey of Access to Information in South Asia*.

◆ **http://faculty.maxwell.syr.edu/asroberts/foi/security.html** is an impressive collection of FOI laws from around the world compiled by Professor Alasdair Roberts of Syracuse University. His online library also includes documents reflecting the impact of NATO directives on the information policies of new NATO member nations, as well as several hard-to-find 'security of information agreements' that govern the exchange of classified information between countries.

3. The prosecution of torturers

As torture is most frequently exercised by intelligence and security agencies it is appropriate to include a section on how these perpetrators may be indicted and charged. The world has made great theoretical strides in bringing torturers to justice. Although the reality, unfortunately, has not yet caught up and there have been relatively few prosecutions, the picture is changing rapidly. The threat of foreign prosecution has already curtailed Israeli security personnel travelling abroad (see *Haaretz*, 25 February 2003: 'Shin Bet Chief Cancelled Trip to Belgium Fearing Arrest').

◆ The **International Court of Criminal Justice (www.icc.int)** has given added impetus to the bringing of torturers and other major abusers of human rights to justice.

◆ **www.iccnow.org** is the website of the coalition for the International Criminal Court which groups over 1,000 NGOs campaigning for an international criminal justice court

> *Address*
> c/o WFM, 777 UN Plaza,
> New York, NY 10017, USA
> Telephone: 1-212-687-2176
> Fax: 1-212-599-1332
> E-mail: cicc@iccnow.org

Other organisations for the international prosecution of torturers

◆ **REDRESS (www.redress.org)** is an internationally focused non-profit human rights/legal organisation based in London, founded on Human Rights Day, 10 December 1992, to help torture survivors obtain justice and reparation. Reparation (including rehabilitation and compensation) plays an important part in the rebuilding of the lives of those who have suffered torture. Seeking legal redress also helps to combat the practice of torture by exposing torturers and the regimes which support them.

> *Address*
> Redress
> 3rd Floor
> 87 Vauxhall Walk
> London SE11 5HJ
> Tel: +44 (0)20 7793 1777
> Fax: +44 (0)20 7793 1719
> Email: redresstrust@gn.apc.org

It may be possible to prosecute torturers in foreign countries. The USA and the UK have domestic legislation which would allow this.

Under the International Convention Against Torture, which the US
and UK have ratified, these governments are obligated to extradite,
surrender or prosecute suspected human rights abusers.

◆ The **Center for Justice and Accountability (www.cja.org)**
focuses on prosecuting torturers in the USA.

Address
870 Market Street, Suite 684
San Francisco, CA 94102
Tel 415/ 544 0444
Fax 415/ 544 0456
Email center4justice@cja.org

◆ **World Organisation Against Torture USA (www.woatusa.
org)** has on its website a section on criminal accountability for human
rights abuse.

Address
1725 K Street NW
Suite 610
Washington DC 20006
Tel 202-296-5702

◆ The **Centre for Human Rights (http://www.essex.ac.uk/
torturehandbook/)** at Essex University has published the *Torture
Reporting Handbook* which shows 'How to document and respond to
allegations of torture within the international system for the protection of human rights'.

INDEX

Abidjan satellite station 121
accountability/transparency 2, 7, 9, 13, 22, 32, 60, 101, 116, 119, 128, 185, 189, 191, 193-4, 207-15
Afghanistan 8, 15-19, 75, 82, 86-92, 112, 179-84
Africa 12, 26, 42, 121-5, 153, 165, 172; Central 122-3; East 15, 122; Francophone 121-5; West 123
African National Congress (ANC) 190-7; Department of Intelligence and Security (ANC–DIS) 190-2, 195
Ahmet, Mahmoud 182-4
Airbus Industrie 55, 77, 92, 120
Aitken, Jonathan 110
Al-Qaida 2, 13, 16, 18, 31, 53, 87-8, 90-2, 124, 126, 175
Albion satellite station 120
Albright, Madeleine 91
Algeria 15, 87, 124. 153, 200
Aliyev, Heydar 144-5
Alluets-le-Roi satellite station 120
Aman (Israeli military intelligence service) 9, 31, 152-4, 157, 159, 161
Americans for Computer Privacy (ACP) 59
Ames, Aldrich 74-5, 145
Ames, Robert 177
Amir, Yigal 155
Angola 123, 125, 200
Anti-Defamation League (ADL) 160
AOL 63
Arafat, Yasser 28-31, 169, 177-8
Armey, Dick 30
Armitage, Richard 89
arms control 3-5, 16, 18, 30, 67, 80, 86, 113-14, 125, 141, 145, 153, 158
arms trafficking 93, 108-10, 114, 159, 166, 173-4, 188, 196
Ashcroft, Attorney General John 31, 65
Asia, 14, 38, 40, 42, 55, 60, 78; Central 9, 15-16, 19, 47, 87, 96, 144, 159; South 12, 165, 172; South-east 159
Asia Pacific Economic Conference (APEC) 78

Assad, Bashar al- 167-8, 170-1
Assad, Basil al- 171
Assad, Hafiz al- 84, 166-71
Assam 179, 184
assassinations 94, 96, 142, 153-8, 169-72, 174, 176, 178, 181-2, 196-9
Association of South-East Asian Nations (ASEAN) 187
Astra Holdings 109-10
AT&T 43-4
Aung San Suu Kyi 186
Australia 4, 38-41, 45, 56, 105, 191, 209-10, 213; Australian Secret Intelligence Organisation (ASIO) 209; Australian Secret Intelligence Service (ASIS) 209-10; Defence Signals Directorate (DSD) 112; Inspector General of Intelligence and Security (IGIS) 209-10
Ayyash, Yahya 154

Bad Aibling satellite station 39, 45, 125
Baer, Robert 82-4, 86, 111
Bahrain 61, 200
Bakatim, Vadim 136-7
Bangladesh 180, 185; war 180
Banko Nazionale de Lavoro (BNL) 79-80
Banna, Sabri al- see Nidal, Abu
Barak, Ehud 29, 177
Barbar, Naseerullah 182
Barghouti, Marwan 28
Barnard, Neil 190
Barranikov, Victor 137-8
Baruskov, FSB Director 148
Barzani, Massoud 82, 86
Bashir, General Omar 123-4
Beirut 20, 158, 169-70, 174, 177
Bell Laboratories 50
Bengali people 179-80
Berezhovski, Boris 139-42
Berger, Sandy 89
Bhutto, Benazir 181-2
Bhutto, Murtaza 182
Bhutto, Shah Nawaz 181
Bhutto, Zulfikar Ali 180

Participating Organisations

Both ENDS: A service and advocacy organisation which collaborates with environment and indigenous organisations, both in the South and in the North, with the aim of helping to create and sustain a vigilant and effective environmental movement.
Damrak 28-30, 1012 LJ Amsterdam, The Netherlands
Tel: +31 20 623 0823   Fax: +31 20 620 8049
Email: info@bothends.org • Website: www.bothends.org

Catholic Institute for International Relations (CIIR): CIIR aims to contribute to the eradication of poverty through a programme that combines advocacy at national and international level with community-based development.
Unit 3 Canonbury Yard, 190a New North Road, London N1 7BJ, UK
Tel: +44 (0)20 7354 0883   Fax: +44 (0)20 7359 0017
Email: ciir@ciir.org • Website: www.ciir.org

Corner House: The Corner House is a UK-based research and solidarity group working on social and environmental justice issues in North and South.
PO Box 3137, Station Road, Sturminster Newton, Dorset DT10 1YJ, UK
Tel: +44 (0)1258 473795   Fax: +44 (0)1258 473748
Email: cornerhouse@gn.apc.org • Website: www.cornerhouse.icaap.org

Council on International and Public Affairs (CIPA): CIPA is a human rights research, education and advocacy group, with a particular focus on economic and social rights in the USA and elsewhere around the world. Emphasis in recent years has been given to resistance to corporate domination.
777 United Nations Plaza, Suite 3C, New York, NY 10017, USA.
Tel: +1 212 972 9877   Fax: +1 212 972 9878
Email: cipany@igc.org • Website: www.cipa-apex.org

Dag Hammarskjöld Foundation: The Dag Hammarskjöld Foundation, established 1962, organises seminars and workshops on social, economic and cultural issues facing developing countries with a particular focus on alternative and innovative solutions. Results are published in its journal *Development Dialogue*.
Övre Slottsgatan 2, 753 10 Uppsala, Sweden.
Tel: +46 18 102772   Fax: +46 18 122072
Email: secretariat@dhf.uu.se • web site: www.dhf.uu.se

Development GAP: The Development Group for Alternative Policies is a Non-Profit Development Resource Organisation working with popular organisations in the South and their Northern partners in support of a development that is truly sustainable and that advances social justice.
927 15th Street, NW - 4th Floor, Washington, DC 20005 – USA
Tel: +1 202 898 1566   Fax: +1 202 898 1612
Email: dgap@igc.org • Website: www.developmentgap.org

Focus on the Global South: Focus is dedicated to regional and global policy analysis and advocacy work. It works to strengthen the capacity of organisations of the poor and marginalised people of the South and to better analyse and understand the impacts of the globalisation process on their daily lives.
C/o CUSRI, Chulalongkorn University, Bangkok 10330, Thailand
Tel: +66 2 218 7363 Fax: +66 2 255 9976
Email: Admin@focusweb.org • Website: www.focusweb.org

Inter Pares: Inter Pares, a Canadian social justice organisation, has been active since 1975 in building relationships with Third World development groups and providing support for community-based development programmes. Inter Pares is also involved in education and advocacy in Canada, promoting understanding about the causes, effects and solutions of poverty.
58 rue Arthur Street, Ottawa, Ontario, K1R 7B9 Canada
Tel: + 1 613 563 4801   Fax: + 1 613 594 4704

Public Interest Research Centre: PIRC is a research and campaigning group based in Delhi which seeks to serve the information needs of activists and organisations working on macro-economic issues concerning finance, trade and development.
142, Maitri Apartments, Plot No. 28, Patparganj, Delhi: 110092, India
Tel: + 91 11 2221081, 2432054   Fax: + 91 11 2224233
Email: kaval@nde.vsnl.net.in

Third World Network: TWN is an international network of groups and individuals involved in efforts to bring about a greater articulation of the needs and rights of peoples in the Third World; a fair distribution of the world's resources; and forms of development which are ecologically sustainable and fulfil human needs. Its international secretariat is based in Penang, Malaysia.
228 Macalister Road, 10400 Penang, Malaysia
Tel: +60 4 226 6159   Fax: +60 4 226 4505
Email: twnet@po.jaring.my • Website: www.twnside.org.sg

Third World Network–Africa: TWN–Africa is engaged in research and advocacy on economic, environmental and gender issues. In relation to its current particular interest in globalisation and Africa, its work focuses on trade and investment, the extractive sectors and gender and economic reform.
2 Ollenu Street, East Legon, P O Box AN19452, Accra-North, Ghana.
Tel: +233 21 511189/503669/500419   Fax: +233 21 511188
Email: twnafrica@ghana.com

World Development Movement (WDM): The World Development Movement campaigns to tackle the causes of poverty and injustice. It is a democratic membership movement that works with partners in the South to cancel unpayable debt and break the ties of IMF conditionality, for fairer trade and investment rules, and for strong international rules on multinationals.
25 Beehive Place, London SW9 7QR, UK
Tel: +44 (0)20 7737 6215   Fax: +44 (0)20 7274 8232
Email: wdm@wdm.org.uk • Website: www.wdm.org.uk

The GLOBAL ISSUES Series

Already available in English

Walden Bello, *Deglobalization: Ideas for a New World Economy*

Robert Ali Brac de la Perrière and Franck Seuret, *Brave New Seeds: The Threat of GM Crops to Farmers*

Oswaldo de Rivero, *The Myth of Development: The Non-viable Economies of the 21st Century*

Joyeeta Gupta, *Our Simmering Planet: What to do about Global Warming?*

Nicholas Guyatt, *Another American Century? The United States and the World after 2000*

Martin Khor, *Rethinking Globalization: Critical Issues and Policy Choices*

John Madeley, *Food for All: The Need for a New Agriculture*

John Madeley, *Hungry for Trade: How the Poor Pay for Free Trade*

A. G. Noorani, *Islam and Jihad: Prejudice versus Reality*

Riccardo Petrella, *The Water Manifesto: Arguments for a World Water Contract*

Peter Robbins, *Stolen Fruit: The Tropical Commodities Disaster*

Vandana Shiva, *Protect or Plunder? Understanding Intellectual Property Rights*

Harry Shutt, *A New Democracy: Alternatives to a Bankrupt World Order*

David Sogge, *Give and Take: What's the Matter with Foreign Aid?*

Paul Todd and Jonathan Bloch, *Global Intelligence: The World's Secret Services Today*

In preparation

Peggy Antrobus, *The International Women's Movement: Issues and Strategies*

Amit Bhaduri and Deepak Nayyar, *Free Market Economics: The Intelligent Person's Guide to Liberalization*

Greg Buckman, *Globalization: Shrink or Sink?*

Julian Burger, *First Peoples: What Future?*

Graham Dunkley, *Free Trade: Myths, Realities and Alternatives*

Ha-Joon Chang and Ilene Grabel, *Reclaiming Development: What Works, What Doesn't – an Economic Policy Handbook*

Susan Hawley and Morris Szeftel, *Corruption: Privatization, Transnational Corporations and the Export of Bribery*

Damien Millet and Eric Toussaint, *Who Owns Who? 50 Questions About World Debt*

Roger Moody, *Digging the Dirt: The Modern World of Global Mining*

Kavaljit Singh, *The Myth of Globalization: Ten Questions Everyone Asks*

Nedd Willard, *The War on Drugs: Is This the Solution?*

For full details of this series and Zed's other subject and general catalogues, please write to: The Marketing Department, Zed Books, 7 Cynthia Street, London N1 9JF, UK or email Sales@zedbooks.demon.co.uk

Visit our website at: http://www.zedbooks.demon.co.uk

THIS BOOK IS ALSO AVAILABLE IN THE FOLLOWING COUNTRIES:

CARIBBEAN
Ian Randle Publishers
11 Cunningham Avenue
Box 686, Kingston 6,
Jamaica, W.I.
Tel: (876) 978 0745, 978 0739
Fax: 978 1158
e-mail: ianr@colis.com

EGYPT
MERIC (The Middle East
Readers'
Information Center)
2 Bahgat Ali Street,
Tower D/Apt. 24
Zamalek
Cairo
Tel: 20 2 735 3818/736 3824
Fax: 20 2 736 9355

FIJI
University Book Centre
University of South Pacific,
Suva
Tel: 679 313 900
Fax: 679 303 265

GHANA
EPP Book Services
P O Box TF 490
Trade Fair
Accra
Tel: 233 21 773087
Fax: 233 21 779099

MAURITIUS
Editions Le Printemps
4 Club Road
Vacoas
Tel: 696 1017

MOZAMBIQUE
Sul Sensacoes
PO Box 2242,
Maputo
Tel: 258 1 421974
Fax: 258 1 423414

NAMIBIA
Book Den
PO Box 3469
Shop 4, Frans Indongo Gardens
Windhoek
Tel: 264 61 239976
Fax: 264 61 234248

NEPAL
Everest Media Services
GPO Box 5443, Dillibazar
Putalisadak Chowk
Kathmandu
Tel: 977 1 416026
Fax: 977 1 250176

NIGERIA
Mosuro Publishers
52 Magazine Road
Jericho, Ibadan
Tel: 234 2 241 3375
Fax: 234 2 241 3374

PAKISTAN
Vanguard Books
45 The Mall
Lahore
Tel: 92 42 735 5079
Fax: 92 42 735 5197

PAPUA NEW GUINEA
Unisearch PNG Pty Ltd
Box 320, University
National Capital District
Tel: 675 326 0130
Fax: 675 326 0127

PHILIPPINES
IBON Foundation , Inc.
3rd Floor SCC Bldg.,
4427 Int. Old Sta. Mesa,
Manila, Philippines 1008
Tel.: (632) 713-2729 / 713-2737
Fax: (632) 716-0108

RWANDA
Librairie Ikirezi
PO Box 443,
Kigali
Tel/Fax: 250 71314

TANZANIA
TEMA Publishing Co Ltd
PO Box 63115
Dar Es Salaam
Tel: 255 51 113608
Fax: 255 51 110472

UGANDA
Aristoc Booklex Ltd
PO Box 5130, Kampala Road
Diamond Trust Building
Kampala
Tel/Fax: 256 41 254867

ZAMBIA
UNZA Press
PO Box 32379
Lusaka
Tel: 260 1 290409
Fax: 260 1 253952

ZIMBABWE
Weaver Press
PO Box A1922
Avondale
Harare
Tel: 263 4 308330
Fax: 263 4 339645